Implementing Change

Implementing Change

Patterns, Principles, and Potholes

Gene E. Hall
University of Nevada, Las Vegas

Shirley M. Hord
Southwest Educational Development Laboratory

Allyn and Bacon

Boston • London • Toronto • Sydney • Tokyo • Singapore

Series Editor: Arnis Burvikovs
Marketing Manager: Kathleen Morgan
Editorial Assistant: Patrice Mailloux
Composition Buyer: Linda Cox
Manufacturing Buyer: Julie McNeill
Editorial-Production Service: P. M. Gordon Associates
Production Administrator: Deborah Brown
Cover Administration: Jenny Hart

Copyright ©2001 by Allyn and Bacon
A Pearson Education Company
160 Gould Street
Needham Heights, Massachusetts 02494

Internet: www.abacon.com

Library of Congress Cataloging-in-Publication Data

Hall, Gene E., 1941–
    Implementing change : patterns, principles, and potholes / Gene E. Hall, Shirley M. Hord.
      p. cm.
    Includes bibliographical references and index.
    ISBN 0–205–16222–3
    1. School improvement programs—United States.   2. Educational leadership—United
States.   I. Hord, Shirley M.   II. Title.
LB2822.82.H355   2001
371.2′00973—dc21   00–025429

Printed in the United States of America

10 9 8 7 6 5 4 3 2   05 04 03 02 01

We wish to thank the many teachers, school and district leaders, and business leaders, who have willingly shared their experiences with and befuddlements about change. We also are indebted to our CBAM colleagues around the world who have contributed to our learning about change and who have shared CBAM ideas with others.

CONTENTS

7 Defining Change Facilitator Style: Different Approaches Produce Different Results   126

PREFACE

We welcome you, the reader, to this book about the *Concerns-Based Adoption Model* (*CBAM*) for understanding and facilitating the change process in organizational and educational settings. The ideas, research findings, and case examples presented here represent our cumulative understanding of the change process after more than thirty years of first-hand experiences as participants, facilitators, and researchers. One clear conclusion is that we should be able to predict much more about what truly happens during this process than is typically the case. We also should be much better at attending to the needs of the people involved and preventing much that often goes wrong. Hopefully, our attempt to pass on some of what we have learned will be of help to you and the others with whom you are engaged during change.

For the past several years our colleagues, our students, and interested others have repeatedly asked us, "Is the new CBAM book out yet?" At first we would say, "We are close." Over time our answers became more evasive, although we kept writing and believing (or hoping) that the completion was near. We even started feeling that we should hide from Ray Short, former editor of educational administration at Allyn and Bacon, since we had promised the final submission for so long. With more time we accepted the fact that the demands of our other work was one reason we did not feel that we had the perfect manuscript. Another reason for the delay was that for the past several years, we and a number of our colleagues have been engaged in some very interesting change projects whose findings are just now coming in. These results have improved our understanding about several issues, which have been included in this book. We also have gained new clarity regarding current enigmas about change, which we are sharing here as well.

The title of this book—*Implementing Change: Patterns, Principles, and Potholes*—is fittingly representative of its content. One of the problems in the field of change is that there is no agreement on the meaning of commonly used terms. For example, the word *change* itself can be a noun (e.g., the change that is being attempted), or a verb, (e.g., changing the culture). The word also can be used to represent the whole of a change effort, (e.g., "We have a big change underway!"). The terms *patterns*, *principles*, and *potholes* have been carefully chosen as well. There are patterns in change processes, and most of this book is about describing and naming those patterns. In the study of change, as in the so-called hard sciences, there are a number of points, or principles, on which there is widespread agreement. We certainly do not know all that we should; however, some elements of change are understood and agreed upon by many of us. All of us know full well that "potholes" may be encountered throughout a change process. While too often there is the inclination to give too much attention to these problems, it is foolish to ignore them.

We begin in Chapter 1 by presenting a list of change principles that we believe should be accepted as givens. All of change should not be a surprise. There are certain things about it that we know, and they should not be well-kept secrets. Reading this chapter alone should lead to fewer surprises and more success in your change efforts. Chapters 2 through 10 deal with different patterns of the change process that we and our colleagues have studied. Each chapter presents a basic pattern, construct names for this phenomenon, examples of what it looks like, descriptions of how to measure it, and implications for achieving change success. Each chapter also has a number of purpose-built features that are intended to help you draw connections between what you know now and what we would like you to understand when you are done reading. To help ground the basic pattern being presented, each chapter begins with several quotes, which will probably be familiar to you. The ideas presented in the chapter illustrate how these quotes can be analyzed in terms of their meaning for change process success. To help you focus on some of the key topics in each chapter, a set of Focus Questions is offered near the beginning. Each chapter, except Chapter 11, also has a short case study, or Vignette, that illustrates its pattern in action. To aid in remembering key points, a set of Guiding Principles is presenting following the Summary section in each chapter, except for Chapters 1 and 11. At the end of each chapter are a number of Discussion Questions and Fieldwork Activities designed to bring each of the patterns to life and to provide opportunities for you to test the constructs presented. Each chapter concludes with a reference list for you to consult for more information.

As you will discover quickly, our particular perspective for viewing change, the Concerns-Based Adoption Model or CBAM (pronounced "see-bam"), offers a number of important ways for understanding what change is about, especially as it relates to the people involved. There is a personal side to change, even when it is taking place in organizational settings. Our presentation of CBAM begins in Chapter 3 with the patterns and construct that explains this aspect of change. The chapters then build from the individual to the group to the whole organizational setting. In Chapters 7 and 8, change leadership is examined. In Chapter 10 the topic is the importance of understanding the culture of an organization that is engaged in change. In the last chapter, Chapter 11, we outline a systemic view of change along with examples of how a number of the constructs presented in the earlier chapters can be used simultaneously. We also use these constructs to examine the potential potholes in more depth. As we end the book, we explore some of our current enigmas as well, hoping to entice you into helping us learn by designing your own studies of change.

A large portion of this book was written with the assumption, and the expectation, that it is possible to be proactive in facilitating the change process. However, there are parts of the process that even the change leaders do not control. We call one key component the uncontrollable "mushrooms," which is the topic of Chapter 9. Some change facilitators are skilled at detecting and addressing mushrooms, while others fail to see them at all. Although we think that this chapter will be of particular interest, an important caution is necessary. The chapter on mushrooms comes after eight other chapters, each of which presents a construct that needs to be understood *before* it is possible to explore the dynamics of mushrooms and what can be done about them.

So here it is. The new CBAM book is out! We hope that it will help you improve your understanding of the change process and how to facilitate change in ways that are responsible and beneficial. If you are interested in research, there are plenty of ideas scattered throughout that need to be systematically examined. Let us know what you are thinking of studying and what you learn.

We gratefully acknowledge the help of the following reviewers of this manuscript: Stephen E. Burris, Hope International University; Boyd Dressler, Montana State University–Bozeman; Carolee Hayes, Kaleidoscope Associates; and Robert K. James, Texas A & M University.

Gene E. Hall, Ph.D.
Shirley H. Hord, Ph.D.

PART ONE

The Context for Implementing Change

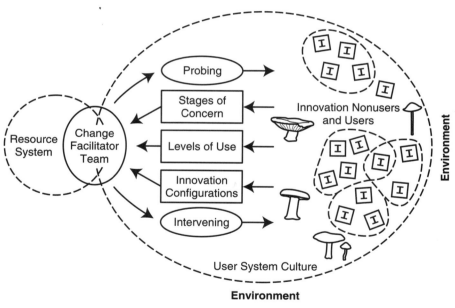

Environment

THE CONCERNS-BASED ADOPTION MODEL

The graphic on the opposite page illustrates the major elements of the Concerns-Based Adoption Model (CBAM): the individuals who implement a change, the change facilitators who provide assistance, and the resource system from which supports are drawn. Within the user system of individuals there is a particular organizational culture. The change facilitators can probe using three CBAM diagnostic tools: Stages of Concern, Levels of Use, and Innovation Configurations. The resulting information can be used to match resources with the needs of the users and thus provide interventions. Surrounding this system are the environmental factors, which are the school, district, community, state, federal, and global forces that influence the change process in any setting.

In Chapters 1 and 2, we describe the setting from which our perspectives on change processes emanate. In essence, Part One is an attempt to set a macro context for change, which is necessary for discussing and examining the dynamics of change in Parts Two to Four.

In Chapter 1, we set forth some basic principles about what is important to know and accept about the process of change. In this way, our perspectives (and biases) are openly and honestly communicated.

Looking at change from a historical perspective in Chapter 2 offers the reader a sense of the perspectives of other researchers and scholars and their approaches to studying, conceptualizing, and constructing theories of change.

In each of the succeeding parts of this book, particular elements of this CBAM diagram are highlighted to indicate the focus of attention for each chapter in that section. In this way, we try to aid the reader in understanding how the discussion of each specific topic relates to the overall picture of change.

1   Implementing Change

Patterns, Themes, and Principles

Here we go again. You know how change is. It is like a pendulum, swinging back and forth.

We know from past experience that it is important to stay the course. It takes time to institutionalize new practices.

This sounds like it would be very good for my students. I think it is worth a try.

After all this research on classrooms, the inescapable conclusion is that building leadership makes a big difference.

Change has to hurt; it never is easy.

When everything comes together right, change is an energizing and very satisfying experience. Just think back to the times in your career that were the most fun.

—Familiar quotations about change

There is an ancient Chinese curse that represents an excellent starting signal for our exploration of change. But before introducing this oft-quoted saying, take a minute to reflect about ancient times. We think of lives being simpler then. Most people lived on small plots of land, grew their own food, and had no education. All they knew about the world beyond the perimeter of their compound was what was told to them through myths, songs, and the occasional wanderer. In China all of society was controlled by the emperor. There was stability, continuity, and predictability not only from year to year, but from generation to generation. In such a society, one of the worst things that you could say to someone was:

May you live in a time of change.

Now, think about life today. Change is everywhere. No one can escape change in his or her work or personal life. We are continuously bombarded with eighteen-second sound bytes about change: *the information age, downsizing, standards, diversity, substance abuse, violence, the economy, the environment, technology, change in schools.* It has gotten to the point where a popular saying is, "The only person who likes change is a baby with a wet diaper!"

As inescapable as change is in today's world, we still tend to hope that change will avoid us personally and professionally. Further, when confronted with change there is a natural tendency to focus on how to defend ourselves from it instead of on how to use and succeed with it.

Comments such as those presented at the beginning of this chapter are typical of those heard when a new change initiative is proposed. Do they sound familiar? Of course they do. Every time we are engaged in change we have similar types of reactions and reflections about past experiences and perceptions of what the new will represent. The fact that all of us have heard such statements indicates that there are certain predictable themes and patterns to change. Perhaps, if we were to study such comments systematically, we could develop descriptions of what typically happens during change, which is the goal of this book.

For the past twenty-five years the authors have been leaders of an international team of researchers studying the change process in schools, colleges, businesses, and government agencies. We have been systematically charting what happens to people and organizations when they are involved in change. Our research approach is different from that of others in a number of ways, including our primary focus on the people at the front lines who have to implement the expected change. Our secondary focus has been on how leaders can and do facilitate change.

The original team for these research efforts came together in the late 1960s at The University of Texas at Austin. From 1970 to 1986 this group studied the change process in schools and universities as part of the agenda of the Research and Development Center for Teacher Education. Along the way researchers from around the United States, Belgium, the Netherlands, Australia, Canada, and several other countries joined in verifying the concepts and extending the research agenda. Now there is an international network of change process researchers who have conducted studies related to the concepts and principles presented here.

FOCUS QUESTIONS

1. Take a few minutes to think about change efforts that you have experienced. What are some of the things that you learned from them?
2. What three to five "principles" of change would you propose?

3. Can teachers initiate and successfully implement change regardless of the amount of administrative support?
4. Does change have to hurt?

Principles of Change

One important result of this long-term collaborative research agenda is that we now can draw some conclusions about what happens when people and organizations are engaged in change. A number of patterns have been observed repeatedly, and some have developed into major themes, or basic *principles,* and we do mean *principles.* As in the so-called "hard" sciences, there is now enough known about some aspects of the change process that we can state a series of principles that will hold true for all cases.

The change principles presented in this chapter are the givens underlying all that is presented in the subsequent chapters. From our point of view, these principles are no longer debatable points, for they summarize predictable aspects of change.

Before introducing selected principles about change, a caveat is needed: each principle is not mutually exclusive, and at first reading some may seem inconsistent with others. Also, these principles do not cover all aspects of change. (Otherwise we would not need the other chapters in this book!) Instead, they address selected aspects of the change process in which the patterns are clear. Acknowledging that these principles are foundational to our way of thinking about change will save you time in trying to discover our implicit assumptions. In addition, understanding them should help you in predicting key aspects of change efforts with which you are engaged.

Also, we need to emphasize that at all levels—the individual, organizational, and system—change is highly complex, multivariate, and dynamic. If it weren't so complicated, it would not be nearly as much fun to study, facilitate, and experience. So let's begin our journey of bringing order to change by introducing a set of principles about change that each of us has understood implicitly, but probably not verbalized. Interestingly, we predict that you will be able to describe personal change experiences in which each of these principles has been ignored or violated. Certainly, your future change efforts can be more successful if these principles are acknowledged.

Change Principle 1: Change Is a Process, Not an Event

The very first assumption in our studies of change in the early 1970s was that change is a process, not an event (Hall, Wallace, & Dossett, 1973). In other words, change is not accomplished by having a one-time announcement by an executive leader, a two-day training workshop for teachers in August, and/or the delivery of the new curriculum/technology to the school. Instead change is a process through which people and organizations move as they gradually come to understand, and become skilled and competent in the use of new ways.

Our research and that of others documents that most changes in education take three to five years to be implemented at a high level (for example, see Hall & Loucks, 1977; Hall & Rutherford, 1976). Further, for each new unit (e.g., school, district, or state) that undertakes the change, the process will take three to five years, to a very large extent. For each new adopting unit, the clock begins at the beginning. There are very few shortcuts. However, the use of the concerns-based approach presented in this book will significantly reduce the time needed to achieve a higher level of implementation. Failure to address key aspects of the change process can either add years to, or even prevent, successful implementation.

Unfortunately, too many policy-makers at all levels refuse to accept the principle that change is a process, not an event, and continue to insist that *their* changes be implemented before their next election, which typically is within two years. This "event mentality" has serious consequences for participants in the change process. For example, the press to make change quickly means that there is no time to learn about and come to understand the new way, nor time to grieve the loss of the old way.

Have you ever realized that grief is a key part of change? Chances are that when people must change, they have to stop doing some things that they know how to do well and in fact like doing, which creates a sense of sadness. What many leaders see as resistance to change may in large part be grief over the loss of favorite and comfortable ways of acting. This personal side of change will be examined in depth in Chapter 4 on the Stages of Concerns about an innovation.

Although many other implications of this first principle will also be developed in subsequent chapters, one that is important to note here has to do with planning for change. The strategic plan for change will look very different depending on whether there is an assumption that change is a process or an event. If the assumption is that change is a process, then the plan for change will be strategic in nature. It will allow at least three to five years for implementation, and will budget the resources needed to support formal training and on-site coaching for the duration of this phase. There will be policies that address the need for multiyear implementation support, and data will be collected each year to inform the planners and further assist implementation in subsequent years.

If the assumption is that change is an event, however, the plan for implementation will be tactical in nature. It will have a short-term focus typically centering around one formal training session for teachers before school begins, no on-site coaching or follow-up, and perhaps a first-year evaluation to see if the new approach is making a significant difference. As will be described in later chapters, one usual consequence of not finding any significant differences in the first or second year of implementation is the mistaken conclusion that the new approach does not work, when in fact there was not enough time and support for implementation.

Examples of an event mentality can be seen also in the formal steps taken in the typical school improvement process. There will be several steps for developing the plan and then a single step for implementing it. If school improvement were being thought of as a process, instead of an event, it would be called school "improving." Such an event mentality was well expressed by one assistant superintendent, who exclaimed in the spring of the first year of implementation, "What do you mean that teachers need more training!? We bought them the books. Can't they read?"

Change Principle 2: There Are Significant Differences in What Is Entailed in Development and Implementation of an Innovation

Development and implementation are two sides of the same coin. Development entails all of the activity related to creating an innovation, while implementation addresses establishing the use of the innovation in adopting sites. Development includes all of the steps and actions involved in creating, testing and packaging an innovation, whereas implementation includes all of the steps and actions involved in learning how to use it. These two halves of the change process equation can be viewed as opposite ends of a balance. As is illustrated in Figure 1.1, the typical pat-

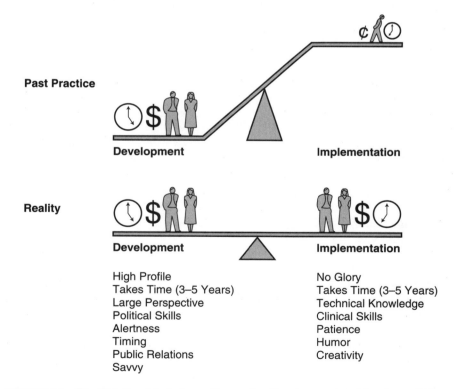

FIGURE 1.1   **The Relationship between Innovation Development and Implementation**

tern is to invest heavily, in terms of people, time, and resources, on the development side. This is true for both relatively simple innovations (such as new curriculum materials), complex innovation bundles, and large-scale policy changes (such as systemic reform). This creates an imbalance, since attention and investment are heavily loaded on the development side, and fails to acknowledge that implementation requires an equal investment of time and money.

However, there are some very important differences in how the development and implementation phases unfold. For example, the style of the change facilitators needs to be different. Change facilitators on the development side tend to be very visible and dynamic, while implementation facilitators need to have the patience to work daily with teachers who are attempting to figure out how to use the innovation.

There are other differences between the development and implementation of change facilitation as well. Leaders on the development side, such as policy-makers, often lose interest once development is done and implementation begins. They are ready to move on to the next initiative, which frequently leads to loss of support for the implementation of the first initiative. By contrast, change facilitators on the implementation side have to have a great deal of patience and persistence. For example, they are frequently required to answer the same question from different individuals and to give each an appropriate response. Their patience is really tested when the same person asks the same question more than once! But to achieve implementation success, a change facilitator must properly deal with each question to prevent small problems from turning into large ones.

Change Principle 3: An Organization Does Not Change until the Individuals within It Change

Although everyone wants to talk about such broad concepts as policy, systems, and organizational factors, successful change starts and ends at the individual level. An entire organization does not change until each member has changed. Another way to say this is that there is an individual aspect to organizational change. Even when the change is introduced to every member of the organization at the same time, the rate of making the change and of developing skill and competence in using it will vary individually. Some people will grasp the new way immediately, while most will need some additional time, and a few will avoid making the change for a very long time. Rogers (1995) calls this third group "laggards." Even when the change is mandated, some individuals will delay implementation. One implication of this principle is that leaders of organizational change processes need to devise ways to anticipate and facilitate change at the individual level.

This principle does not mean that all of the interventions (e.g., on-site coaching or a telephone hot line to address specific questions) in a change process must be addressed at the individual level. Nor does it mean that every individual will be at a different point in the process, for people respond to and implement change, in typical patterns, which will be described in the following chapters. Change process leaders can and should anticipate many of these patterns. Many interventions should be targeted toward subgroups (e.g., by offering in advance principals training in what the change entails), and many others should be aimed at the organization as a whole. Still, since there is an individual element to how the change process unfolds, many of the interventions must be done with and for individuals.

Change Principle 4: Innovations Come in Different Sizes

As this chapter unfolds, we are gradually introducing key terms that will be used in the other chapters and that will add to your understanding of how the change process works. The concept of an *innovation* is one of these. When most people think or talk about change, they focus on what will be changed; in other words, the innovation. But other than being aware that there is an innovation, most leaders do not seem to consider that there are ways to characterize innovations, and that they can vary in the amount of time, resources, and effort required for implementation.

For example, innovations can be either *products*, such as computers, curriculum texts, or assessment techniques, or *processes*, such as constructivist teaching techniques, principles of self-esteem in character education, or student teamwork. Depending on the type of innovation and its characteristics, the change process can require more time and be more resource consuming or relatively quick and simple to implement.

Another important implication of the innovation concept is that change initiatives are not typically centered around a single innovation but rather a bundle of innovations. In other words, several innovations will be frequently masquerading as one. Although a single name may be used—such as magnet schools, inclusion, literacy programs, restructured high schools, and integrated use of technology—each of these innovations in fact is a bundle of smaller innovations. For example, the integrated use of technology in reading and science instruction might entail the use of word processing, spread sheets, e-mail, the World Wide Web, laptops, and CD-ROMs, each an innovation with its own requirements for implementation, training, and user supports.

Size is another important characteristic of innovations. Some are relatively small and simple, such as using a new edition of a standard curriculum text, while others are enormous in terms of their complexities and demands on prospective users. Van Den Berg and Vandenberghe (1986) have proposed the concept of *large scale* to describe very complex school- and system-wide changes. Large-scale innovations require major changes in the roles of teachers, principals, and schools; take five to eight years to implement; and demand specialized training and ongoing consultation. In the United States even larger innovations are implied in the term *systemic reform,* whose goal includes simultaneously changing all parts of curriculum and teaching in an entire state.

One way to keep in mind considerations of the relative size of innovations is the Hall Innovation Category (HiC) Scale, which was created following the example of the Richter scale, which ranks earthquakes in terms of the amount of movement that occurs. The HiC Scale rates innovations by the amount of effort required to achieve successful implementation and the number of changes produced in people, organizations, and systems (see Figure 1.2).

Change Principle 5: Interventions Are the Actions and Events That Are Key to the Success of the Change Process

As people plan and lead change processes, they tend to be preoccupied with the innovation and its use. They often do not think about the various actions and events that they and others take to influence the process, which are known as *interventions*. Training workshops are perhaps the most obvious type of intervention. Although workshops are important, the research studies cited in this book document that many

	Level	Name	Examples
Talking	0	Cruise Control	1950s Teacher in same classroom for many years
	1	Whisper	Pronouncements by officials Commission reports
	2	Tell	New rules and more regulations of old practices
	3	Yell	Prescriptive policy mandates
Thinking	4	Shake	New text Revised curriculum
	5	Rattle	Change principal Team teaching
	6	Roll	Change teacher's classroom Change grade configurations
Transforming	7	Redesign	Evening kindergarten Integrated curriculum
	8	Restructure	Site-based decision making Differentiated staffing
	9	Mutation	Teachers and principals belong to the same union Changing the role of school boards Coordinated services
	10	Reconstitution	Local constitutional convention *Glasnost*

FIGURE 1.2 The HiC Scale of the Relative Size of Innovations

From *Examining the Relative Size of Innovations: A Scale and Implications* (pp. 24–26) by G. E. Hall, 1993, Greeley, CO: College of Education, University of Northern Colorado.

other kinds of interventions are significant also, and that some are even more crucial to achieving change success!

Interventions come in different sizes. Interestingly, the most important interventions are the little ones, which most leaders forget to do or forget about having done. When change is successful it is the quantity of the little things that makes the final difference. One of the major types of small interventions is what we call the "one-legged interview." One frequent opportunity for one-legged interviews occurs when a teacher and a principal meet in the corridor. If they do not talk or if they have a social chat, this does not count as an innovation-related intervention. However, if the principal or teacher initiates a brief discussion about the innovation, then it is a one-legged interview type of intervention.

We use the name "one-legged" to indicate that these interventions are brief (most people can't stand on one leg very long), since both the teacher and the principal probably have to be somewhere else when the next bell rings. Yet a moment was taken to talk about the teacher's involvement with the innovation. The research reported in later chapters consistently indicates that teachers are more successful with change in schools where there are more one-legged interviews.

We will talk more about one-legged interviews in Chapter 6 on interventions. Here the point is that it is critical to distinguish between the concepts of innovations and interventions. Change process leaders tend to think only about the innovation and not to think sufficiently about interventions in terms of an overall plan for and during the unfolding of the change process; and many fail to appreciate the value of the little interventions.

Change Principle 6: Although Both Top-Down and Bottom-Up Change Can Work, a Horizontal Perspective Is Best

People seem to prefer to maintain a vertical perspective when thinking about organizations and how they work. For example, teachers see themselves as being at the "bottom" of the organization, with principals and superintendents at the "top." Policy-makers such as state legislators and members of Congress are viewed as being still higher up. Currently, most changes are initiated from the top, thus the phrase "top-down." Increasingly this is the case as more and more mandates are passed down by federal, state, and local policy-makers. Even the moves toward block grants and devolution are directed from above. Even though there is an abysmal track record of top-down initiatives succeeding at the local level, the preferred mode continues to be top-down change.

Occasionally, either through a glimmer of understanding or an attempt to be politically correct, there will be talk of making change from the "bottom-up." The implication here is that people at the bottom—the teachers—should have a role in shaping the change process, since they are closer to the action. But ironically, even bottom-up change frequently tends to be directed from the top! An example of this

TABLE 1.1 The Policy-to-Practice Continuum

Federal	State	District	School	Classroom
President	Governor	Superintendent	Principal	Teacher
Secretary of Education	Commissioner of Education	Board of Education	Site Council	
Congress	Legislature			

oxymoron is the state policies that mandate that all schools will have "site-based" councils. In most instances, however, the state system is not restructured so that it too operates with a similar council that includes representatives from the various constituencies. Bottom-up change has not worked well for several reasons: because the top rarely relinquishes control in those areas that are most important; because the bottom has neither the ideas nor the time to initiate change; and/or because the top does not support the change efforts of the bottom.

For change to succeed, a major shift in thinking by *all* the participants is needed. The vertical paradigm must be replaced with a horizontal perspective in which all of the actors are viewed as being on the same plane, with none higher or lower than any others. One way to represent this is with the Policy-to-Practice Continuum outlined in Table 1.1. Rather than viewing the education system as a vertical top-down or bottom-up world, all of the participants need to recognize that they are members of *one* system, and that the only way that change is going to succeed is if everyone does his or her job well and learns to trust that members at other points along the continuum can and will do their jobs well.

Trust is a key to system change that appears to be in short supply. Currently it seems as if everyone at each point across the system not only does not trust and respect persons at other points along the continuum, but also is cynical about the intents of those other people. The metaphor of looking down the railroad tracks can be used to illustrate this problem and the needed solution. As is illustrated in Figure 1.3, when you look down railroad tracks, the two rails do seem to come together to a point in the far distance. Up close you can see the rust on the rails, and the weeds and trash on the rail bed. As you look farther and farther away, these problems become less obvious.

Metaphorically, the same thing happens to participants at different points along the Policy-to-Practice Continuum. Teachers can see their end of the continuum very well, but they do not recognize what work is like at other points along the continuum. They think that district superintendents and state policy-makers have easy jobs, "They are given cars, and all they do is mandate things for teachers to do; they have no idea what life is like in the classroom." Policy-makers at the other end of the continuum have a similarly limited view. They feel harried and pressured, and do not see themselves as being able to influence much of anything. They see the

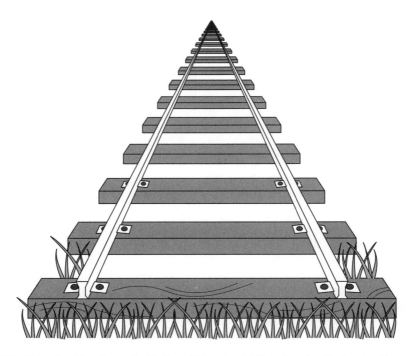

FIGURE 1.3   Looking down the Railroad Tracks: A Metaphor for Understanding What One Sees Depends on Where One Looks

complexity of their work and believe that no one understands their approach to education. Many of them view teachers as having the easy job. As can be seen in these simplistic examples, two important pieces are missing in the vertical (top-down/bottom-up) way of thinking: (1) a lack of accurate knowledge and understanding about the jobs of people at different places across the continuum; and (2) an absence of mutual trust and respect.

In summary, currently there is a self-centeredness of thinking and action as well as a distrust of others among members at each point along the Policy-to-Practice Continuum. Meaningful change is not going to be possible until people at *all* points come to understand the whole system and begin to trust members at other points. In addition, those at each spot along the continuum need to focus on doing their own jobs well, and to stop trying to force accountability in members elsewhere in the system, especially when they themselves have limited knowledge of how other parts of the system work. Through some sort of systemwide community-building processes, respect and trust must be developed for all along the Policy-to-Practice Continuum, together with an understanding that the system will not change until everybody along the continuum does his or her part.

Change Principle 7: Administrator Leadership Is Essential to Long-Term Change Success

A central theme of advocates for bottom-up change is that those nearest the action have the best ideas of how to accomplish the change. There are many implementors who believe that they do not need any involvement from or with those above them. But here again, the findings of research and experience argue for a different conclusion.

Many of us have had first-hand experience with trying to implement some sort of innovative effort from the bottom. A classic example for the co-authors of this book was when we first worked together as teacher education faculty members. We were hired to create and implement an experimental teacher education program based on the teacher concerns model of Frances Fuller (1969). We and several others formed a multidisciplinary faculty team that developed and operated an experimental teacher education program that was truly an innovation bundle, one that included innovations such as professor teaming, an all-day blocked schedule for students, early field experiences, and a partnership of principals and teachers. In short, it incorporated many of the innovations that are found in what are now called "professional development schools."

Although the teacher education program was very successful and became well known nationally and internationally, it died after five years. It did not become the regular teacher education program at our university, nor did it have much direct influence on the traditional teacher education program.

We relate an anecdote on pp. 16–17 to illustrate several of the principles about change that we have described above and to document the importance of Principle 7. As faculty, we were at the proverbial bottom of the organization. As long as we had the energy, we were able to work collaboratively to develop and implement an innovation bundle. Although that bundle turned out to be successful, over time our faculty colleagues in the regular programs and the administration of the university did not actively support the continuation of the bundle nor the implementation of any of the specific innovations into the regular programs. Without their long-term support, the innovation withered and was forgotten.

The point here is not to analyze what we might have done to garner more administrator support (which we will do in other chapters). Rather, our goal is to use a first-hand experience that shows that while the "bottom" may be able to launch and sustain an innovative effort for several years, if administrators do not engage in ongoing active support, it is more than likely that the change effort will die.

In many ways Principle 7 is a corollary of Principle 6, since everyone along the Policy-to-Practice Continuum has a role to play if change is going to be successful. Yes, teachers and professors can create and implement new practices. Yes, administrators have to do things on a day-to-day basis that are supportive. (Remember those one-legged-interviews?) Administrators also have to secure the necessary infrastructure changes and long-term resource supports if use of an innovation is to continue indefinitely. And finally, yes, policy-makers need to design polices that legitimize the infrastructure changes and innovative practices and encourage the continued use of the innovation.

Change Principle 8: Mandates Can Work

Principle 5 introduced the concept of interventions and gave special attention to a category of small interventions called one-legged interviews/conversations. Among the number of other types of interventions that will be described in later chapters, one of the more common is known as a *strategy*. A mandate is one kind of strategy that is used widely. Although mandates are continually criticized as being ineffective because of their top-down orientation, they can work quite well. With a mandate the priority is clear, and there is an expectation that the innovation will be implemented. The mandating process falls down, however, when the only time that the change process is supported is at the initial announcement of the mandate. When a mandate is accompanied by continuing communication, ongoing training, on-site coaching, and time for implementation, it can operate quite well. As with most change strategies, the mandate has gotten a bad name not because the strategy itself is flawed but because it is not supported with the other interventions that are necessary.

Change Principle 9: The School Is the Primary Unit for Change

Although we have and will continue to emphasize the importance of understanding the dynamics of individuals in change, the key organizational unit for making change successful is the school. The school's staff and leaders will make or break any change effort, regardless of whether the change is initiated from the inside or outside. However, the school is not an island, but rather part of a district, state, and federal system of education. The school can and must do a lot by itself, but it also needs to move in concert with and be supported by the other components of the system.

   Note the assertion that schools need outside support. Change is a complex, dynamic, and resource-consuming endeavor. No single organization, be it a school or a national corporation, is likely to have all the expertise and resources needed to succeed in change. As will be emphasized in later chapters, *external* change facilitators, as well as supports from other parts of the system, are necessary. This is why the concept of "local control" does a disservice to organizations such as schools. Change processes are easier and chances of sustained success are increased as the school staff understands more about how to use external resources and as those external to the school recognize the importance of their roles in facilitating each school in achieving change success.

   Everyone, teachers and principals in a school and personnel in the district office, must consider and view how a school advances as a change process unfolds. Many of the same interventions, such as training teachers (and principals) in their roles with the innovation, can in fact be made throughout a district, especially during the first year of implementation. However, by the second year different schools will be moving at different rates and will have different change successes and challenges. Thus at least some of the key interventions will need to be targeted specifically for each school.

Change Principle 10: Facilitating Change Is a Team Effort

In this book we will emphasize repeatedly the importance of facilitating the change process, which means that there must be ongoing leadership for change to be successful. In Chapter 7 we will describe different Change Facilitator Styles and the significance of each. Embedded in all of this and in many of the principles presented above is the core belief that change is a team effort. Just as in Principle 6 we described the importance of developing trust across the Policy-to-Practice Continuum, and in Principle 9 we stressed that no school is an island, we argue here that collaboration is also necessary among those responsible for leading change efforts.

Although in Principle 7 we described the crucial role of the school principal, we want to emphasize that many others also have a responsibility to help change processes be successful. Indeed, other administrators play important roles, as do front-line users and nonusers of the innovation. Teachers, for example, play a critical leadership role in whether or not change is successful. We really are in this phenomenon together, and all must help to facilitate the change process.

Change Principle 11: Appropriate Interventions Reduce the Challenges of Change

Several contemporary writers have stated in one way or another that change is painful, and assert that this pain must be endured as a natural part of the change process. They might leave you feeling that only the masochist likes change. But this does not have to be the case. *If* the process is facilitated well, change can be fun, and it certainly does not have to hurt or even be dreaded. Of course, there are moments of frustration and times of grieving over what is being lost. However, if there is major pain in change, chances are strong that the leadership for the change process has not understood what is entailed and required to facilitate the process. In each of the following chapters, basic concepts, measures, research findings, and case examples are introduced and used to describe ways of more effectively facilitating change. If these concepts are understood and used well, there should be little pain and large gains in change.

Change Principle 12: The Context of the School Influences the Process of Change

Considering the school as the unit of change, we can think of it as having two important dimensions that affect individuals' and the organization's change efforts:

1. The *physical features,* such as the size and arrangement of the facility, and the resources, policies, structures and schedules that shape the staff's work
2. The *people factors*, which include the attitudes, beliefs, and values of the individuals involved as well as the relationships and norms that guide the individuals' behavior

An increasing body of literature on the influence of workplace culture has evolved from both educational writers who study school improvement and from members of the corporate sector who are concerned with quality and its relationship to profits. Interestingly, these two rather disparate worlds share common views about desirable organizational conditions that result in effective staff performance and customer satisfaction/high-level learner outcomes.

In schools that have created such organizational conditions, the staff collectively reflects on its work with students and assesses its influence on student results. In this collegial inquiry, the staff may identify areas for improvement. Interestingly, addressing these improvement targets begins with the staff's identification of what *they* must learn in order to more effectively help students become more successful learners. This community of "professional learners" (Hord, 1997) embodies individuals who value change and who seek change in order to increase their efficacy as teachers. Having such a learning-oriented staff can contribute profoundly to how the change process unfolds and ultimately succeeds in a given school.

One attribute of these change-ready staffs is shared and supportive leadership. Such a community demands a sharing principal who is working participatively with the teachers in their quest for high-quality learning.

In Chapter 10, we briefly review the literature and describe additional characteristics of these professional learning community schools, whose culture embodies those conditions that are conducive to and supportive of change. The operationalization of these factors in a school makes a significant difference in the staff's concerns about change and in how the staff moves to higher quality implementation of change. The Vignette below presents a brief change story as a way to summarize what these change principles are like in action.

VIGNETTE

A Districtwide Change Initiative: Principles Addressed, Principles Missed

During the writing of this book, one of the authors was invited to conduct a CBAM training workshop for a medium-size school district. While the district leaders were facilitating change in ways that were consistent with most of the principles outlined in this chapter, several of the principles were being violated, with predictable results.

The district teachers had been engaged in implementing a well-known model of teaching for three years (Principle 1). This initiative was a districtwide mandate of the superintendent (Principles 6 and 8). The teachers, as well as the district office curriculum and staff development personnel, had received extensive training in the use of the teaching model (Principles 3 and 5).

As in most school districts, a number of other change initiatives and mandates were being advanced in the district at the same time. For example, each school was engaged with school improvement plans, annual standardized testing, inclusion, technology, a new mathematics curriculum, and the elementary schools were engaged in restructuring the primary grades (Principle 4). Ironically, even with all of these change initiatives at work in the schools, the principals were only allowed to leave their schools for training in the teaching model; they had not received training in what any of the other innovations entailed. The change facilitation training was done with all the central office professionals, but no principals (Principle 7). The teachers received extensive training through workshops, but there were no specialized interventions to help teachers individually (Principles 3 and 5).

Further, although implementation of the teaching model had been underway for three years, there were no efforts by the district leadership to adjust change-facilitating interventions on a school-by-school basis. All schools were being treated in the same way (Principle 9).

As could be predicted, there was an undercurrent of talk about how too much attention had been given to the teaching model and not enough to a number of the other priorities. There also was dismay over the fact that principals were not permitted to leave their buildings for training in how to help teachers implement any of the other innovations.

Three principles were not supported in this situation: Principle 6, which emphasizes trust; Principle 9, which argues that each school be seen as a unit of change; and Principle 10, which underlines the need for a team to facilitate change. As a result, the teaching model was being used well in some classrooms and some schools but not in others.

What was needed next was a process that would help all of the system's professionals—the district staff, principals, and teachers—realize that they were part of the same team and that they all had role responsibilities. The verticality of the superintendent's centralized directives was not allowing for a horizontal policy-to-practice perspective to develop. The need for each role group to do its own jobs well was being eroded. There was training of some, but the sense of a team effort was not being developed. The key to forming a horizontal/teaming approach was missed by prohibiting principals from participating in learning about what teachers were doing with the other innovations and about how to use change-facilitating concepts. An additional change leadership objective was missed by not assuring that all district change facilitators developed a common language about the change process and ways to facilitate it. A shared language gives those who have the opportunity to facilitate change a better understanding of how to do so, which means that teachers will have more success in implementing the various innovations that have been introduced.

1. If Principles 6, 9, and 10 had been in place in this district, what specific differences would they have made?
2. How would you facilitate the next steps in this district?
3. Think about a systemwide change process you have experienced. Which change principles were present and absent? Which, in your opinion, were key to its success and/or failure?

Summary

The main reason for writing this book was to describe what has been learned about facilitating the change process. This knowledge, if used well, can reduce, if not avoid altogether, the apprehension and dread associated with change, and lead to successful results. The primary source of the concepts, research findings, and experiences presented is our work and that of our colleagues with the Concerns-Based Adoption Model (CBAM). In this chapter we have laid the foundation by summarizing a set of change principles that represent some of the predictable patterns about change in organizational settings. A very important next step is to develop an understanding and appreciation of the personal side of change, which we will address with the concept of Stages of Concern. The fact that leaders do make a difference will be addressed through our research on Change Facilitator Style. The leaders' actions, known as interventions, will be reviewed as well. Don't forget that the change process we are describing is taking place inside an organizational setting. The people in each organization have constructed a culture based on values and norms that represent the beginning context for change. Consideration of this culture will be explored as well.

We will constantly be asking you to think about situations that you are experiencing and about how you can facilitate change. This is done throughout to help you tie the various ideas together and to learn how to make them useful in your setting.

We are living in a time of change. But rather than viewing it as a painful curse, let's figure out how it works, how to facilitate the process, and how to learn from our experiences. To accomplish these outcomes, the following chapters are organized around key change process concepts. Each chapter includes research findings and examples of how the concepts can be used to facilitate change. Occasionally we point out areas where more research is needed. The primary purpose, though, is to introduce ways to understand how the change process works, and how to be most effective in influencing and facilitating that process.

DISCUSSION QUESTIONS

1. With which of the change principles presented in this chapter do you strongly agree? With which do you strongly disagree? Why?

2. Does change have to hurt?

3. Principle 6 argues for a horizontal perspective across the Policy-to-Practice Continuum, in which there is trust and understanding among the various role groups. Describe what you know about what members of other role groups value and understand about change. How have these perspectives affected the change process for you and your colleagues?

4. Describe a change process that you have had or are experiencing. Point out where the different principles fit. Do any of them explain why certain things have gone well and what is, or was, problematic?

FIELDWORK ACTIVITIES

1. Interview a person in a leadership role in a school district office. Ask him or her to propose three to five principles they have learned about change. How do their principles compare with those presented in this chapter?

2. Select a school and a major innovation that it is implementing. Make a chart of the leaders of the change process inside and outside the school. What types of expertise does each bring to the process?

3. Review all the available information about a change process that failed. Which of the principles outlined in this chapter were in place? Which were not? Does your analysis lead you to suggest additional change principles? If so, what are they?

REFERENCES

Fullan, M. G. (1993). *Change forces: Probing the depths of educational reform.* Bristol, PA: Falmer Press.

Fuller, F. F. (1969). Concerns of teachers: A developmental conceptualization. *American Educational Research Journal, 6*(2), 207–226.

Hall, G. E., & Loucks, S. F. (1977). A developmental model for determining whether the treatment is actually implemented. *American Educational Research Journal, 14*(3), 263–276.

Hall, G. E., & Rutherford, W. L. (1976). Concerns of teachers about implementing team teaching. *Educational Leadership, 34*(3), 227–233.

Hall, G. E., Wallace, R. C., & Dossett, W. A. (1973). *A developmental conceptualization of the adoption process within educational institutions* (Report No. 3006). Austin: The University of Texas at Austin, Research and Development Center for Teacher Education. (ERIC Document Reproduction Service No. ED 095 126)

Hord, S. M. (1997). *Professional learning communities: Communities of continuous inquiry and improvement.* Austin: Southwest Educational Development Laboratory.

Rogers, E. M. (1995). *Diffusion of innovations* (4th ed.). New York: Free Press.

Van Den Berg, R. M., & Vandenberghe, R. (1986). *Large-scale change and school improvement: Dilemmas and solutions.* Leuven, Belgium: Acco.

ADDITIONAL READINGS

Fullan, M. G. (1991). *The new meaning of educational change.* New York: Teachers College Press.

Reigeluth, C. M. & Garfinkle, R. J. (1994). *Systemic change in education.* Englewood Cliffs, NJ: Educational Technology Publications.

Sarason, S. B. (1996). *Revisiting "The culture of the school and the problem of change."* New York: Teachers College Press.

CHAPTER

2

Examining Initiatives and Innovations

A Historical Perspective

I am so excited—inquiry-oriented process science that I began teaching in the sixties has come into vogue again. This time it is [called] the constructivist approach to science!

Now, let's see, help me to understand how today's mastery learning differs from competency-based education of some years ago.

My principal reported that our district will drop our effective schools/school improvement approach and move into standards-based education.

It's been said that practices in education swing back and forth like a pendulum. What's hot today is not hot tomorrow. New bandwagons beckon policy-makers and educators to jump on for the latest "fads" (as some are irreverently named) that will cure the problems faced by educators at all levels of the system.

While there may be a back-and-forth rhythm to the pendulum of education practices, we believe there also is a spiral. A change is adopted, tried out, and subsequently rejected—only to cycle around and be readopted some years later in a "new and improved" form. There is growth and new understanding reflected in each swing of the pendulum. For example, the competency-based education of the 1970s in many ways returned as outcomes-based education of the 1990s. An area of increased understanding reflected in standards-based education is the constructivist approach to teaching and learning.

Further, there seem to be patterns to each cycling of new practices, with each promising to improve schools. For example, in the 1960s there was a focus on developing discipline-specific curricular programs for use by individual teachers: math and science were emphasized especially, but language arts and social studies were also included. The 1970s saw a quantitative research and development focus on teacher behaviors and teaching strategies that were associated with increased student learning as measured by standardized tests. The direct instruction model (Brophy & Good, 1974; Brophy & Evertson, 1986) was preeminent. In the 1980s attention shifted to effectiveness and improvement of the whole school as the unit for change (Lezotte, 1984; Lezotte, 1986; Sparks, 1993), and in the 1990s the cry was for systemic change (Fuhrman, 1994).

This never-ending quest to improve schools is supported by theoreticians, researchers, policy-makers, practitioners, parents, and the business community, all of whom have a stake in educating our children. As the quotes at the beginning of this chapter suggest, the array of improvement possibilities—past and present—can be quite baffling. Therefore, we believe it is useful to explore briefly some of the kinds of changes that have been offered to schools and school districts during the past thirty years or so, and consider why there has been this continuing search for what programs, pieces of programs, people, or parts should be changed in order to increase effectiveness. The focus questions guide this review.

FOCUS QUESTIONS

1. How has the perspective on recommended changes for schools differed over time?
2. How have analysts and policy-makers advised and expanded the size or scope of improvement efforts?
3. How unique are current educational improvement initiatives?
4. Why have innovations and initiatives largely failed to improve the effectiveness of schools?

How Changes for Schools Have Evolved

Any reader of educational journals will discover a plethora of articles describing recommended changes for schools and districts. Such articles report about how the changes can benefit various clients of the schools, and why schools should adopt them. These changes frequently include program changes, such as curriculum, process changes, such as instructional strategies or discipline procedures, and governance or structural changes, such as shared decision-making. Whether program, process, or other kind of change, the particular time period in which the change is introduced seems to shape its philosophical perspective as either *behavioral, cognitive,* or *socially responsible.*

The Behavioral Perspective

Behavioral objectives (Mager, 1962; Richey, 1996) were the hallmark of curricular programs and instructional processes of the 1970s. Prospective teachers were coached ad nauseum by education departments on developing lesson plans that were initiated by a statement identifying the specific behaviors that students should exhibit. The assertion was that the only way to know what students had learned was to observe specified behaviors. These statements were to assess the degree to which students were able to name, order, distinguish, and "behave" in specified ways. Being able to demonstrate particular behaviors was both the objective and the accountability measure of teaching.

During the 1970s (and in some cases continuing today, we might add), this objective and concrete means for defining learning provided a relatively straightforward way to test students and to identify which students were successful and which were not. In this period, students were grouped and separated into college-bound and otherwise. This separation of students who could use "their head well" and others who could use "their hands well" was a source of considerable consternation to some educators. But to economists and American business, the scheme fit the need for supplying the workers needed in the industrial age of the time.

Thus, new programs were created that fit this behavioral model, whether it was a science curriculum based on a learning hierarchy, wherein students were to be able to classify ten objects in three groups based on their attributes, or a home economics course, wherein students were to be able to classify ten swatches of fabric based on their fiber content. In the main, learning was expressed as the acquisition of describable behavior. It was in the next period that creating knowledge and applying knowledge became goals for student learning.

The Cognitive Perspective

Because the United States in the early 1980s was moving into the postindustrial information age, it was deemed important that students learn to use, process, and apply knowledge in meaningful ways. Thus, expectations for student outcomes began to focus on higher level skills: critical thinking and problem solving, for example. This focus drew the attention of program developers who began to design programs and processes that would engage students at all ages in cognitive-oriented learning, such as the Core Knowledge Curriculum (Hirsch, 1993) and Paideia (Carter, Ensrud, & Holden, 1997; Potter, 1996).

A particular emphasis developed around students' ability to create knowledge and meaning for themselves in what was known as a constructivist approach to learning. Instead of one right answer, students were encouraged to create—construct—their own understanding and meaning. In addition, it was hypothesized that students would learn to learn with less dependence on teachers. While this idea had cycled earlier in the curriculum heyday of hands-on, inquiry-approach science and math reform in the early 1960s, such a major change had not become widely used in classrooms. However, new demands from the marketplace and from international comparisons in the 1980s and 1990s fueled this perspective as a means to prepare all citizens to participate in a high technology society.

If the United States were to regain its position of preeminence in the global economy, it was argued, its students had to become creative, inventive thinkers and problem-solvers. But another national concern began to be expressed, known as social responsibility.

The Socially Responsible Perspective

The increasing pluralism of the nation has been paralleled by the increasing deterioration of productive relationships between many sectors of our society. Like our sociological environment, our physical environment is also in need of attention, and in the early 1990s a new set of programs for schools were being explicitly developed and recommended to focus on such matters as caring for the environment, caring for others, appreciating diverse cultures, and providing community service. Multicultural curricula and cooperative learning strategies are part of the recommended changes now deemed needed for students to become more empathetic world citizens—a recently articulated learner outcome. Community projects and service learning are programs that engage students in sharing and working for the collective good, and in supporting others less fortunate or less able.

This quick review across the history page of school change perspectives shows quite clearly how innovations and policy initiatives for schools reflect the economic and social milieu in which they exist. As conditions in the nation change, so also do the views about how schools should change. However, there are other factors, such as, size or scope, that can be considered in analyzing the patterns in educational change, and a number of analysts have done this.

The Escalating Scope of School Change

The previous section of this chapter examined the *what* of change in schools, vis-à-vis various perspectives. This section looks again at what changes to make, in this case by applying the variable of scope of the change.

Waves of Reform

Just as Sputnik served as the rallying point for demands for change in schools in the late 1950s, the publication of *A Nation at Risk* (National Commission on Excellence in Education (1983) catalyzed a renewal of demands in the 1980s. Various writers (Cuban, 1988; Raywid, 1990) refer to two, three, or four waves of reform beginning in 1982 and continuing to the present. The exact number of reform periods or their boundary years is not important. What is interesting is the trend toward an increasingly broader target for change.

Raywid (1990) labeled an early reform wave in the 1980s that advised repairing the existing school or district a period of "pseudo-reforms." The call was for quick fixes that were cosmetic in approach—shifting schedules, increasing graduation requirements.

The second wave targeted classroom practices—curriculum and instructional strategies—to increase student achievement. The classroom teacher was expected to adopt new curriculum and instructional practices. Raywid (1990) named this type of change "incremental reform," and Cuban (1988) called it "first order change." These changes, again, were designed to fix the existing school and its educational program by changing some of its components. These reforms were characterized by engaging in widespread data collection and analysis, and by planning for change; however, few plans moved beyond the written page.

Because these efforts (mostly never implemented, or implemented poorly) were judged to be less than fruitful, it was thought that changes of greater magnitude would be more successful. Concluding that schools had failed also because of their bureaucratic structure, policy-makers argued that effective reform would necessitate change in the fundamental design of schools and how they operate, thus "restructuring" (Raywid) or "second order change" (Cuban) was the focus. These ever-expanding changes targeted the decentralization of power and authority to the building level and within it to teachers and parents. A widespread example was the innovation of site-based decision-making.

In the late 1980s and early 1990s, new policy-maker targets again emerged because the restructuring of the school was seen as insufficient. The new cycle called for systemwide changes, or in other words, systemic reform. New proposals suggested the "need to alleviate the environmental factors that contribute to the failure of school children and called for redesigning the fundamental structure of schooling" and other services (Bjork, 1993, p. 248). This model envisioned an integration of service delivery systems, including schools, health, and community organizations, to provide services to children and families. At the federal level, one push was for state systemic initiatives. It was believed that such comprehensive models would fundamentally change how schools operate and would have wide (i.e., systemic) impact.

Policy Approaches to Change

In 1992 Sashkin and Egermeier conducted an analysis of the history of policy approaches to school change and identified four. The first was "fix the parts" approach that involved introducing and adopting specific innovations such as curricular programs and instructional practices. This approach was viewed as an exchange of new products (curriculum) or processes (instruction) for old.

Sashkin and Egermeier termed the second approach "fix the people." Training and development were provided to educational personnel to change their practices/behaviors, attitudes, values, and beliefs.

In the third approach—"fix the school"—the school (rather than programs or people) was seen as the unit of change. A school improvement team would guide the school in needs analysis, solution identification, and plans for change. This approach has been widely used throughout the nation.

Sashkin and Egermeier concluded, after analyzing these three approaches, that successful change had not been reached, but that a fourth approach, which they called "fix the system" or restructuring, could do it. Resonating compatibly with the reform waves described earlier, these four approaches range in scope or magnitude from isolated parts to whole system views. There appears to be a trend of wide agreement, especially from writers promoting restructuring, that bigger is better and that if the target for change is sufficient in scope, reform will be successful and schools will be improved. We suspect that before long the pendulum will swing once again to increasing attention on what occurs in individual classrooms.

Much Ado about Changes

During the past several decades, as noted above, a continuing series of changes have been advocated for schools. School districts and state departments of education have directed schools to be involved in particular educational improvement strategies—effective schools process, strategic planning, outcomes-based education (OBE), and state-wide testing, to name a few. Federal legislation has encouraged the adoption and implementation of large-scale changes such as inclusion and comprehensive school reform. Local campuses and school districts are also encouraged to adopt practices imported from the corporate sector, such as site-based management (SBM) and total quality management (TQM).

The abundant possibilities and continuing cycles/waves of changes in the types and levels of advocated changes have been confusing and frustrating for school practitioners. Committed to providing the best possible education to their students, they read and attend conferences and training institutes to learn about SBM, TQM, and a host of other new offerings. But they find it difficult to determine what to bring to the school that will fit its needs and that will be compatible with changes already underway in addition to those mandated by a higher authority. They also realize, since the historical record is so clear, that within a year or two, a new direction will be announced.

Integrating the various initiatives into a coherent vision and plan for improvement has been especially challenging. To support schools' choices of restructuring and reform efforts, an analysis to demonstrate similarities of initiatives, in terms of philosophy and operation, was undertaken by a subgroup of the directors of the national LEAD (Leadership in Educational Administration Development) centers (National LEADership Network Study Group on Restructuring Schools, 1993). This work produced some interesting insights; an early analysis resulted in a matrix (Table 2.1) that permits comparison of five popular initiatives on eight factors selected from Deming's (1982) principles of quality.

TABLE 2.1 Factors Associated with Effective Schools, Site-Based Management, Strategic Planning, Outcomes-Based Education, and Total Quality Management

	Innovations and Initiatives				
Factor	Effective Schools	SBM	Strategic Planning	OBE	TQM
Constancy of purpose	■		■	■	■
Customer-driven focus	■			■	■
Counting	■		■	■	■
Culture	■	■			■
Collegial leadership	■	■	■		■
Decentralization		■			■
Comprehensive					■
Continuous improvement			■	■	■

Note: From *Total Quality Management: A Fad or Fit with Other Educational Initiatives* by J. G. Burnham, S. M. Hord, & L. Roberts, (1992). Paper presented at the Governor's Conference on TQM in Education, Houston.

The matrix can be used as a diagnostic filter to examine the properties of each of the various initiatives and the properties that give a particular initiative added value over others. The factors, briefly defined, are

Constancy of purpose: Organizational commitment to exceeding clients' needs in an environment where all persons work to move the school or district in an identified direction for the long term

Customer-driven focus: Identification of clients' needs and a continuous focus on satisfying those needs

Counting: Utilization of tools and processes by all persons in the organization in order to solve problems and make decisions based on data rather than on opinions, feelings, or yesterday's myths

Culture: Shared understandings and ways of working in an organization, representing the norms, attitudes, and beliefs of the organization

Collegial leadership: Cooperation and teamwork by all people across all divisions of the organization in order to solve problems and pursue quality improvement by all employees

Decentralization: Empowerment of those nearest the action to make decisions for improvement and to solve problems of quality

Continuous improvement: Commitment to ongoing improvement and refinement of services and products for clients, based on review of the system at all times.

This matrix, of course, represents but *one* interpretation of the perceived attributes of these five initiatives. It does, however, provide a means for practitioners and policy-makers to examine programs or processes in order to ascertain their common and unique features, and the contribution each can make to change and improvement. The features of other innovations could be similarly compared on a chart that could then be used as a tool for making decisions about innovation adoption.

In a comparable analysis, Lesley (1993) examined seven educational improvement initiatives that were quite visible in the professional press and found them similar to each other and to the factors found in TQM. She noted the congruence of effective schools correlates with quality factors. For example, in Henry Levin's Accelerated Schools model she found a "unity of purpose" and ongoing examination of data for stock-taking consistent with Deming's (1982) constancy of purpose and use of data for decision-making. Lesley also concluded that a staff's collaboratively developed "covenant" serves as Carl Glickman's League of Professional Schools' constancy of purpose. Further, schools involved in these programs are required to collaboratively develop a charter to identify their decision-making system and commit to critical study of their schools.

Lesley reviewed William Glasser's Quality Schools, which are based on encouraging self-assessment (with elimination of fear and coercion) and supported by leaders' collaborative decision making to reach the desired outcome of self-directing students. Other models (Ted Sizer's Coalition of Essential Schools, John Champlin's Outcomes-Driven Developmental model, Phil Schlechty's Twenty-First Century Schools, and James Comer's School Development Program) were also analyzed by Lesley, who found significant similarities to the programs noted above and to those reviewed in the matrix. It appears reasonably easy to find points of confluence among the streams of school reform initiatives. Study and analysis to identify these points could aid practitioners and policy-makers in understanding and planning for change more effectively. (For further information about these seven models, see the Additional Readings at the end of this chapter.)

But understanding and articulating *what* to change is one thing; understanding and managing *how* to change is quite another. It is this last issue to which the rest of this book is devoted, and a few words about it are appropriate at this time.

Implementation Is the Issue

Abundant rhetoric has been, continues to be, and probably in the future will be given to the reform, renewal, and restructuring of schools to attain better results. Despite all the focus on structures and strategies and other features of schools that could be changed, little attention has been given to the most powerful factor: people. What change is really about is *people* and their implementation of new practices in their classrooms, schools, school districts, and states.

Change is not only, however, about the implementors—those who will change their practices—but also about those who will facilitate the implementors in doing so.

It is quite clear from the disciplined research on change and from accounts of successful school change efforts, that ongoing, well-crafted facilitation must be present for implementing identified programs and practices, either small or systemic in scope. The skilled change facilitator helps people become ready for implementation and change through a personalized approach, and creates a context in which change flourishes.

What form the implementation facilitation should take and who can do it are two vital questions that are addressed in the remainder of this book. A third, very important consideration is the context. Classrooms and schools have an identifiable context in which teaching and learning take place—and in which change and improvement thrive or die. The issue of context and culture is addressed in Chapter 10.

All can agree that increased student gains is the ultimate goal of school improvement endeavors. However, for students to benefit from any new program or practice, the innovation must first be in operation in each and every classroom. As noted, new practices require change in peoples' behavior as well as in their understandings. Thus, a change effort must be humanely oriented and must have a supportive context—both of which require attention by knowledgeable and skilled facilitators, which so frequently has been absent. Because change facilitation is so often lacking, the typical assessment of the change effort is that the selected innovation was poor and thus should be rejected. Such judgments continue to contribute to the decades-old practice of rejecting changes before they've been implemented, leading to the next swing of the pendulum and a new wave of innovations. The Vignette that follows illustrates a number of these points.

VIGNETTE
The Mustard Mill School District

Mustard Mill, a small rural district with 1,100 K–12 students (in a K–2 primary school, grades 3–5 intermediate school, grades 6–8 middle school, and grades 9–12 high school), began an effective schools (ES)/school improvement (SI) process eighteen months ago. The four schools, with their school improvement councils, provided the energy to respond to the superintendent's "suggestion" that they examine their data and plan for improvement. Training for the councils was provided by a regional educational laboratory and an intermediate service agency.

The councils did a substantial amount of work and seemed to be successful in guiding the schools in self-study and analysis. At the end of the first year each of the schools had developed a campus action plan that emphasized the effective schools model for change.

Six months elapsed, but school improvement activities were not very visible in any of the schools, and the rumor mill concluded that the effective schools process was not effective for this district. Meanwhile, the state's education board set a policy requiring every school to be trained for and implement site-based management (SBM). Simultaneously, the Mustard Mill superintendent, with the strong recommendation of a school board member, determined that the schools needed further "challenges" to recharge school change and improvement. The board member was bringing total quality management (TQM) to his factory, and he arranged for a three-day session on TQM for all school and district staff.

At this point the school staffs didn't know what had hit them, and they were, in a word, befuddled over all these new things being directed at them. It was no surprise, then, that the gossip squad shifted into overtime.

Analysis

When word of the schools' consternation reached the central office, the superintendent understood well what had happened and summoned the four school improvement councils to a meeting. She led the councils in articulating the philosophy and operational processes of the effective schools improvement process in which they had been engaged. During the discussion it became suddenly clear why the schools' momentum on their effective schools projects had slowed to a standstill: approval of the school's plans was treated as an event. The plans had given no attention to implementation, which no one seemed to realize was needed to put them into practice in the schools and classrooms. The school improvement plans had met with dry rot.

The superintendent was quick to understand the situation and asked the councils to return the following week for a second meeting.

One + One + One ≠ Three in One

When the councils reconvened, they were provided with the product of their prior meeting: a list of the effective schools operations and guiding principles. In a matching format, the councils were given a listing of the major dimensions of SBM. The superintendent asked the councils to study the two lists and react. The first thing they noticed was that both initiatives used a team approach. In addition, they observed that both had well-articulated values and assumptions that contributed to developing a strong culture. What the councils then recognized was the decentralization of decision-making and authority granted under the aegis of SBM. "Hey," they said, "in this scheme we would have the power to do what our faculties agreed on for our action plans. We could examine our staffing and arrange to release one or two teachers half-time to support the staff in implementation."

Clearly this revelation gave a new light to SBM. The councils saw its strong similarities to their ES work, but took note of the value added by SBM's decentralizing element. They were ready to embrace SBM immediately.

"Let's enrich the mix just a bit more," the superintendent coaxed. "Here is a list of TQM principles and features. Analyze them to see how they stack up with ES and SBM." The rest is history. The councils developed one strong initiative that combined the desired features of ES, SBM, and TQM, while maintaining the integrity of all. Their work was not any less difficult, nor necessarily more arduous, but it made good sense to the council members. "Analyze" became the password of the councils, and their analysis work together strengthened their networking and support of each other. Since they couldn't make a really crisp and clever acronym of ES, SBM, and TQM, they called it "Three in One" and adapted the following logo:

Two Years Later

It would be nice to report that two years after the four councils had enthusiastically embraced their three-year integrated design, significant change had occurred in their schools. Unfortunately, like so many previous efforts that started with a bang, this district's effort floundered. The initial energy was not maintained, despite each school's development of a significant plan for change.

While the campus councils and district administrators assumed that plans were being implemented, attention dissipated, energy waned, and the plans generally gathered dust. No sustained training and development had been provided to those involved. The expectation that some staff would be reassigned to serve as facilitators of implementation was derailed because of a budget crunch. Everyone in the district became distracted by a new mandate from the state board of education.

Since this design hadn't worked, the district leadership declared that "attention will be given to restructuring the schools" in the hope that this new highly touted change would succeed.

1. What factors contributed to the success or failure of Mustard Mill's change effort?
2. This district might be described as having jumped on the bandwagon of change and improvement. What might this metaphor mean for Mustard Mill, and how helpful or detrimental was this strategy?
3. What advice would you give to the central office planners or to the community supporters of the district?

Summary

Over time an unlimited array of suggested changes for what should be done to increase educational effectiveness has contributed to the litany of school change failure. Because schools are pressed to clamor on board for every new innovation, U.S. schools' programs and processes are a mile wide and an inch deep, resulting in a dearth of very promising innovations that have been fully implemented. Various changes have been conceptualized, designed, and delivered to schools in the hope that somewhere along the way the magic bullet—the right program—could be found. But few have had sustained support in the implementation phase.

Over the years a pattern has developed: introduce a new program, give it a year to take hold, immediately assess its effectiveness, and reject it when no increased program outcomes are found. School staffs soon catch on to this annual cycle and conclude, "Don't put any energy into this one; it, too, will go away," And, sure enough, it does.

After continuing cycles of rejecting programs because they are assumed to be ineffective, a new idea emerged: maybe it's not the program but the process. Beginning in the early 1970s, a team of researchers was invited—mandated—to explore this new hypothesis. The researchers had a perspective that differed from those of the past: they viewed change as a process, not an event. They also hypothesized that the change process has a personal side and that change takes place at the individual level but within an organizational context.

Because of the nature of its guiding question—how schools can successfully change and improve—this research team continues to work in the field, focusing on the everyday practices of campus and district staffs, operating alongside state departments of education and colleagues in higher education. Thus was born the body of work known as the Concerns-Based Adoption Model (CBAM), whose concepts and research findings are reported in this book. All address the process of change, especially its relationship to individuals as they personally experience the change process and its implications for implementation at the classroom level.

We have believed, as others are coming to believe, that attention to implementation is an imperative. This book argues that careful and thoughtful personalized attention, coupled with human and material resources, will, over time, achieve the successful *implementation* of change.

Guiding Principles According to Innovations and Initiatives

1. Practitioners and policy-makers, for several decades, have given attention to improving schools through attempts to change programs, processes, and structures.
2. The perspective of what should constitute such change has evolved over time from a behavioral to a cognitive to a socially responsible perspective.
3. When such changes were not widely implemented, it was assumed that the "change of the moment" was too insignificant and that larger, more comprehensive changes would be more successful.
4. At any time, the suggested programs, practices, or models of schooling have many similarities as well as certain unique factors.
5. Whether a proposed change is large or small, or behavioral or cognitive in perspective, its implementation requires the facilitating actions of supportive people.

DISCUSSION QUESTIONS

1. Why has the perspective of recommended changes for schools changed over time? What factors have contributed to the change in perspectives?

2. Explain the four approaches involved in the "fix the parts" to "fix the system" sequence of changes proposed for schools. What might be the advantages and limitations of each approach?

3. A change facilitator engages implementors in analyzing a newly adopted innovation along with other changes already (or recently) installed. What purposes might be served by this strategy?

FIELDWORK ACTIVITIES

1. In a given district, select three initiatives that are currently the focus of adoption and implementation in the schools. Compare and contrast them using a set of variables of your selection.

2. Identify a school that is actively engaged in a change effort. Select a change that is being implemented and interview three persons to ascertain what the change specifically is, what student outcomes are expected, and what perspective directs the change. How similar are the three sets of responses? Is there a pattern?

3. In a state education department of your choice, select four changes mandated for education. After analyzing the related documents and policy statements, develop a matrix that examines the mandates in terms of their similarities and differences.

4. Visit the central office of a district to identify recently recommended changes that represent (a) a "pseudo-reform"; (b) an "incremental" change; and (c) a serious "restructuring" change. Describe how each change fits its scope and size category.

REFERENCES

Bjork, L. G. (1993). Effective schools—effective superintendents: The emerging instructional leadership role. *Journal of School Leadership, 3*(3), 246–259.

Brophy, J. E., & Evertson, C. M. (1986). Teacher behavior and student learning in second and third grades. In G. Borich (Ed.), *The appraisal of teaching: Concepts and process* (pp. 79–95). Reading, MA: Addison Wesley.

Brophy, J. E., & Good, T. L. (1974). *Teacher-student relationships: Causes and consequences.* New York: Holt, Rinehart and Winston.

Carter, M., Ensrud, M., & Holden, J. (1997). The Paideia seminar: A constructivist approach to discussions. *Teaching & Change, 5*(1), 32–49.

Cuban, L. (1988). A fundamental puzzle of school reform. *Phi Delta Kappan, 69*(5), 341–344.

Deming, W. E. (1982). *Out of the crisis.* Cambridge, MA: Massachusetts Institute of Technology, Center for Advanced Engineering Study.

Evertson, C. M., Emmer, E. T., & Brophy, J. E. (1980). Predictors of effective teaching in junior high mathematics classrooms. *Journal of Research in Mathematics Education, 11*(3), 167–168.

Fuhrman, S. (1994). *Politics and systemic education reform* CPRE Policy Briefs. Philadelphia: University of Pennsylvania, Consortium for Policy Research in Education.

Hirsch, E. D., Jr. (1993). The Core Knowledge Curriculum—What's behind its success? *Educational Leadership, 50*(8), 27–30.

Lesley, B. A. (1993, May). Do they hear what we say? Understanding school restructuring initiatives. *Texas ASCD Newsletter.*

Lezotte, L. W. (1984). *School effectiveness research: A tribute to Ron Edmonds.* Paper presented at the annual meeting of the American Educational Research Association, New Orleans.

Lezotte, L. W. (1986). *School effectiveness: Reflections and future directions.* Paper presented at the annual meeting of the American Educational Research Association, San Francisco.

Mager, R. F. (1962). *Preparing instructional objectives.* Palo Alto, CA: Fearon.

National Commission on Excellence in Education (1983). *A nation at risk.* Washington, DC: U.S. Department of Education.

National LEADership Network Study Group on Restructuring Schools. (1993). *Toward quality in education: The leaders' odyssey.* Austin: Texas LEAD Center.

Potter, L. (1996, fall). Reading in a Paideia school. *Reading Improvement, 33*(3), 176–180.

Raywid, M. A. (1990). The evolving effort to improve schools: Pseudo-reforms, incremental reform, and restructuring. *Phi Delta Kappan, 72*(2), 139–143.

Richey, R. C. (1996). *Robert M. Gagne's impact on instructional design theory and practice of the future.* Paper presented at the national convention of the Association for Educational Communications and Technology, Indianapolis.

Sashkin, M., & Egermeier, J. (1992). *School change models and processes: A review of research and practice.* Paper presented at the annual meeting of the American Educational Research Association, San Francisco.

Sparks, D. (1993). Insights on school improvement: An interview with Larry Lezotte. *Journal of Staff Development, 14*(3), 18–21.

ADDITIONAL READINGS

Brandt, R. S. (1986). On improving achievement of minority chidren: A conversation with James Comer. *Educational Leadership, 43*(5), 13–17.

Brandt, R. S. (1992). On building learning communities: A conversation with Hank Levin. *Educational Leadership, 50*(1), 19–23.

Brandt, R. S. (1993). On restructuring roles and relationships: A conversation with Phil Schlechty. *Educational Leadership, 51*(2), 8–11.

Burnham, J. G., Hord, S. M., & Roberts, L. (1992). *Total Quality Management: A fad or a fit with other educational initiatives.* Paper presented at the Governor's Conference on TQM in Education, Houston.

Champlin, J. (1991). A powerful tool for school transformation. *School Administrator, 48*(9), 34.

Glasser, W. (1990). The quality school. *Phi Delta Kappan, 71*(6), 424–435.

Glickman, C. D. (1991). Pretending not to know what we know. *Educational Leadership, 48*(8), 4–10.

Glickman, C. D. (1992). The essence of school renewal: The prose has begun. *Educational Leadership, 50*(1), 24–27.

Glickman, C. D., et al. (1994). Factors affecting school change. *Journal of Staff Development, 15*(3), 37–41.

O'Neil, J. (1995). On lasting school reform: A conversation with Ted Sizer. *Educational Leadership, 52*(5), 4–9.

PART TWO

Tools and Techniques
for Change Facilitators

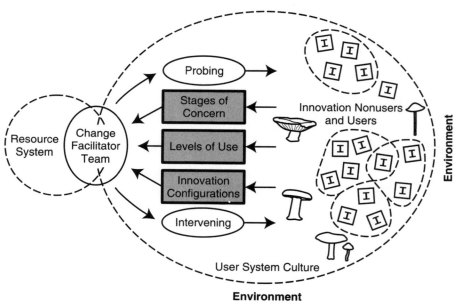

THE CONCERNS-BASED ADOPTION MODEL

The title of Part Two expresses precisely what this part of the book is about: providing change facilitators with *diagnostic* tools and recommendations for their use. Each of the three diagnostic tools has been identified, studied, and verified through twenty-five plus years of research and application by multiple researchers and facilitators globally, as noted in the Preface. In Part Two, a chapter is devoted to each tool, and includes a description of the construct, its measurement devices, and the techniques for employing each tool in facilitating change processes. Every attempt is made to provide sufficient information for understanding each tool and how it may be used. However, as in the case with many new ideas (innovations), the level of information may be just enough to make the user "dangerous." Findings from staff development and change process research indicate that most people need training and development in order to use new ideas, programs, practices, and the like, effectively. With that caveat in mind, a brief description of each of these diagnostic tools is given here as an introduction to this part of the book.

Innovation Configurations, described in Chapter 3, are a means for clarifying the change that is to be implemented. All too often, the picture of change toward which an organization is heading is obscure and ill-defined. Having a shared mental image or vision of the desired change when it has been implemented in a high quality way provides meaning and clarity of understanding for all.

The people who are involved in a change effort have personal reactions and feelings about the change and about their involvement in the process. To say this is stating the obvious, but understanding and using the obvious as a means for anticipating and providing appropriate responses is the goal of Chapter 4. Acknowledging that the successful implementation of any change is highly dependent upon each individual involved and attending to his or her concerns with appropriate assistance are important keys to successful change. Chapter 4 can help facilitators with this task.

An additional way to understand and to provide appropriate assistance to individuals is the focus of Chapter 5. Whereas Chapter 4 looks at feelings, the affective side of change, Chapter 5 explores the behaviors of individuals during change. This chapter suggests ways in which this tool can be used by facilitators as well as evaluators to describe and document each person's increasing competence in using an innovation.

3

Clarifying the Change

Innovation Configurations

Why can't they [instructors] just read the lesson as written and do what it says? When you go out in the field, some of the things that are going on you will not believe!

—Curriculum Developer

The district mathematics liaison stopped by yesterday and said I was doing a good job! To tell you the truth, I still don't know what I am supposed to be doing, so I just make it up as I go along.

—Middle-School Teacher

Well, the teacher's guide is so clear and the training gave me the opportunity to practice, so I understand what is expected. I am able to do all of the activities in each lesson just as they are described in the guide and how I saw them in the video examples.

—Social Studies Teacher

A frequent problem for teachers and others who are expected to implement new practices is that they are not clear about what they are being asked to do. Even when training and materials are provided, there is a big leap from preparing to do something to actually doing it. In the end, what teachers do in the classroom may bear little resemblance to what the creator(s) of the change had in mind originally. All of the teachers may call it the same thing, but in practice what they do may look very different. In this chapter we will examine the *innovation*, or the change itself: how to describe it and how to measure it in classroom use are central themes. A key purpose of this chapter is to identify a concept and tool that can be used to construct a common understanding of the change by everyone involved.

FOCUS QUESTIONS

1. Should all teachers in a school be doing the same thing in their classrooms relative to reading, science, mathematics, and the other subject areas?
2. How do you specify an intended change?
3. What key issues result from a lack of clarity about how to use an innovation?
4. How can a clear vision of a change serve as a road map to successful implementation?
5. How can you determine which classroom practices really make a difference in student learning?
6. What is an Innovation Configuration Map? Who should be involved in developing one?
8. What are some of the uses of an Innovation Configuration Map?

The Change: What It Is and Is Not

A major reason that widespread change often occurs only modestly across a school is that the implementers, change facilitators, and policy-makers do not fully understand what the change is or what it will look like when it is implemented in the envisioned way. When there is such confusion, principals and other facilitators may give conflicting signals, and teachers will create their own versions of the change as they try to understand and use the materials and/or processes that have been advocated. Evaluators then have serious difficulties in appraising whether the new way is better than the old. This is particularly problematic when what is being done under the name of the innovation is different in different classrooms. This phenomenon led those of us working with the CBAM model to add a third diagnostic dimension to the paradigm—*Innovation Configurations* (IC)—which is the topic of this chapter.

Before beginning the description of Innovation Configurations, a definitional issue must be addressed. For any change or innovation there will be one or more architects, or creators, who may be national expert(s) or local developer(s). Frequently the creators of the innovation are curriculum experts from outside the school or district, such as a national project or publishing house. Others are a local team or committee of teachers who have experimented in their classrooms and developed an approach that they wish to share with others. Still other changes are driven by local school boards, state legislative, and federal policies; some are even initiated by court decisions. In the CBAM approach to change, we have used the term *developer* to represent any and all of these sources.

Innovation Adaptation

The concept of Innovation Configurations addresses both the idealized images of a change developer as well as the various operational forms of the change that can be observed in classrooms. The focus in the IC diagnostic dimension is on developing and applying word-picture descriptions of what the use of an innovation can look like.

Previously, a typical means of determining whether a new program or process was being used in classrooms was to count how many classrooms contained the program materials. Alternatively, *use* of the new way would be assumed because the teachers had participated in a workshop or the principal would report that teachers were "doing it."

The uncertainty of whether there was high-quality use of a new program or process was discovered early in the original CBAM verification studies. The implementation of two innovations was being studied: teacher teaming in elementary schools and college professors' use of instructional modules. In each case, when the so-called users were asked to describe what they were doing, a surprising range of practices was outlined, but in all cases the interviewees would claim to be using the same innovation. For example, when teachers in Texas, Nebraska, and Massachusetts were asked to describe their teams, they provided very different pictures of the innovation of teaming:

> *Team Texas* consisted of three teachers and two aides who served approximately 110 students. They "teamed" all day and were housed in a pod that was equivalent to three classrooms in size. The students were taught by all of the teachers, and each teacher took the lead in planning for one subject area.
>
> *Team Nebraska* consisted of three teachers, each of whom had a homeroom class. For half the day, students would move from classroom to classroom as they were grouped and regrouped for lessons. Teachers kept their own students for the afternoon. Teachers specialized in teaching all students particular subjects.
>
> *Team Massachusetts* consisted of two teachers, each of whom had a regular classroom with twenty-five to thirty students. The teachers exchanged lesson plans once a month, but each kept and taught their own students all day.

As these examples illustrate, how the change is thought about in theory may bear little resemblance to the activities that are done in classrooms under the name of that innovation. In each of the schools described above, the teachers were quick to say, "Oh, yes, we are teaming," but what they were doing under the name of teaming was very different.

An early conclusion in our studies was that users of innovations tend to adapt and, in many cases, mutate innovations! In other words, the innovation in action can take on many different operational forms, or configurations. Once the phenomenon of Innovation Configurations is recognized and accepted as a natural part of the change process, a number of implications emerge. For example, the outcomes from the use of different configurations of an innovation will likely vary. Users of some configurations will be associated with higher outcomes than those using other configurations. Also, training and coaching users to further their implementation will need to target different aspects of the innovation, depending on which configuration is in use. There is a philosophical issue here too. To what extent is there a need to advocate for close adherence to the developer's intended model, i.e., a "fidelity" approach? When, or should, all users be doing the same thing? In other words, how necessary and appropriate is a fidelity model of change? The concept of IC and its related measurement procedure help address these questions.

The purpose here is not to make judgments about how good or bad it may be to adapt an innovation. Instead the goal is to point out (1) that in most change efforts, innovation adaptation will occur; (2) that there is a way to chart these adaptations; and (3) that these adaptations have direct and indirect implications for facilitating and assessing change processes. In the concluding section of this chapter we will return to issues related to fidelity and some of their implications, but first Innovation Configurations as a concept and its mapping procedure need to be described.

Innovation Configurations as a Concept

Anyone who has been involved in change recognizes the phenomenon of Innovation Configurations. The tendency to adapt, modify, and/or mutate aspects of innovations is a natural part of the change process; it is neither malicious nor even explicitly planned. It happens for a number of interrelated reasons, beginning with uncertainty about what is supposed to be done. Most people, especially teachers, want to do the "right" thing. Therefore, when teachers are asked to use an innovation, they will try. The problems begin when the details of how to do it are not made clear.

In nearly all cases the innovation as operationalized by different users will vary along a continuum from being very close to what the developer had in mind to a distant zone where what is being done is nearly unrecognizable. Creating different configurations of an innovation is not unique to education. For example, consider cars as the innovation. As Figure 3.1 illustrates, and as any parking lot confirms, a car can be and has been significantly adapted from the initial conception of a two-door sedan. A whole range of "configurations" can be observed ranging from changes in color, to the addition of mag wheels, to rebuilding as a race car, to some forms that some might claim are cars that the rest of us would say, "No, those are not cars!"

This same continuum of configurations exists for educational innovations, only determining what is and is not the innovation is more difficult than with the car example. All too frequently the developers of an educational innovation have not thought clearly about what the use of their change will really entail. They have thought more about what is needed to support its implementation, such as training and materials. In addition, because teachers, like the rest of us, are always short on time, they will tend to reduce the amount of change and effort they have to invest

FIGURE 3.1   A Continuum of Innovation Configurations for a Car

whenever they can. If there is limited training and support for the change, it is likely that it will not be fully implemented. Although the teachers may genuinely believe that they are using the innovation, an expert observing their classroom may conclude, "Hmm, is that the way it should be done?"

The different configurations of educational innovations are easy to picture. Take, for example, the innovation of integrated use of technology. What is envisioned here is classroom use by students and teachers of various forms of technology for information retrieval, processing, and communication. Some of the relatively simple configurations that could be observed are as follows: (1) classrooms with only a few computers with no Web access, which are used mainly for drill and practice; (2) classrooms with computers that are linked within the school and include CD-ROM databases, but no Web access; (3) classrooms with computers with Web access, projection devices, and video, where students work individually and in groups to research, plan, develop, and communicate presentations about their learning; and (4) schools in which all computers are in a lab or media center and used on an assigned schedule for groups of students.

Once it is recognized and accepted that there will be different configurations of an innovation, an important next issue is how to describe those configurations. Answering this question entails development of an Innovation Configuration Map (IC Map).

Mapping Innovation Configurations

The scenarios described above are very familiar to teachers, principals, and other leaders. The situation in which teachers are not sure about what they are to do occurs in part because innovation developers have a hard time imagining the extent to which their innovation can be adapted. Another reason for the uncertainty is that change facilitators and teachers do not have clear images and descriptions about what the use of the innovation can look like. To address these needs, we have developed a process and tool that can be used to visualize and assess the different configurations that are likely to be found for any particular innovation. We call the process Innovation Configuration Mapping and the resultant tool an Innovation Configuration Map.

Innovation Configuration Maps

The concept of a map was deliberately chosen for this work because, just as a road map shows different ways for getting from one place to another, so does an Innovation Configuration Map. A highway map will picture interstate highways, U.S. highways, and county roads. These are alternate routes, all of which make it possible to complete the trip. The IC Map does the same thing for change facilitators and users of innovations by identifying the major components of an innovation and then describing the observable variations of each component. The IC Map is composed of "word picture" descriptions of the different operational forms of an innovation or change.

IC Map Components   Consider the very simple IC Map component presented in Figure 3.2, which describes the units that a teacher presents. In the *a* variation, all units and most activities is taught. The quantity of units and activities that are taught decreases in the other variations, with the *e* variation describing the classroom where none of the units or activities is taught. Even without naming a specific program, it is possible to use this component with its different variation descriptions to visualize different degrees of coverage of units and activities. It is part of the "map" just as is a highway map.

The purpose of the IC Map is to present carefully developed descriptions of different ways of doing the innovation. An IC Map will have a number of components (typically eight to fifteen), and each component will have a number of variations (typically two to six). The number of components will vary depending on the complexity of the innovation and the amount of detail needed. There is a dynamic trade-off between the number of components and the level of detail represented.

Component 1:   Units Taught

(a)	(b)	(c)	(d)	(e)
All units and most activities are taught	Most units and activities are taught	Some units are taught	A few selected activities are taught	No units or activities are taught

FIGURE 3.2   A Simple IC Map Component (from The Science Program)

Normally, in an IC Map with fewer components, each component will have more information, which at some point makes the descriptions too dense and difficult to visualize. On the other hand, in an IC Map with many components, each one may be too finely ground to be useful. In the end, the team that develops an IC Map has to decide what is best for its situation.

The major goal in writing each component description and each variation description is to be as visual as possible. The better the word pictures, the easier it will be for teachers, principals, and others to see what successful use of the innovation entails.

Developing Clear Word-Picture Descriptions   The IC Map component presented in Figure 3.2 was deliberately chosen because of its simplicity. A more typical IC Map would have much richer component descriptions, as shown in Figure 3.3. These components were selected from the Instructor Profile for Fast Trac II (Novak, 1992), a ten-week course for business entrepreneurs. In this project, which was done by the Center for Entrepreneurial Leadership of the Kauffman Foundation, there was interest in developing an IC Map that depicted the role of the course instructor that could be used as part of the quality control check as the course was disseminated nationally. The resultant IC Map was used also to select content for instructor training, since instructors were to be skilled in doing each of the map's components. The map was also used by the instructors in planning and self-reflection, and by trained assessors in determining instructor certification by viewing videotapes of their classes.

One of the interesting aspects of the Fast Trac IC Map was that the innovation was the role of the course instructor. An IC Map could also have been developed around the role of workshop participants or around what they, as entrepreneurs, applied from the course to their businesses. Deciding which innovation will be the focus for IC Mapping is a critical first step.

Note, in Figure 3.3, how the component and variation descriptions in Component 2 have been stated. The basic component is the same, but more information is presented for the component than in Figure 3.2. However, as IC Mapping expert Paul Borchardt would say, this is still a "boring" component, since it basically just evolves from "a lot" (*a*) to "a little" (*d*). A component of this type could be made much richer by adding a second dimension, or practice, that increased in occurrence from *a* to *d*. For example, the dimension of excessive time being spent on one or two modules could gradually increase across the variation descriptions.

A much higher quality example of an IC Map component and its variations is Component 11 in Figure 3.3. Note how the word-picture descriptions of each variations are richer, and how four different dimensions—variety, type, relevance, and length—are addressed in each variation. An IC Map notation technique is to present a key word for each dimension within brackets following the component label.

Indicating Ranges of Quality and Fidelity   Figures 3.2 and 3.3 illustrate a number of additional features of IC Map components as well, including the implicit value

FAST TRAC II COURSE
INNOVATION CONFIGURATION MAP

Site _____ Session _____ Instructor _____ Observer _____ Date _____

A. FULL COURSE OVERVIEW

2) Balanced Coverage of the Six Core Modules — Entrepreneurial Mind Set — Management & Organization — Finance   [6 covered, equal emphasis]
— Legal Entities — Marketing — Negotiations

(a)	(b)	(c)	(d)	(e)	(f)
All six modules are developed and with equal emphasis.	All six modules are developed but with one or more given less emphasis.	One or more modules is not systematically addressed.	One or two modules become the course.		

LECTURE SEGMENT

11) Use of Examples by the Instructor during the Lecture   [Variety, type, relevance, and length]

(a)	(b)	(c)	(d)	(e)	(f)
Examples are used throughout. Examples are interesting, varied, to the point, and congruent with the issue or topic at hand Examples include retail/ service/manufacturing & integrate participant's expertise with examples from their businesses.	Examples presented are to the point and congruent. There is limited variety in terms of retail/service/ manufacturing and participant's businesses.	Examples and stories are not always relevant to the issue or topic at hand and tend to be drawn out, or a few businesses are overused as examples. Examples may not be clearly explained.	So many examples and war stories shared that complete coverage of the points is hindered.	So many examples and war stories particular to the Instructor's personal experience are shared that there is little variety and complete coverage of the point is hindered.	There are few examples and/or all of the examples are based in one or two businesses.

FIGURE 3.3   Two IC Map Components for the Instructor's Role in the Fast Trac II Course for Business Entrepreneurs

Reprinted by permission from the Kauffman Center for Entrepreneurial Leadership at the Ewing Marion Kauffman Foundation.

in the sequencing of the variations. As one moves from the "e" variation toward the "a" variation, the behaviors and practices described increasingly approach the more ideal practices as viewed by the innovation developer or some consensus group, usually those who developed the IC Map. Laying the component variations along such a continuum from more to less desirable can be very helpful. Note that this IC Mapping technique can only be used to implicitly signify when some variations are valued more highly than others. The authors of this text are not arguing for or against such a fidelity perspective, but merely showing how it can be noted on the IC Map.

Another IC Mapping technique that can be helpful with a fidelity perspective is use of what we call *fidelity lines*, which are represented by the vertical dashed and solid lines between certain of the variations of the components in Figure 3.3. A solid line signifies that all of the variations to the right have been judged to be "unacceptable" ways of doing that component; all of those to the left of a dashed line are considered "ideal" practices, while those between the solid and dashed lines are viewed as "acceptable." Determining the placement of these lines in this case was done by the Fast Trac course developers. Whether to have lines and where to place them are important decisions for IC Mapping groups. No matter who is to make the decision about the inclusion of fidelity lines, *no lines should be added until after the IC Map has been through several versions and has been used in data collection.* The insertion of fidelity lines should not be arbitrary or capricious. There should be a very good rationale and, hopefully, empirical data to support their placement.

Student Roles in IC Maps   One of the first decisions in IC Mapping is to determine which role(s) will be the focus of the map. For example, as was mentioned above, the Fast Trac map shown in Figure 3.3 could have focused on the participants or the regional dissemination administrators instead of the instructors. Normally, a complete IC Map will deal not just with the role of the teachers and their use of the materials but with the role of the students too. For example, Figure 3.4 describes one aspect of student performance in a constructivist approach to teaching mathematics (Alquist & Hendrickson, 1999), which is based on the National Council of Mathematics Standards. Figure 3.5 is a student component from the IC Map for standards-based education of the Douglas County School District in Colorado. The rich and observable descriptions of each variation in these examples were the result of intense and sustained effort.

More Complex and Richer IC Map Components   When there is the need and time, IC Map components can be made even more complex and richer. In one such project the innovation itself was very subtle and complex, and developing each component had to be done in ways that built in the nuances of the philosophy of the developer as well as clear descriptions of how this approach would be seen in classroom practices. The innovation, the ESSENTIAL Curriculum, is an educational program that provides children and young people with the knowledge and skills that will directly assist them in their development as capable and ethical people (Dunn & Borchardt, 1998). Although there are lessons and activities in the program, its philosophy

INNOVATION CONFIGURATION MAP FOR THE TEACHING AND LEARNING OF MATHEMATICS

DoDDS-Hessen District Superintendent's Office
Rhein Main, Germany

B. Engagement with Task/Investigation

3) Student Engaged in Mathematical Tasks throughout the Lesson {engagement, time}

a	b	c	d
Most students are engaged in mathematical tasks, most of the time.	Most students are engaged in mathematical tasks, part of the time.	Some students are engaged in mathematical tasks. Many are off task most of the time.	Few students are engaged any of the time.

4) Students' Understanding of Problem-Solving Strategies {knowing your goal, where you are now, knowing the steps to get to the goal, reflection}

a	b	c	d	e
Students view the open-ended problem as a whole and analyze its parts. They create, select, and test a range of strategies. Students reflect upon the reasonableness of the strategies and the solution.	Students grasp the open-ended problem as a whole and analyze its parts. Students pick an established/traditional strategy to try to solve the problem, which is applied without considering alternatives. Students reflect upon the reasonableness of the solution but not the strategy.	Students approach the open-ended problem as a whole but do not have a clear understanding of the parts. The primary focus is on getting an answer. The students' reflection is on whether the answer is right rather than the reasonableness of the strategy.	Students approach open-ended problems as unconnected/unrelated parts and do not see the problem as a whole. Students may manipulate materials and numbers, but are not clear about the reason/purpose. If observable, reflection is about procedures.	Students calculate and compute using rote and routine procedures. Students are not clear about the final goal or the relationship of the tasks to that goal. There is little or no reflection about what is being learned.

DRAFT

FIGURE 3.4 Student IC Map Components

From "Mapping the Configurations of Mathematics Teaching" by A. Alquist and M. Hendrickson, 1999, *Journal of Classroom Interaction*, 34(1), 18–26.

DOUGLAS COUNTY SCHOOL DISTRICT—LEARNING SERVICES
STANDARDS-BASED EDUCATION—CONFIGURATION MAP

Component #5—Student Ownership and Understanding of Learning: (understanding of standards or checkpoints, understanding of progress in relation to standards or checkpoints, understanding of what is needed to improve performance in order to achieve standards or checkpoints)

(I)	(II)	(III)	(IV)	(V)
Students' focus is on the current activity.	Students' focus is on the **requirements of the class** and **grade** they receive.	Students can use the **"language" of standards**. They can state **the standards and checkpoints** that they are expected to learn, but are **unclear about where they are** in meeting the standards or checkpoints or **what they need to do** to achieve them.	Students **understand** what they **are expected to know and be able to do** and can **articulate in specific terms** what it means to reach the standards or checkpoints. They can **describe where they are** in regard to the standards or checkpoints but are **unclear what they need to do** to achieve them.	Students **understand** what they **are expected** to know and **be able to do** and can **articulate in specific terms** what it means to reach the standards or checkpoints. They can **describe where they are** in regard to the standard and know what they **need to improve** to achieve it.

Examples:

"We are reading *The Diary of Anne Frank*, and I will be writing some kind of report when we are finished."	"We are studying how to use primary source materials. I need to get at least a B on the final report."	"I know that we are studying how to select and evaluate primary source materials as related to the Holocaust. I'm not sure exactly what I'll need to know about primary sources, or if I am any good at using them."	"I know that we are studying primary source materials as related to the Holocaust, and that's why we are reading *The Diary of Anne Frank*. I know that we will be evaluating and interpreting sources for their usefulness in understanding the Holocaust. I can find sources, but I am not sure how to evaluate their relevance and quality. I am not sure what I'll need to do to become proficient in evaluating these sources."	"I know that we are studying primary source materials as they relate to the Holocaust and that's why we are reading *The Diary of Anne Frank*. I know that we will be evaluating and interpreting sources for their usefulness in understanding the Holocaust. I am pretty good at locating primary sources, but I have trouble knowing whether they are really quality sources. My teacher has shown some interesting ways to judge the quality of a source, but I need some more practice with them."

Douglas County School District Re-1

April, 1999

FIGURE 3.5   Student IC Map Component for Standards-Based Education (Douglas County School District, Castle Rock, Colorado)

Reprinted by permission.

of how people should treat each other is expected to be expressed in the classroom throughout the day. Because of this, the IC Map included components that described practices during a lesson as well as others that addressed practices to be used throughout the day.

To help teachers, change facilitators, and evaluators assess implementation of the ESSENTIAL process, the IC Map components became much more complex. One of those components is presented is Figure 3.6. There are a number of readily apparent differences between this IC Map component and the earlier examples. First, the range of variations is greater, and there is a common dimensionality built into each one that deals with how holistically the teacher is integrating use of the program's principles. The f variation, for example, describes the case when nothing that is related to that component is observed. The g variation addresses behaviors and actions that are actually *antithetical* to the intent of the program, information that can be very helpful. Another important addition to this component is the open-ended list of examples under each variation description. While they will not represent all that is in a particular variation, nor will they necessarily be exclusive to that variation, they do describe the kinds of behaviors that are indicative of it.

The Process of Developing an IC Map   Developing an IC Map is a challenging endeavor. It also is energizing for those who really are interested in having implementation of an innovation succeed. There are moments of discovery about the intent of a particular innovation and how it should be used. There is also the initial struggle to figure out what the components are and then to develop useful word-picture descriptions for each variation. Additional rewards come when the first draft of the IC Map is shared with interested teachers, principals, and other change facilitators. Often, this is the first time they will have seen written descriptions of what they can do when using the innovation.

Often the first reaction of people who examine an IC Map is to do a self-assessment of where they would place themselves on each component. A second reaction is to consider some of the other variation descriptions and whether they should try them. The IC Mappers receive very helpful feedback from these dialogues, which can be used in further refining the map.

Developing an IC Map is definitely an interactive process. An individual working alone is very unlikely to construct a map that is as useful as one that evolves from a team effort. Typically three to seven key people work together for five or six days to devise a complete first draft of an IC Map. One of the major outcomes of this interactive process is that the IC Mappers develop a consensus about what the innovation should look like when it is in use. Up to that time, they likely will not have been using the same terms and detailed images of use. This regularly observed lack of explicit agreement in understanding adds greatly to teachers' confusion about what they are supposed to be doing.

The general process that is followed in developing an IC Map is presented in Figure 3.7. The beginning steps entail reviewing all of the available printed material and then interviewing the innovation developer and/or experts. Following this, a

THE ESSENTIAL CURRICULUM IC MAP

II. All Day in the Classroom

D. Teacher

6) The Principles and Concepts are applied throughout the day by the teacher [*teacher application, all*]

Consistent reliance on and integration of program	Deliberate and conscious application of principles and concepts	Emphasizes selected principles and concepts	Program delivery as designed	Presentation of parts and pieces at random	Non-use	Opposition to principles and concepts
(Complete Integration)	(Deliberate Application)	(Selected Emphasis)	(Motions)	(Parts & Pieces)	(Nothing)	(Antithesis)
(a)	(b)	(c)	(d)	(e)	(f)	(g)
Principles and concepts are integrated without conscious effort into activities of the day. • Teacher and students acknowledge mistakes in words including "oops, I goofed." • Teachers teach students through steps of correcting errors seamlessly. • Students have "Driver's Licenses" and "Drive" to other parts of the building using self-control. The license can be suspended for lack of self-control.	All principles and concepts are developed and consciously applied throughout the day. • When opportunities arise, teacher and students draw connections to and apply specific principles and concepts. • When faced with opportunities, teacher and students talk out loud about the relevant Principle or Concepts.	Selected principles and concepts are emphasized and applied appropriately throughout the day. • Teacher leads students in applying principles of "self control," but does not refer to other concepts. • Teacher recognizes opportunities around "making mistakes," but misses opportunities related to other Principles and Concepts.	Lessons are taught, but no extrapolations to situations outside the Essential lesson context. • When obvious opportunities to refer to principles and concepts arise, teacher does not make connection. • Teacher handles fight on playground without reference to any Essential principle.	Some activities are purposefully selected to teach the concept. • Tap and Trade game is played without Principles being taught. • Social studies curriculum happens to lend itself to the selection of Essential lessons.		Principles and concepts applied in classroom are antithetical to Essential. • Indiscriminate use of praise (unearned). • Self esteem activities teaches principles and concepts counter to Essential's Principles and Concepts. • "In this classroom we wil not make mistakes." • "I can give my students self esteem." • Mistakes are punished without any processing.

FIGURE 3.6   A Dense and Complex IC Map Component with Indicators

From *The Essential Curriculum*, The Teel Institute, Kansas City, Missouri. Reprinted by permission.

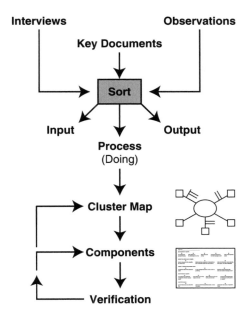

Note: This is a dynamic, interactive, consensus-building process.

FIGURE 3.7   The IC Mapping Process

range of classrooms where the innovation and like practices are in use should be observed. It is important to observe a variety of classrooms, because an IC Map needs to have word-picture descriptions that cover all possible variations. Three key questions that should be asked throughout this process are:

1. What does the innovation look like when it is in use?
2. What would I see in classrooms where it is used well (and not as well)?
3. What will teachers *and* students be doing when the innovation is in use?

A key part of IC mapping is the orientation that is taken. The focus is on developing pictures of the operational forms of the innovation, not statements of its philosophy or a listing of its implementation requirements. Innovation creators have a tendency to focus on implementation requirements. They may say something like, "You have to use these materials and spend at least thirty minutes doing so every day." However, this is the wrong answer for those building the IC Map, who instead need to know *how* those materials are being used and *what* happens in the classroom when they are.

The initial document review, interviews, and observations should lead to the development of a *cluster map*, which is a schematic map of the array of possible components, their clustering, and some of the possible variations for certain components.

The first goal is to develop a holistic organizing scheme of possible components and clusters of components that represent what the innovation is like when it is used.

Following this is the task of agreeing on which components are key and should be developed. Then comes the intense work of negotiating the wording of components and component variations. Once there is a draft, it needs to be tested in what we call the first "dose of reality." Without exception, when IC Mappers try out their first full draft, they discover a number of points that need clarification. They also are likely to discover that other components need to be mapped.

Developing an IC Map is a highly interactive and iterative process. Our experience has been that innovation developers cannot develop high-quality IC Maps by themselves. Also, it is always best to have three or more people drafting an IC map. An earlier technical document on IC Mapping (Heck et al., 1981) may be of some help. The Guiding Principles of IC Mapping presented later in this chapter also provide additional technical information and tips to consider in reviewing map drafts.

Innovation Configurations: Applications and Implications

There are many applications and implications of the Innovation Configuration concept and IC Maps. We have selected a few to introduce here to stimulate further thought about this important aspect of the change process. The points included address some facets of facilitating change processes, conducting research, and drafting IC Maps.

Using IC Maps to Facilitate Change

Once an IC Map is developed, it should not be kept a secret. Share it with all of the potential and current users of the innovation and with all change facilitators. This was done, for example, for the nine innovation bundles in the Kentucky Education Reform Act. Under the leadership of Roger Pankratz and the Kentucky Institute of Education Research, nine cross-state constituent teams of six to ten members each, met for a week to develop the first drafts of the IC Maps. Each team was assigned to one bundle. Copies of their IC Maps were then sent to all 1,230 schools in the state. This was the first time that teachers and principals had word-picture descriptions of what they could be doing under the labels of each of the reform initiatives.

An IC Map is also a diagnostic tool for planning training and development. For example, a large number of teachers could be observed and an IC Map completed for each, with the information then summarized by component. The summary would be a tally of how many teachers were at each of the variations for each component. Then it would be possible to identify those components where implementation was going well (i.e., many teachers using "a" and "b" variations) and any components where implementation was lagging (i.e., many teachers using "d" and "e" variations). This information could be used to plan a training workshop to address less well implemented components.

IC Maps can be a useful coaching tool as well. Principals and other change facilitators could observe classrooms to provide help to teachers, but often they are not given guidelines and specifics about what to look for. The IC Map provides a set of descriptions that can be used to focus their observations. There might also be a preobservation discussion where the teacher and the facilitator agree that certain IC Map components will be targeted during the observation. Since many of the components focus on what the students are doing, teachers are less likely to perceive the use of an IC Map during an observation as an evaluation threat. In all cases, if the focus is kept on the innovation instead of the teacher, personal concerns will be lower.

Using IC Maps in Research, Evaluation, and Implementation Assessments

A serious problem in most research and evaluation studies has been the failure to document implementation before making judgments about the effects of various treatments, programs, and innovations. Typically, implementation is assumed to have occurred if teachers were trained or the materials were purchased. An IC Map provides one clear and direct way to record the actual extent and quality of what has been implemented.

In a number of research studies, IC Maps have been developed and data collected to assess implementation. For example, Bridge (1995) conducted a number of studies of the implementation of the Integrated Primary program in Kentucky. The *a* variations were formulated using the state's reform initiative and the standards of the National Association for the Education of Young Children. Bridge found that children had higher achievement in primary grade classrooms where there were higher levels (i.e., more *a* and *b* variations) of implementation of the developmentally appropriate practices. Koon (1995) had similar findings in a study of the extent of implementation of YESS! Mini-Society (Kourilsky, 1983), an innovation designed to introduce concepts of business and entrepreneurship to students.

The Fidelity Enigma

The work of both Bridge and Koon had a fidelity orientation, or an established vision of which practices were more preferable. In both studies, the IC Maps were developed accordingly, and higher student outcomes were associated with higher fidelity implementations. An issue that needs discussion is whether it is appropriate to ask for or insist on high-fidelity use of an innovation. From one point of view, teachers are being told what to do, which reduces their teaching freedom. On the other hand, if student gains are higher when the innovation is used in specified ways, should not teachers be expected to use the verified practices? Although we do not have a simple or universally applicable answer to this critical question, we believe that it needs to be openly asked, discussed, and addressed in each change effort. The following Vignette illustrates how an IC map could serve as a guide for teacher reflections.

VIGNETTE

Using an IC Map Component for Reflection and Peer Observation

Two teachers are discussing their understanding of standards-based education (SBE) and what they think their students understand about it.

JOSÉ: *I think that I am finally understanding what SBE is about. It really has been a big change for me. I have been use to providing information and teaching with the discovery approach. The idea that I should make sure up front that the students understand the desired outcome has been a big change for me.*

MARY JO: *I know what you mean. I have always wanted my students to learn, but I too thought that they should have to figure it out from scratch.*

JOSÉ: *I still don't think my students get it. They can give me a general idea about the standards and the specific benchmarks we are working on, but they don't seem to be very clear about it. I wish I could somehow get them to understand what their responsibilities are.*

MARY JO: *I know what you mean. Do you remember that implementation rubric handout that Elliott [the district SBE coordinator] gave us last August? There was a student component. Maybe we should look at that.*

JOSÉ: *I know what you mean. I just happen to have a copy in my file. I am going to look it over and see if it gives me any ideas.*

MARY JO: *Why don't you pull a copy and then tomorrow, when you have your break, come observe my physical science class and see what you think? Don't use the whole thing, just the component that focuses on student learning.*

This story points out two important applications of an IC Map. First, it can be used by teachers for self-reflection. Teachers can read each component, assess where they are, and then think about what they wish to continue doing and what they might want to change. An IC Map can also be used for peer observation, as teachers observe each other's classrooms using an IC Map as the rubric. They can focus the observation through preobservation discussion, and then debrief one another afterward.

Note that only one component of the IC Map was used as the focus for the planned peer observation in this case. This is a very efficient and useful way to go about it. The selected component was one that dealt with student behaviors, which was a very good choice. When teachers focus on what they would like students to accomplish, there can be a very direct connection back to what the teachers need to do to help students succeed in the desired ways.

1. Think about using an IC Map for teacher self-improvement. Under what conditions would you want to use the whole IC Map? When would it be best to use one or two components?
2. Would you ever want to share the IC Map with students? Why or why not?
3. Would you ever consider sharing an IC Map with parents? Why or why not?

Summary

In this chapter we have introduced the idea that an innovation can be made operational in many different forms or configurations. We have advocated developing Innovation Configuration Maps and openly sharing the drafts with all parties. Along the way we have pointed out some of the conceptual, operational and philosophical implications of this process. Key points to remember from this chapter are summarized as Guiding Principles on the following page.

One of the important benefits of developing an IC Map is the consensus-building that it encourages. Without such agreement, the various leaders and change facilitators all too frequently deliver different messages to the nonusers and users, which adds to the confusion and frustration about the change. It sometimes also leads to early adopters of the innovation establishing practices (i.e., configurations) that are later determined to be inappropriate or even not in keeping with the original design. Change processes will be more efficient and effective when there is careful consideration of the possible components, variations, and clusters from the outset. This is not to say that images and values of the innovation cannot change with time. In fact, this is one of the reasons why it is important to type "draft" on each page of the IC Map. Still, it is better to begin with the best possible estimate of a shared vision rather than starting with conflicting conceptions.

In conclusion, efforts to implement changes in schools—new processes, practices, organizational structures, and the like—have long been highly ambiguous. We believe that the typically elusive visions of what the use of an innovation entails has been a primary reason for the lack of widespread successful change. When a variety of configurations are implemented, there is little likelihood that significant gains in student learning will be detected across all classrooms. As has been described in this chapter and illustrated in the Vignette, the Innovation Configuration Map is a multipurpose tool that change leaders and implementers can use to improve this situation. Evaluators and researchers have also found it to be valuable in promoting specificity and unstacking innovation bundles. As one constituent enthusiastically reported, "The IC Map is the best thing since sliced bread!"

Guiding Principles of IC Mapping

1. Always type the word "draft" on each page of your IC Map.
2. Always type your name and the date of the current draft on each page. This will reduce confusion over whether someone is referring to the most recent version of the IC Map.
3. Watch out for IC Map components that simply taper off as they move from the *a* to the final variation. If this is happening to one dimension, make sure you have a second dimension that increases from *a* to the final variation. After all, if the ideal dimension is decreasing, some other practice is taking its place.
4. Remember that the *d* and *e* variations are not "bad" or simply pejorative descriptions, they should be descriptions of alternatives that represent other ways of doing things.
5. A completed IC Map should serve as a record of how an innovation is being used; its purpose is not to explain how the information about practice is to be collected, which may be done by interview, observation, or user self-assessment. Some caution is needed in terms of reliability and validity, especially for certain types of IC Map components. For example, there will be much lower validity for a teaching process component that is self-assessed than one that is recorded by a trained observer.
6. An IC Map is only good for the innovation for which it was designed. With a different innovation, the map-building process will have to be done again.
7. Strive to have very descriptive word pictures for each variation. Address the presence or absence of each dimension in each variation.
8. Be careful about having too few and too many dimensions in a component. Very rarely should a component consist of only one dimension or more than four.
9. Remember that the consensus-building process and debate among the mappers is key. The talk, about "what you mean" and "what I mean" is critical to developing a useful and valid IC Map.
10. Do not insert fidelity lines until after the IC Map has been through several generations of drafts and there are clear reasons to do so.

D I S C U S S I O N   Q U E S T I O N S

1. Describe an experience that you have had where the innovation as used was different from what the developer had intended. Why did this occur?
2. What key steps would you take to introduce the idea of developing an IC Map to a school/district staff?
3. How could a teacher use an IC Map?
4. How could a principal use an IC Map?
5. What do you see as an important implication of Innovation Configurations for evaluation and research studies?

FIELDWORK ACTIVITIES

1. Develop two or three configuration components, with their variations, for an innovation that you know. Try to draft your IC Map by observing or interviewing someone who is using the innovation. What did you learn about the innovation and its implementation from this experience?

2. Critique an IC Map that someone else has developed. Can you visualize the ideal use of the innovation from studying the map? Which variation descriptions present clear word pictures? Do any of the components taper off from the *a* variation? Does each component contain an appropriate number of variations? Which would you suggest be changed or clarified?

3. After studying all of the available materials related to a particular innovation, sketch a cluster map of possible components and some of the variations. Then interview or observe someone who is using the innovation. How does you cluster map need to be changed?

REFERENCES

Alquist, A., & Hendrickson, M. (1999). Mapping the configurations of mathematics teaching. *Journal of Classroom Interaction. 34*(1) 18–26.

Bridge, C. A. (1995). *The progress of implementation of the K–3 primary program in Kentucky's elementary schools.* Paper presented at the annual meeting of the American Educational Research Association, San Francisco.

Dunn, L., & Borchardt, P. (1998). *The ESSENTIAL Curriculum.* Kansas City, MO: The Teel Institute.

Heck, S., Stiegelbauer, S. M., Hall, G. E., & Loucks, S. F. (1981). *Measuring Innovation Configurations: Procedures and applications* (Report No. 3108). Austin: The University of Texas at Austin, Research and Development Center for Teacher Education. (ERIC Document Reproduction Service No. ED 204 147).

Koon, S. L. (1995). *The relationship of implementation of an entrepreneurial development innovation to student outcomes.* Unpublished doctoral dissertation, University of Missouri–Kansas City.

Kourilsky, M. L. (1983). *Mini-society: Experiencing real-world economics in the elementary school classroom.* Menlo Park, CA: Addison-Wesley.

Novak, A. (1992). *The entrepreneur's Fast Trac II handbook.* Denver: Premier Entrepreneur Programs.

CHAPTER

4

Understanding Feelings and Perceptions about Change

Stages of Concern

You see. She wasn't interested in what we think. They have already decided what is going to happen.

—A teacher's comment following an exploratory school staff meeting with the superintendent

I don't have time to go see what someone else is doing; I have more than I can get done right here.

—Reaction to a curriculum consultant's suggestions that a teacher observe another teacher's class

My kids have been doing terrific things with manipulative materials in mathematics. Now José and I are talking about bringing our two classes together to do some cooperative groups.

—One teacher's thoughts in the third year of use of a new approach to teaching mathematics

The above quotes are all too familiar to those of us who have spent time in schools talking with teachers as they have been engaged in change. Many feelings and perceptions are expressed, and many more are only whispered or left unspoken. No matter how promising and wonderful the innovation, no matter how strong the support, teachers will still have moments of self-doubt about whether they can succeed with this new way, and whether they even want to. There are also moments of euphoria when the change works well, as well as times it seems it will never succeed.

We all know what it is like during that first year of doing something new and different. We tire more easily. We need more time to prepare. And we can't predict everything that will happen. We never feel like we are really on top of things.

56

Yet, after several years, the new becomes familiar and readily doable. Our thoughts shift from the struggles of figuring out what to do to the satisfactions of seeing what happens with students, and of talking with other teachers about the benefits of the change and about how to fine-tune it to work even better.

Across all of these experiences, there is an affective dimension, for we are not just doing but continually thinking and feeling about how the change is working, how well we are doing, and what effects it is having. Although we will limit our examples here to schools, this personal side of change is experienced by everyone—executives, parents, students, sales representatives, secretaries, and governors—whenever we are involved in change.

FOCUS QUESTIONS

1. How do you handle those personal feelings and perceptions that come out as part of the change process? Should they be ignored?
2. Do all of the teachers in a building or district have the same types of concerns, or are they different for everyone?
3. When you are talking to a teacher, how can you discover what his or her concerns are?
4. Is there a predictable pattern to the feelings and perceptions that people have as the change process unfolds?
5. Do the Stages of Concern always move forward, or can they be arrested or move backward?
6. How fast can teachers move through the Stages of Concern?

The Personal Side of Change

Feelings and perceptions about the innovation and the change process can be sorted and classified in to what we call *concerns*. In fact there is a developmental pattern to how our feelings and perceptions evolve as the change process unfolds, which we have named the *Stages of Concern*. These stages give us a way of thinking about people's feelings and perceptions about change. Additionally, through our research we have developed a set of techniques for assessing concerns.

Understanding the Stages of Concern and using the assessment techniques can result in significantly more effective one-on-one coaching sessions, more relevant workshops, and strategic plans that take into account the personal side of the change process. In this way, the process can be both facilitated and increasingly personalized. A description of the Stages of Concern, the assessment techniques, and their applications is the central topic of this chapter. In subsequent chapters we build on this idea, especially as it relates to the design and delivery of facilitating interventions.

Stages of Concern about an Innovation

The idea of calling one's feelings and perceptions *concerns* was originally proposed by Frances Fuller (1969), a counseling psychologist at the University of Texas at Austin, who took an interest in student teachers as a result of teaching their required educational psychology course. When she started teaching the course, she worked diligently to make it a good one, but the evaluations at the end of the semester showed that ninety-seven out of the one hundred students rated it "irrelevant" and "a waste of time."

Fuller was an exceptional educator. As Howard Jones, a colleague of ours from the University of Houston likes to tell, she did not react as you might expect to the students' evaluation of her course. Instead of being completely discouraged, she asked, "What did I do that turned those three students on?" This was a breakthrough question. When she looked at the three students who had rated the course positively she found that they, unlike the other ninety-seven, had had some sort of previous experience with children. They had either taught a church class or were parents already. Thus they had a different background with which to understand and appreciate the introductory course on educational psychology. Fuller hypothesized that their *concerns* were different as a result of their experiences.

Fuller's Unrelated, Self, Task, and Impact Concerns

Fuller proceeded to conduct a series of in-depth studies of the concerns of student teachers. She then proposed a model outlining how, with increasing experience in a teacher education program, the student teacher's concerns moved through four levels: *unrelated, self, task,* and *impact.*

Unrelated concerns are found most frequently among student teachers who have not had any direct contact with school-age children or clinical experiences in school settings. Their concerns do not center on teaching or teaching-related issues. Instead they more typically focus on college life (e.g., "I hope I can get a ticket to the U2 concert") and college studies removed from professional education courses (e.g., "I hope I pass that geography course"). These students do have concerns, but they are not teaching-related concerns.

Self concerns tend to be most prevalent when student teachers begin their student teaching or other, more intense clinical work. Now they have concerns about teaching, but there is an egocentric frame of reference in terms of what the experience will be like for "me" and whether "I" can succeed. Beginning student teachers with self concerns will be asking questions such as: "Where do I park my car when I get to the school?"; "Can I go in the teachers' lounge?"; and "I hope that I can get along with my cooperating teacher so that I get a good grade." These expressions indicate a concern about teaching, but with a focus on the teacher rather than on the act of teaching or the needs of children.

Task concerns show up quite soon after the start of student teaching, as the actual work of teaching becomes central. Typical expressions include: "Oh! I am so tired, I had to stay up until midnight grading papers"; "When three groups are going at once, my head is spinning; I don't know where to turn next!"; and "These materials break too easily—there are pieces everywhere, and they just play with them!"

Impact concerns are the ultimate goal for student teachers, teachers, and professors. At this level the concerns focus on what is happening with students and what the teacher can do to be more effective in improving student outcomes. Improving teaching and student learning are what the talk and thought are about: "My kids are doing great; they understood what I was trying to do!"; "I am thinking of adding some new interest centers. They might attract those children who don't seem to get it this other way."; and "There is a workshop next Saturday on involving special-need kids in cooperative groups. I am going to take it."

In her studies, Fuller found that over two-thirds of the concerns of preservice teachers were in the self and task areas, while two-thirds of the concerns of experienced teachers were in the task and impact areas. She also observed that at any given time teachers may have concerns at several levels, but that they tend to concentrate in one particular area.

Connecting Concerns to Teacher Education

Fuller next began to examine the relationship between the concerns of student teachers and the content and sequence of their courses and field experiences. Guess what she found? There was not a good match, because the sequence of the courses paralleled the professors' concerns rather than the student teachers' concerns.

The typical teacher education program began with a required course in the history and philosophy of education, because the professors believed that future teachers needed to have an understanding of the background and underlying rationales for why we have K–12 schooling for all children. One innovative professor offered beginning education students twelve hours of training in Flanders's system of Interaction Analysis, which is a way to observe, code, and count the types of questions and statements teachers make during a lesson. This professor's decision was based on the belief that education students needed a structured system of observation to understand what teachers were doing.

As important as these pieces of knowledge may be from the professors' point of view, how well do they match with the beginning education students' concerns? Not at all! If the students have unrelated concerns about getting tickets for rock concerts and learning where to park their car at the school, they will probably not find a series of lectures on colonial schools and John Dewey very useful. So what is the answer?

In response to this dilemma, Fuller (1970; Fuller & Bown, 1975) proposed a different model for the content and flow of a teacher education program, which she named *personalized teacher education*. In such a program, the courses and field experiences are linked with the developing concerns of the students. She believed that becoming a teacher entailed *personalogical development*, or the development of one's own style and philosophy, and that the best way to achieve this end was to address the student's concerns when she or he had them. In the design of a teacher education program, this means offering the courses and field experiences in a sequence that parallels the developing concerns of the students, rather than a sequence that parallels the professors' concerns.

Thus, when teacher education students have self concerns, this is the time for early field experiences, low-ratio teaching activities, and educational psychology courses on children of the same age as those being observed. For students with task concerns, the timing is ripe for the "how-to" components of methods courses. The history and philosophy aspects of teacher education are seen by the students as being much more relevant when offered to parallel the development of their impact concerns, which typically occurs near the end of their program. This personalized approach does not mean that all content that is important from the professors' point of view is left out. Instead, the information is provided *when* it is most relevant to the students' developing interests and perceived needs. In terms of cognitive psychology it means that the students have accumulated sufficient prior knowledge, or have schema constructed so that they are able to draw connections between what they currently understand and what they need to be learning next.

Concerns and the Change Process

As you may have already seen, our research on the concepts and issues related to change has clearly documented that the concerns phenomena that Fuller identified are not limited to college students going through teacher education programs nor to teachers. In fact, everyone involved in change exhibits the same dynamics seen in the education students confronted with the "innovation" of student teaching.

The same *unrelated, self, task,* and *impact* pattern of concerns is found in people involved with all types of innovations and change processes. In addition, choosing the types of "interventions" that are to be done to facilitate the change process is based on the same personalization model. What facilitators of the change process do needs to be reflective of the concerns of those engaged with the innovation and those considering its use. In fact, if the example is simply changed from teaching to a school innovation, the same types of expressions of concerns are typically heard:

> *Unrelated*: I am not really interested in _____ [this innovation]. My mind is on. . . .

> *Self*: I don't know if I can do this. Also, I am concerned about what the principal thinks.

> *Task*: Using this material is taking all of my time. You can't imagine all the pieces and steps that are entailed in just doing one lesson!

> *Impact*: Yesterday, I was talking with Mary. Both of us have found that with this approach, all of the students are engaged in and picking up on the concepts much more quickly.

As these quotes illustrate and the findings from our research and that of our colleagues document (Van den Berg & Vandenberghe, 1981; Persichitte & Bauer, 1996; Shieh, 1996), the same types of concerns exist when people are engaged with any change. Further, the personalized idea about what the leaders need to say and do is the same. Interventions to facilitate change need to be aligned with the concerns of those who are engaged with the change. For example, when teachers are in the first year of implementing an innovation such as whole-language or interdisciplinary curriculum, and they have many task concerns, the most valued and effective facilitator is a teacher or consultant who is highly experienced with the details and mechanics of using the innovation and can offer specific "how-to" tips. Teachers with intense task concerns don't want to hear about the philosophy; they want help in making the innovation work more smoothly. The more abstract and subtle aspects of innovation use are of greater interest to teachers with impact concerns.

Identifying the Stages of Concern

Through our research, we have identified and confirmed a set of seven specific categories of concerns about the innovation that we call *Stages of Concern*, or *SoC* (pronounced "ess-oh-see;" not "sock"!), as presented as in Figure 4.1.

We also developed a more comprehensive definition of the term *concern*:

> The composite representation of the feelings, preoccupation, thought, and consideration given to a particular issue or task is called *concern*. Depending on our personal make-up, knowledge, and experiences, each person perceives and mentally contends with a given issue differently; thus there are different kinds of concerns. The issue may be

FIGURE 4.1   Stages of Concern: Typical Expressions of Concern about the Innovation

	Stages of Concern	Expressions of Concern
IMPACT	6 Refocusing	I have some ideas about something that would work even better.
	5 Collaboration	I am concerned about relating what I am doing with what my co-workers are doing.
	4 Consequence	How is my use affecting clients?
TASK	3 Management	I seem to be spending all of my time getting materials ready.
SELF	2 Personal	How will using it affect me?
	1 Informational	I would like to know more about it.
	0 Awareness	I am not concerned about it.

interpreted as an outside threat to one's well being, or it may be seen as rewarding. There may be an overwhelming feeling of confusion and lack of information about what "it" is. There may be ruminations about the effects. The demand to consider the issue may be self-imposed in the form of a goal or objective that we wish to reach, or the pressure that results in increased attention to the issue may be external. In response to the demand, our minds explore ways, means, potential barriers, possible actions, risks, and rewards in relation to the demand. All in all, the mental activity composed of questioning, analyzing, and re-analyzing, considering alternative actions and reactions, and anticipating consequences is *concern*.

To be concerned means to be in a mentally aroused state about something. The intensity of the arousal will depend on the person's past experiences and associations with the subject of the arousal, as well as [on] how close to the person and how immediate the issue is perceived as being. Close personal involvement is likely to mean more intense (i.e., more highly aroused) concern which will be reflected in greatly increased mental activity, thought, worry, analysis, and anticipation. Through all of this, it is the person's perceptions that stimulate concerns, not necessarily the reality of the situation. (Hall, George, & Rutherford, 1979, p. 5)

With further study and application in schools, colleges, and, to a lesser extent, business, we and our colleagues developed paragraph definitions for each of the Stages of Concern, which are presented in Figure 4.2. Note that the original ideas of unrelated, self, task, and impact have been preserved, but, based on the research findings, the self and impact areas have been clarified by distinguishing stages within each. Self concerns are now divided into two stages—informational and personal—and impact concerns into three—consequence, collaboration, and refocusing.

If you think about it, these stages make intuitive sense, and you certainly hear people express these kinds of concerns. For example, at the beginning of the change process teachers (and others) say:

Well, at this point I don't know much about it, other than we have been told that we will be adopting it (Stage 1 Informational). I don't know what the principal thinks about our doing this (Stage 2 Personal), or if he even knows about it (Stage 1 Informational). I just hope that I don't have to stop doing what I have been doing and start all over again (Stage 2 Personal). I hope that we learn more at the next faculty meeting (Stage 1 Informational).

All of these concerns are in the self area, but they represent two component parts. The person knows a little, but would like to know more (Stage 1 informational), but is also concerned about where he or she stands in terms of the principal's knowledge and position and what he or she will have to give up when the innovation arrives (Stage 2 Personal).

Impact concerns are even more complex. Stage 4 Consequence deals with increasing effectiveness and impact in one's own classroom; Stage 5 Collaboration focuses on concern about working with one or more colleagues; and Stage 6 (Refocusing) indicates that the person has ideas about a more effective alternative. Remember, however, that the overarching theme of Stages 4, 5, and 6 is always concern about improving the impact of the innovation on students.

FIGURE 4.2 Stages of Concern about the Innovation: Paragraph Definitions

6 Refocusing: The focus is on the exploration of more universal benefits from the innovation, including the possibility of major changes or replacement with a more powerful alternative. Individual has definite ideas about alternatives to the proposed or existing form of the innovation.

5 Collaboration: The focus is on coordination and cooperation with others regarding use of the innovation.

4 Consequence: Attention focuses on impact of the innovation on clients in his or her immediate sphere of influence. The focus is on relevance of the innovation for clients, evaluation of outcome including performance and competencies, and changes needed to increase client outcomes.

3 Management: Attention is focused on the processes and tasks of using the innovation and the best use of information and resources. Issues related to efficiency, organizing, managing, scheduling, and time demands are utmost.

2 Personal: Individual is uncertain about the demands of the innovation, his/her inadequacy to meet those demands, and his/her role with the innovation. This includes analysis of his/her role in relation to the reward structure of the organization, decision-making, and consideration of potential conflicts with existing structures or personal commitment. Financial or status implications of the program for self and colleagues may also be reflected.

1 Informational: A general awareness of the innovation and interest in learning more detail about it is indicated. The person seems to be unworried about himself/herself in relation to the innovation. She/he is interested in substantive aspects of the innovation in a selfless manner, such as general characteristics, effects, and requirements for use.

0 Awareness: Little concern about or involvement with the innovation is indicated.

From *Measuring Stages of Concern about the Innovation: A Manual for Use of the SoC Questionnaire* (Report No. 3032) (p.000) by G. E. Hall, A. A. George, and W. L. Rutherford, 1979, Austin: The University of Texas at Austin, Research and Development Center for Teacher Education (ERIC Document Reproduction Service No. ED. 147 342).

Why Are They Called "Stages" of Concern?

The research studies clearly document that there is a quasi-developmental path to the concerns as a change process unfolds. However, the flow of concerns is not always guaranteed, nor does it always move in one direction. *If* the innovation is appropriate, if the principal is initiating, and if the change process is carefully facilitated, then teachers will move from early self concerns to task concerns (during the first years of use), and ultimately to impact concerns (after three to five years).

Unfortunately, all of these "ifs" are not always present in a school, school district, or state. More often than not, the support needed for the change process over the years is not forthcoming, or the principal fails to facilitate effectively, or the district and state annually add more innovations to the point that none are being fully implemented. In these situations, concerns do not progress from self to task to impact in the prescribed stages. Instead, progress is arrested, with Stage 3 Management concerns continuing to be intense. If these conditions do not change, in time many teachers return to self concerns.

In the first conception of the Concerns-Based Adoption Model, the term *Stages of Concern* was deliberately chosen to reflect the idealized, developmental approach to change that we value (see Hall, Wallace & Dossett, 1973). Unfortunately, in most instances, as we pointed out in Chapter 1, change is not viewed and treated as a process but as an event. When this event-mentality is applied, the stages model breaks down, and people are forced into sustained self and/or task concerns.

Can There Be Concerns at More Than One Stage?

When presenting the Stages of Concern, we are frequently asked if it is possible to have concerns at more than one stage at the same time. Of course it is possible. In fact, most of the time a person will have intense concerns at more than one stage. For example, although a teacher may have intense task (Stage 3 Management) concerns, concerns about students are still influencing his or her instructional decision-making. In general teachers will have a conglomeration of concerns representing several of the stages, with some more strongly felt than others, and some absent all together.

Graphically, we represent this conglomeration or array of concerns of varying intensities by using a *concerns profile*. By representing the Stages of Concern on the horizontal axis and the relative intensity of concerns on the vertical, a general picture of a person's concerns can be displayed. The peaks indicate stages that are more intense, while the valleys show those that are less intense.

Different, commonly observed scenarios can be envisaged using concerns profiles. For example, we have already described the first-year user of an innovation with intense Stage 3 Management concerns. That person's concerns profile would have a peak on Stage 3, while the other stages would be lower. If the person were also a first- or second-year teacher, he or she might have more intense Stage 2 Personal concerns about surviving the evaluation process and receiving tenure. In this case the concerns profile would likely have peaks, one for Stage 3 Management concerns and a second peak for Stage 2 Personal.

Another teacher might be very experienced and truly a master teacher. His or her concerns profile would be most intense on Stage 3 Management concerns too, relative to first-year use of the innovation. But her or his second-highest stage could be Stage 4 Consequence, indicating more concern about how use of the innovation is affecting his or her students.

Many combinations of concerns can be imagined and have been observed. In each case, once the profile of concerns has been identified, the important work can begin. As interesting as it is to see and attempt to analyze a concerns profile, the crucial step is in using it to make concerns-based interventions that will be able to resolve the concern and move the person toward more advanced use of the innovation.

Are There Typical Concerns Profiles?

Stages of Concern profiles are a very informative way to illustrate movement and nonmovement during a change process. When concerns profiles are collected at different points in time, each is a snapshot of that moment. The time series of profiles becomes a motion picture of how concerns evolved and hopefully developed.

As the name *stages* implies, and as the numbering of the stages suggests, there is a hypothesized pattern in the concerns profiles when the change process unfolds successfully. This progression takes the form of a "wave motion" of intensity that begins with self concerns being more intense prior to first use of the innovation. Then, as implementation begins, task concerns become more intense, and there is a gradual reduction in self concerns. With time (three to five years), impact concerns can increase in intensity as the self and task concerns decrease. A graphic representation of this wave motion pattern is presented in Figure 4.3.

As we have pointed out, this idealized evolution does not always occur. Attempting to change humans in an organizational context is a very complex, dynamic, and, in many ways, subtle enterprise. However, by looking for the patterns, being knowledgeable about what has been learned about change, and being grounded in the uniqueness and intricacies of the situation, it is indeed possible to plan and facilitate a change process that will unfold in the manner shown in Figure 4.3. But since there is a high likelihood that there will be convoluted turns and unexpected happenings along the way, change facilitators must continuously engage in monitoring and adjusting.

Techniques for Assessing Stages of Concern

The monitoring of the change process should include regular and ongoing assessment of the Stages of Concern of all participants, including the change facilitators. There are three ways to assess concerns:

1. One-Legged interview
2. Open-Ended concerns statement
3. Stages of Concern questionnaire

Each of these techniques has its strengths and appropriate uses, as well as its inherent weaknesses.

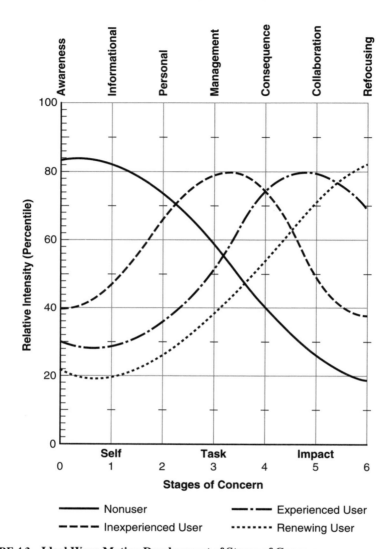

FIGURE 4.3   Ideal Wave Motion Development of Stages of Concern

The One-Legged Interview

Many of the CBAM research studies have carefully documented the numerous interventions that school principals, school improvement teams, lead teachers, staff developers, and others have used to facilitate an innovation (Hall, Hord, & Griffin, 1980; Vandenberghe, 1988; Entrekin, 1991; Schiller, 1991; Stassens, 1993; Shieh, 1996). One of the major findings has been that schools that are more successful in change have statistically significantly more of the very small, almost unnoticed interventions that we call *incidents*. Most of these take the form of a brief conversation between a change facilitator and an implementor about use of the innovation, known as a one-legged interview (OLI).

In the busy work of schools, there is little time for extended conversation; everything happens on the run. The clock is ticking, the bells are ringing, and the students are moving. When the adults do meet, their available time is short. Maybe there are a couple of minutes for a quick chat as they pass in the hall, go to the office to pick up their mail, or grab a few minutes in the lounge during the lunch period.

CBAM research shows that these brief moments are *critical opportunities*, whose frequency will determine the final degree of implementation success. Because the time available is so brief, you must make it count.

One interesting insight into the concept of the one-legged interview came when a principal suggested that we should call them "flamingo interviews." This seemed like a good idea until, when telling a Floridian about the suggestion, she pointed out that, yes, a flamingo does stand on one leg, but it also puts it head under its wing! This would not be a very effective way to assess concerns.

The important beginning of a one-legged conference is to encourage the client (i.e., the teacher) to describe what he or she is doing and how he or she feels about what they are doing, or thinking of doing, with the innovation. The facilitator should not assume that he or she understands the situation, but instead should ask and listen. The trained facilitator can quickly hear, and if necessary probe lightly to clarify, the concerns

Following this quick diagnosis, the second part of the OLI is for the facilitator to do something to address in some way the indicated concerns. This is an important time to keep the "wave motion" in mind. The focus of the intervention needs to be on helping to resolve current concerns as well as anticipating the potential arousal of others.

There are advantages and disadvantages to using the one-legged interview to assess concerns. Advantages include that it can take place whenever you are in conversation, whether it is face-to-face or by telephone. Also, it is unobtrusive, with none of the obvious probing involved in paper-and-pencil methods. Another strength is that the facilitator shows interest in what the teacher is doing, which in and of itself is supportive.

The major disadvantage is accuracy. Different facilitators can hear the same words and offer very different interpretations, especially without training. So be very careful about leaping to conclusions based on a diagnosis derived from a one-legged interview. Things must be checked out and, as with all concerns-based diagnoses, treated as tentative until more is known.

The Open-Ended Statement

The first systematic measure of concerns that Fuller used was to ask teacher education students to write a description of their concerns, which was then content analyzed. This open-ended statement has continued to be helpful. Collecting the information is straightforward. Teachers are given a blank piece of paper that has the following written at the top:

> When you think about [the innovation] what concerns do you have? Please be frank, and answer in complete sentences.

These papers are then collected and content analyzed as described in a manual by Newlove and Hall (1976). The first step is to read the statement to determine if the overall theme is unrelated, self, task, or impact concerns. The statement is then reread, and a Stage of Concern is assigned to each sentence in order to make a holistic assessment. Note that the individual sentence scores are not totaled and averaged. There is no such thing as a "3.5 concern" or a "5.7 average concern." Instead, the entire statement is judged.

This technique has a number of strengths. An obvious one is that the concerns are in the respondents' own words. Also, this technique can be used at any time. For example, if a staff meeting or workshop is coming up, ask the participants to submit an open-ended concerns statement two weeks in advance. This information can then be used to plan the meeting or workshop so that it responds to the expressed concerns. Teachers can thus have input in a nonthreatening way.

As with the one-legged interview, there are disadvantages with the open-ended format. One is that different respondents will provide different amounts of information. One person may write three paragraphs, while another may write only one sentence. Some people will only provide a list of topics instead of complete sentences, which means that there is no concerns statement to be scored. And some people will turn in a blank page, which is very hard to interpret. The other major problem with open-ended concerns statements is reliability. Even thoroughly trained judges have difficulty in agreeing on how to rate them. But for most staff development and meeting situations, where an estimate of concerns is useful, the open-ended statement is an excellent tool.

The Stages of Concern Questionnaire

The most rigorous technique for measuring concerns is the Stages of Concern Questionnaire (SoCQ), which is a thirty-five-item questionnaire that has strong reliability estimates (test/retest reliablities range from .65 to .86) and internal consistency (alpha-coefficients range from .64 to .83). The SoCQ was constructed to apply to all educational innovations. The questionnaire items stay the same, with the only change being the insertion of the name of the specific innovation on the cover page.

It is possible to use the SoCQ to construct concerns profiles. Because the questionnaire has been designed so that there is a raw score for each stage, a graphic representation of the data can be made using a percentile table for conversions. Study and practice, as well as training, will develop one's skill in interpreting these profiles.

Copies of the SoC Questionnaire and the SoC Quick Scoring Device are included as Appendixes to this book. A technical manual (Hall et al., 1979), which includes additional scoring and interpretation information, as well as guidelines for appropriate applications, should also be studied closely by those who wish to use the SoCQ. No one should consider using the SoCQ without study and direct access to this important reference. There is also a specially designed questionnaire for assessing the concerns of change facilitators and a technical manual for its use (Hall et al., 1991).

The advantages of the SoCQ technique for assessing concerns include strong reliability and validity, and the capability of using it to develop concerns profiles. The SoCQ is particularly useful for formal implementation assessment efforts. One disadvantage is that teachers often do not want to fill out this questionnaire, or any other. This most formal way of assessing Stages of Concern should thus be used sparingly. Normally in our school studies we will use the SoCQ twice a year (e.g., early October and late April). Sometimes we have gone to a third assessment in January. We always include space for an open-ended statement on the last page to give the respondents another opportunity to point out something they may think is being missed.

Characteristic Stages of Concern Profiles

Many of the commonly observed SoC profiles are easy to interpret by studying the technical manuals and developing an understanding of concerns theory. Some profiles are in fact "classic"; we have seen them many times, and their meaning is well understood. A couple of these are presented below to illustrate our thinking about diagnosis and implications for concerns-based intervening.

Remember that one of the keys to interpreting concerns profiles is to look for the peaks and valleys. It does not matter if the overall profile is at the eightieth percentile or the twentieth, it is the overall shape that must be considered first. It is the high and low points on that profile that serve as the beginning frame of reference.

The second step is to study closely the full definitions of each stage presented in Figure 4.2. A peak on a profile indicates that the type of concerns that are described for that stage are intense, whereas a valley shows that there is little or no concern for that stage. When there is a peak at more than one stage, the profile must be interpreted by combining the definitions for those stages. In most cases this level of interpretation will serve well.

However, to illustrate that there is always more to be learned about concerns theory and assessment, a couple of the more interesting variations in concerns profiles are described next. For each profile we offer a brief interpretation and ideas about the types of interventions that would make sense.

One, the "Big W" Concerns Profile (so named for its configuration of peaks and valleys), has been observed all too frequently (see Figure 4.4). In this profile Stage 3 Management concerns are very intense, while Stages 1 Informational, 2

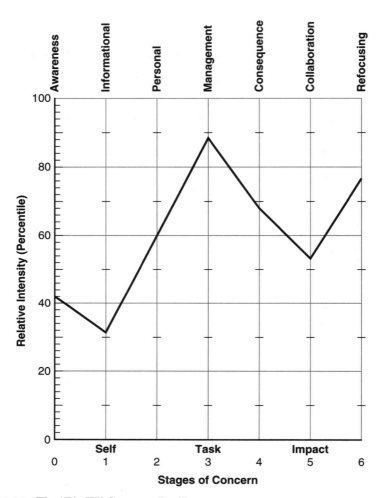

FIGURE 4.4   The "Big W" Concerns Profile

Personal, 4 Consequence, and 5 Collaboration are of much lower intensity. This profile would not be so significant if it were not for the "tailing up" on Stage 6
Refocusing. This combination of peaks and valleys indicates that there are strongly
held ideas about what ought to be done with this innovation (Stage 6) that are related to the very high (and unresolved) management concerns. Teachers with this profile can be quite adamant about their situation and are not as favorably disposed
toward the innovation.

More than a one-legged conference will be needed to address the underlying
cause of such high management concerns. We know from a number of studies that
this concerns profile is frequently found in schools where the principal has displayed

the Responder Change Facilitator Style (see Chapter 7). Part of the strategic action may thus be to strengthen the principal's support of the teachers' use of the innovation.

High Stage 4 Consequence and Stage 5 Collaboration concerns in a concerns profile (see Figure 4.5) represent the ideal goal of a concerns-based implementation effort. After all, the essence of good schooling is teachers with high impact concerns about the effects of the use of the innovation in their classroom (Stage 4 Consequence) and about linking with other teachers in using the innovation (Stage 5 Collaboration). The research of Judith Warren Little (Little & McLaughlin, 1993) on

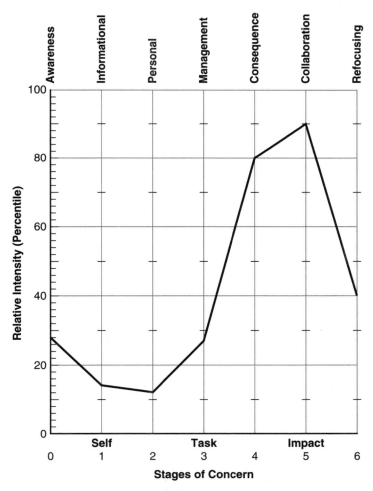

FIGURE 4.5 The Goal of Concerns-Based Implementation Expressed in an Impact Concerns Profile

teacher collegiality confirms the importance of this dynamic for teachers and their students. Unfortunately, finding individual teachers and school staffs that reflect this concerns profile is very rare. To develop to this point means that change truly has been treated as a process, that the innovation has been given sufficient time to be implemented, that there has been a principal with an Initiator Change Facilitator Style, and that the innovation, or more likely an innovation bundle, was significant and matched the school's vision well.

Intervening on this profile should include a celebration. Clearly the teachers and the principal have been hard at work and doing some special things. They should be congratulated, supported, and cherished. Also, this is a fragile system state. A change in a key player (e.g., the superintendent, or the principal), or the arrival of some new mandate from the school board, state, or federal government, can sidetrack and undercut the energy and momentum that have been built. Therefore, a second set of interventions would be to protect and encourage the continuation of the impact concerns, with a special emphasis on facilitating the development of collaborative work for impact concern reasons.

Implications of Resistance in Stages of Concern Profiles

We haven't yet talked about resistance, which is a natural part of change. In the CBAM work, most of what is called *resistance* will show up in the Stages of Concern diagnostic dimension, especially self concerns. Here again, we advocate listening before intervening. Often, what change facilitators see as resistance are aspects of Stage 2 Personal concerns. There is an uncertainty about what will be expected and self-doubts about one's ability to succeed with the new way. There may also be some grieving over the loss of things that were currently being done successfully. Another aspect of this, which is all too frequently overlooked, is the failure to have addressed, early on, Stage 1 Informational concerns. When people don't know what is happening, it is perfectly normal for Stage 2 Personal concerns to become more intense. The less information that is provided, the higher the Stage 2 Personal concerns will be.

At the beginning of a change process, when self concerns are more intense, be sure to use many channels to communicate what is coming. Communication needs to start during the spring, before implementation is to begin. Also, don't simply make a one-time announcement and expect everyone to get the message. People with Stage 1 Informational concerns need to receive small bits of information, repeated across time. They do not want all of the details at once. And don't forget their Stage 2 Personal concerns; they want to hear enthusiasm and promises of continuing commitment to and support for the change.

Of course, there always are real resistors. The reasons for their position are varied. Some may simply not understand the proposed innovation. Others may have a different agenda or a real philosophical disagreement with the innovation. Sadly, there may be one or two who have serious problems elsewhere in their lives, which none of us are equipped to handle. In a concerns profile, especially high personal concerns (Stage 2) in what would otherwise be a nonuser profile (remember Figure 4.4), and a slight "tailing up" of Stage 6, are the indications of what typically is called a "hostile" nonuser.

Let's look more closely at these dynamics. Figure 4.6 presents both the typical positive nonuser profile and the typical hostile nonuser profile. Consider some of the standard comments of the hostile nonuser:

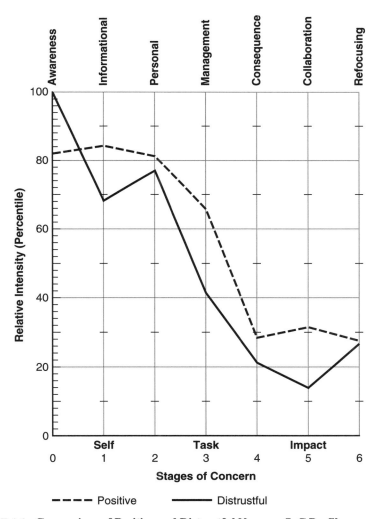

FIGURE 4.6   Comparison of Positive and Distrustful Nonuser SoC Profiles

"Where is the research to show that this is better?"

"We've always done it this way. All you have done is put a new name on it."

"Ah. This is just old wine in new bottles. You know how education is. It's just a pendulum swinging back and forth from fad to fad."

The tendency of change facilitators is to react to such attitudes by saying something like, "Oh, no. This really *is* different." However, from a concerns profile perspective, this is the wrong intervention. What the facilitator is hearing is the "tailing up" on Stage 6 Refocusing, that is, strongly held ideas about how things ought to be different. But which concerns are the highest? Stage 2 Personal, and right behind these are Stage 1 Informational. This indicates that the so-called resistor actually does not have enough information about the innovation and thus is personally uncomfortable about it. So telling this person that this innovation really is different is *interpreted* (see Chapter 9) as follows: "You are telling me that I don't know what I am talking about and that further threatens me." The result is less ability to listen, still higher personal concerns, and probably stronger "tailing up" on Stage 6 Refocusing.

A better intervention approach (although there is no quick cure once this profile is established) would be to express empathy and understanding for the person's concerns. Don't attempt to explain a lot in the first contact. Try to have a series of one-legged conferences to get a sense of what is producing this concerns profile, and then gradually provide pieces of information about the change, the change process, and how they will be supported. There is no simple remedy for this, or for many other concerns profiles. However, what needs to be done to facilitate change in most cases is relatively straightforward: provide information, resources, and support that are aligned with the person's concerns. Read the Vignette presented here to see how Stages of Concern can be used in a districtwide change process.

VIGNETTE

A Districtwide Use of Stages of Concern

In one large suburban school district, the science department coordinators and staff developers engaged in a collaborative project with CBAM researchers to do a concerns-based implementation of their Revised Science Curriculum. Ultimately, this project was very successful in terms of teacher success in implementing the curriculum and was recognized with a special award from the American Educational Research Association based on the practitioner-researcher partnership.

The Implementation Game Plan
From the beginning, an accepted assumption was that change is a process, not an event. Further, the Stages of Concern were used as the guiding dimension when planning training workshops, newsletter content, and other interventions.

The SoCQ was administered twice a year (in early October and late April) for three years, and science facilitators were trained in doing one-legged conferences.

Due to the large size of the district (eighty elementary schools plus many secondary schools), it did not seem reasonable to expect that all schools could be supported in implementation at the same time. So the district was divided into thirds, and there was a phased implementation for one-third of the schools at a time, beginning at six-month intervals. (There were many year-round schools in this district, so the traditional nine-month school year did not apply throughout.)

Addressing Task Concerns
The school board had budgeted for three all-day inservice sessions. Rather than holding all of these at the beginning, they were distributed over the first year and a half of use of the curriculum. This made great sense from a concerns-based perspective, since Stage 3 Management concerns last for at least a year. Also, task concerns are most clear and intense when teachers are engaged in teaching specific lessons. By stretching the time between the inservice days, it was possible to offer each near the time when teachers would have questions about specific lessons they were about to teach.

A cadre of lead teachers was identified and trained to design and conduct the inservice workshops. These teachers had field-tested the materials and were experienced science teachers. They were trained in the Stages of Concern, in how to interpret SoCQ and open-ended data, and in doing one-legged conferences.

The lead teachers established an overall design for workshop days as well as a special version for each grade level. Then teachers from across the district were brought together by grade for the workshops. A newsletter was used to guide teachers in pacing themselves from lesson to lesson and to alert them about upcoming logistical steps. A special class of interventions was the "comfort and caring" sessions, which were hosted by an experienced science teacher after school. Here again, face-to-face opportunities were provided to address the "how-to" questions (Stage 3 Management) as they arose.

Self Concerns and the Principal
The important role of the school principal was anticipated as well. All too frequently the principal is bypassed, and only teachers are trained. Most principals, however, like to know what the teachers are being asked to do. In addition, the change facilitator role that the principal assumes makes a major difference in how successful teachers will be with implementation (see Chapter 7). Remember, one of the early concerns is Stage 2 Personal, when a common question is where the principal stands. Having principals know what is expected and anticipated can help them be more supportive.

Thus early in the district project it was decided that principals should be given information first, before their teachers, although they did not receive as much information, nor the same information. A half-day session was held with the principals, who were shown the materials, the teacher's guide, and sample lessons. All of this addressed their self concerns. They were also told about some of the questions and problems that their teachers would likely have. They were introduced to the lead teachers, and to the special telephone hot line and the other implementation support resources that were designed to help them and their teachers implement the Revised Science Curriculum.

Early Self Concerns of Teachers

According to concerns theory, teachers are likely to have some kinds of self concerns in the school year prior to implementation of the innovation (remember the "wave motion" shown in Figure 4.3?). To address these early nonuser Stage 1 Informational and Stage 2 Personal concerns, a one-and-a-half hour afterschool meeting was held in the spring before implementation was to begin. As the staffs from two neighboring schools met at one of the schools, one of the science department coordinators and a lead teacher hosted an introductory session about the new curriculum, what would be expected, the time line, and the availability of supplies.

These briefing sessions were conducted in an upbeat tone. The expectation was made clear: "Use of this curriculum is board policy." The time line for inservice sessions and the resources that would be available to help teachers were described briefly. Remember, at this point teachers do not want all of the detail. They instead need positive reinforcement and a general picture of what will be happening. At this time, Stage 1 Informational concerns are being addressed, and Stage 2 Personal concerns are being anticipated. If the dispersing of information is paced well, and if the support is in place, the intensity of Stage 2 Personal concerns should not increase disproportionately.

At the end of the introductory sessions, teachers were offered the opportunity to take the teacher's guide with them: "I know that some of you will want to do some preplanning this summer. In case you do, here is a copy of the teacher's guide. You don't have to look at it before the first workshop, but it is here if you would like it."

Impact Concerns?

It was expected that more intense impact concerns would be felt by some teachers, such as those who had field-tested the innovation and those who were experienced science teachers. Although they still had to learn about the curriculum, they were ready to consider some of the more advanced and subtle aspects of innovation use. Interventions for them had to be different in some ways.

To address the varying levels of teachers' concerns, the workshops were designed with alternate routes for parts of the day. One route, which allowed teachers to stay in a small-group setting and to work with an experienced teacher on specifics of lesson preparation, materials, and activities, was chosen by teachers with more self and task concerns. The second route, which gave teachers the choice to work independently or in pairs through a series of self-paced modules, films, and exercises, was selected by teachers with higher impact concerns.

Another strategy that focused on impact concerns was to wait three years before training all teachers in some of the more subtle aspects of the innovation. It was decided at the outset that the first goal was to have all teachers teaching science, instead of having just some teaching science very well. Given the limits on resources and the large size of the district, it would not have been possible to achieve both outcomes at once. It was also not possible from a concerns perspective. As a result, a new round of workshops was started in the third year to prepare all teachers to use cooperative groups in science teaching. Although this had been planned from the beginning, it was not emphasized until after the task concerns about materials, lessons, and scheduling had been resolved.

In summary the first three years of the implementation were designed to have all teachers teaching science by addressing their self and task concerns. During the next three years, other innovations (e.g., cooperative learning), in what was now an innovation bundle, were introduced and supported. With this phasing approach an entire district came to have quality science teaching in most of its elementary classrooms.

1. What characteristics of the interventions used in this district made them especially relevant to each identified Stage of Concern?
2. What would need to happen in a school that continued to have task concerns?
3. Typically, it takes three years for a school staff to resolve their task concerns. What should be done in the third year of implementation to facilitate the arousal of impact concerns?

Summary

In this chapter we have introduced and briefly illustrated the Stages of Concern diagnostic dimension of the CBAM. It is clear that Stages of Concern can be experienced, observed, and documented in most change processes. We also know that it is a cross-cultural phenomenon. For example, Shieh (1996) has observed the same categories of concerns in teachers in Taiwan that we have seen in the United States and that Van den Berg and Vandenberghe (1981) have documented in Belgium and the Netherlands. The various technical manuals and research reports should be studied before launching a major Stages of Concern initiative. Talking with experts and participating in training sessions are important steps too. At all times keep the Guiding Principles in mind as a guide to thinking about using SoC as a diagnostic approach to making facilitating interventions.

Guiding Principles of Concerns Theory

1. We all have personal concerns (Stage 2) when first confronted with change. Rather than condemning someone who has a high level of personal concerns, you first need to be empathetic and work to determine why these concerns are so intense. Then efforts can be made to resolve them.

2. When you find teachers with impact concerns, be sure to take time to encourage him or her. Although these are the types of concerns that we wish educators had all the time, they are unfortunately less frequent than we would like. Spend more time with teachers who have impact concerns. They will find your interest supportive, and you will feel better by being around such positive teachers.

3. Stage 5 Collaboration concerns are very rare in any organization, including schools. When a number of teachers in a building have such concerns, it strongly indicates that the principal has been doing something special. In terms of interventions, do all that you can to nurture and support collaboration concerns. A school where both Stage 5 concerns and Stage 4 Consequence concerns are intense truly exhibits an interest in students and collegiality about teaching.

4. The Stages of Concern can be applied to both individuals and to groups. In fact, throughout this chapter we deliberately did not identify which we were discussing. The concepts and thinking are the same for both. However, because group SoCQ profiles are by definition an average, they can mask individual differences.

DISCUSSION QUESTIONS

1. Think about someone you have talked with recently. What were his or her concerns? What did you say or do in response?

2. What was something that someone did for you when your concerns were really high? At what stage were they?

3. What could be done to help teachers with intense Stage 4 Consequence concerns?

4. What happens to your concerns when your supervisor has high Stage 2 Personal concerns?

5. Think about one of the great teachers you have had. Generally, what were his or her most intense Stages of Concern?

6. Which workshops have you considered to be the best and the worst? How did each match with your concerns at the time?

FIELDWORK ACTIVITIES

1. Attend a workshop and observe the concerns of the participants. How well did the content and process of the workshop match those concerns?

2. Collect and analyze open-ended concerns data from people who are attending a staff meeting or workshop. (Obtain a copy of Newlove and Hall's 1976 manual to help with this.) Develop a recommendation about what should be done and how to address the participants' concerns.

3. Conduct a one-legged conference with a person, and then ask someone else who understands Stages of Concern to do the same, with the same individual. See how well you both assess concerns.

4. Collect Stages of Concern Questionnaire data about a particular innovation for a school or other population. Do this before and after a workshop, or at two points during the semester. Analyze the interventions that were done, and how they relate to changes and nonchanges in the concerns profiles. Be sure to refer to the technical manual for the SoCQ (Hall et al., 1979).

REFERENCES

Entrekin, K. M. (1991). *Principal Change Facilitator Styles and the implementation of consultation-based prereferral child study teams*. Unpublished doctoral dissertation, Temple University, Philadelphia.

Fuller, F. F. (1970). *Personalized education for teachers: An introduction for teacher educators*. Austin: The University of Texas at Austin, Research and Development Center for Teacher Education.

Fuller, F. F., & Bown, O. H. (1975). *Becoming a teacher: Teacher education 1975*. Chicago: The National Society for the Study of Education.

Hall, G. E., George, A. A., & Rutherford, W. L. (1979). *Measuring Stages of Concern about the innovation: A manual for use of the SoC Questionnaire* (Report No. 3032). Austin: The University of Texas at Austin, Research and Development Center for Teacher Education. (ERIC Document Reproduction Service No. ED 147 342).

Hall, G. E., Hord, S. M., & Griffin, T. H. (1980). *Implementation at the school-building level: The development and analysis of nine mini-case studies* (Report No. 3098). Austin; The University of Texas at Austin, Research and Development Center for Teacher Education. (ERIC Document Reproduction Service No. ED 207 170).

Hall, G. E., Newlove, B. W., George, A. A., Rutherford, W. L., & Hord, S. M. (1991). *Measuring change facilitator Stages of Concern: A manual for use of the CFSoC Questionnaire*. Greeley, CO: University of Northern Colorado, Center for Research on Teaching and Learning.

Hall, G. E., Wallace, R. C. & Dossett, W. A. (1973). *A developmental conceptualization of the adoption process within educational institutions* (Report No. 3006). Austin: The University of Texas at Austin, Research and Development Center for Teacher Education. (ERIC Document Reproduction Service No. ED 095 126).

Little, J. W. & McLaughlin, M. W. (1993). *Teachers' work: Individuals, colleagues and contexts*. New York: Teachers College Press.

Newlove, B. W., & Hall, G. E. (1976). *A manual for assessing open-ended statements of concern about the innovation* (Report No. 3029). Austin: The University of Texas at Austin, Research and Development Center for Teacher Education. (ERIC Document Reproduction Service No. ED 144 207).

Persichitte, K. A., & Bauer, J. W. (1996). Diffusion of computer-based technologies: Getting the best start. *Journal of Information Technology for Teacher Education, 5* (1–2), 35–41.

Schiller, J. (1991). Implementing computer education: The role of the primary principal. *Australian Journal of Educational Technology, 14*(4), 36–39.

Shieh, W. H. (1996). *Environmental factors, principal's Change Facilitator Style, and implementation of the cooperative learning project in selected schools in Taiwan*. Unpublished doctoral dissertation, University of Northern Colorado, Greeley.

Staessens, K. (1993). Identification and description of professional culture in innovating schools. *Qualitative Studies in Education, 6*(2), 111–128

Van den Berg, R., & Vandenberghe, R. (1981). *Onderwijsinnovatie in verschuivend perspectief*. Amsterdam: Uitgeverij Zwijsen.

Vandenberghe, R. (1988). *Development of a questionnaire for assessing principal Change Facilitator Style*. Paper presented at the annual meeting of the American Educational Research Association, New Orleans. (ERIC Document Reproduction Service No. ED 297 463).

CHAPTER

5 Exploring the Use of Innovations

Levels of Use

I am happy to report that I have worked the bugs out of how to use math manipulatives with third-graders, and I have a system that works!

Can you help me order the equipment for the sophomore's earth science units? I'm getting things ready to start in September.

I telephoned a colleague at another school to inquire about the problem-based social studies program his school is using and whether it stimulates the kids in critical thinking.

Another teacher and I have worked together with this approach. The changes that we have made this year are really helping students to succeed.

Through our research studies we have learned that use of a new program is not automatic, nor is it a matter of some persons using it and others not. Using new programs or processes is not a simple case of, "Yes, he's using it," or "No, she is not." In any given change effort, implementors will be operating in very different ways with new practices, thus, the real question is, "How is she or he using it?"

Before we began to address this question, use of new curriculum, instructional methods, or organizational structures was assessed in terms of whether the materials and/or equipment required were present in the classroom. Little attention was given to whether the materials ever left the storage closet.

The implicit assumption was that initial training plus materials equaled use. Instead, our observations and studies document a number of different behavioral patterns for nonusers and users. To understand this phenomenon of the change process, the diagnostic dimension of Levels of Use (LoU) was born.

Stages of Concern. Levels of Use. The terms have a deceptively similar ring. However, we are about to make a significant conceptual switch, for whereas Stages of Concern (SoC) addresses the *affective* side of change—people's reactions, feelings, perceptions, and attitudes—Levels of Use has to do with *behaviors* and portrays *how* people are acting with respect to a specified change.

This chapter explores the behaviors of people as they seek to learn about new practices for their classrooms and schools or perhaps ignore such matters entirely. It also examines individuals' behaviors as they adopt and implement new ideas and innovations. Eight Levels of Use will be explained, and examples and applications will be given. Levels of Use is a second diagnostic dimension of the CBAM, and the behaviors of so-called users and nonusers are the basis for describing where people are in the change process and for diagnosing their progress in implementing a change project.

Further, the LoU framework makes it possible to understand and predict what is likely to occur with people in change. Facilitators who understand and apply the LoU concept and its measures are able to provide appropriate interventions that will be relevant and helpful to those involved, or expected to be involved, in change. LoU is a very important concept for evaluators, too. A critical step in determining whether a new approach is making a difference is to determine first if the innovation is being used. Otherwise, as Charters and Jones (1973) observed, there is a risk of evaluating "nonevents."

FOCUS QUESTIONS

1. What is the concept of Levels of Use?
2. How can an individual's Levels of Use be assessed?
3. How can a person be further described by categories at each Level of Use?
4. What does a person look like at each Level of Use?
5. How can Levels of Use be applied to change efforts?

The Levels of Use Concept

Eight classifications, or levels, of how people act or behave with a change have been identified and verified through our research. Since Levels of Use deals with behaviors, it was possible to develop operational definitions of each level (see Figure 5.1). These definitions enable a change facilitator or evaluator to place an individual at one of the levels (Hall et al., 1975). However, the individual assessments can be aggregated for a school- or systemwide view of the extent of use of a particular change.

The first distinction to be made is whether the individual is a user or a nonuser. Three nonuse and five use levels have been identified. Each is described

FIGURE 5.1   Levels of Use of the Innovation

<table>
<tr><td rowspan="6" style="writing-mode: vertical-lr;">Users</td><td>VI</td><td>**Renewal:** State in which the user re-evaluates the quality of use of the innovation, seeks major modifications of or alternatives to present innovation to achieve increased impact on clients, examines new developments in the field, and explores new goals for self and the system.</td></tr>
<tr><td>V</td><td>**Integration:** State in which the user is combining own efforts to use the innovation with related activities of colleagues to achieve a collective impact on clients within their common sphere of influence.</td></tr>
<tr><td>IVB</td><td>**Refinement:** State in which the user varies the use of the innovation to increase the impact on clients within immediate sphere of influence. Variations are based on knowledge of both short- and long-term consequences for clients.</td></tr>
<tr><td>IVA</td><td>**Routine:** Use of the innovation is stabilized. Few if any changes are being made in ongoing use. Little preparation or thought is being given to improving innovation use or its consequences.</td></tr>
<tr><td>III</td><td>**Mechanical Use:** State in which the user focuses most effort on the short-term, day-to-day use of the innovation with little time for reflection. Changes in use are made more to meet user needs than client needs. The user is primarily engaged in a stepwise attempt to master the tasks required to use the innovation, often resulting in disjointed and superficial use.</td></tr>
</table>

<table>
<tr><td rowspan="3" style="writing-mode: vertical-lr;">Nonusers</td><td>II</td><td>**Preparation:** State in which the user is preparing for first use of the innovation.</td></tr>
<tr><td>I</td><td>**Orientation:** State in which the user has recently acquired or is acquiring information about the innovation and/or has recently explored or is exploring its value orientation and its demands upon user and user system.</td></tr>
<tr><td>0</td><td>**Nonuse:** State in which the user has little or no knowledge of the innovation, no involvement with the innovation, and is doing nothing toward becoming involved.</td></tr>
</table>

From *Measuring Levels of Use of the Innovation: A Manual for Trainers, Interviewers, and Raters* (pp. 171–195) by S. F. Loucks, B. W. Newlove, and G. E. Hall, 1975: Austin: The University of Texas at Austin, Research and Development Center for Teacher Education.

briefly in the following paragraphs, and suggestions about appropriate interventions are offered.

Nonusers

Rather than classifying all nonusers in the same way, three very different types have been identified. It is important to understand the behavioral distinctions between them, since the support and assistance that is appropriate for each will vary accordingly. And although the behaviors of each are quite different, all three describe nonusers of the change from an evaluation perspective.

Level of Use 0 Nonuse   When a person knows very little or nothing at all about an innovation or change, and exhibits no behavior related to it, that person is said to be at Level of Use 0 Nonuse. Further, the LoU 0 person will not display any knowledge of or interest in the innovation, and will take no action to learn about it. If such a person receives a brochure in the mail, it is not read. If there is an orientation presentation about the innovation, he or she does not attend, or, if required to attend, grades papers or engages in some other form of off-task activity. Again, there is no action related to the change.

It is not important for such an individual to become involved with the particular change, a facilitator may ignore this person. However, if the person is expected to be involved, the facilitator's challenge is to design and deliver interventions that stimulate interest and support movement to learn about the change. Level of Use 0 Nonuse people are potentially an excellent source of data for the evaluator who is looking for a comparison or control group. However, much to the chagrin of change facilitators and evaluators, significant proportions of LoU 0 people are found in the *treatment* schools.

Level of Use I Orientation   When a person takes action to learn about an innovation, or exhibits interest in knowing more about it, he or she is characterized as being at LoU I Orientation. Typical LoU I behaviors include attending an overview session about the innovation, examining print materials displayed by a vendor, asking questions of colleagues, or writing to a vendor for descriptive materials about various approaches that might work. The behaviors of the individual are related to learning more about the innovation, but no decision has been made to use it.

The facilitator will find it easy to respond to such a person, since he or she is actively looking for information. Thus, relevant interventions include providing information in the most provocative and interesting manner possible, so that adoption and use will be encouraged.

Level of Use II Preparation   An individual who has decided to use the new program or process and names a time to begin is at LoU II Preparation. At this level, use has not started, but the intention and a specific start-up time have been indicated. The person typically is preparing materials and him- or herself for initial use.

It could be that the decision to begin use has been made for the individual—for instance, by a state or district policy that mandates action, or by the principal in concert with faculty peers who are pressing for use. In any case, while how the decision is made is of interest, it does not figure into Levels of Use, which focuses on behaviors. Obviously, the facilitator's role is to be as supportive as possible, providing assistance so that when use does begin, it can proceed as efficiently and smoothly as possible.

The three classifications of nonusers have been verified through studies of change efforts in K–12 schools, universities, medical schools, and business settings. Because the three levels represent three different behaviorial profiles, they provide understanding and guidance to change facilitators in supporting each individual in his or her actions to learn about, consider, and prepare for first use of an innovation. Strategic planners should keep in mind that in order for an entire organization or macrosystem to change, the individual members will need time and appropriate interventions to move beyond these nonuse levels.

Users

Implementation may be said to start in earnest when users and their clients (i.e., teachers and students) begin interacting with it in the classroom or other setting. Five Levels of Use of users have been identified and described. A key in making these distinctions is the type of adaptations that are being made by the user in use of the innovation or in the innovation itself. How this plays out will be discernible as each of the five levels is described below. Keep in mind that although these descriptions are presented in a sequence that is logical, each person will not necessarily follow the sequence. Each LoU is independent of the other; LoU is not a straight-line hierarchy.

Level of Use III Mechanical   At this level the user is actively engaged with the innovation in the workplace. This LoU is characterized by experimentation by the user as he or she endeavors to make the change work for him or her. Adaptations are made in managing time, materials, and other logistics. There is a short-term day-to-day focus on planning and a general inefficiency in how the innovation is used. If it is a classroom innovation, the implementor is making adaptations in its use or in the innovation itself in order to master use of the new practice.

The facilitator's task is to help implementing teachers with the frequently harrowing experiences of finding and organizing materials and scheduling time to plan for use, while they manage classrooms and students and experience the use of the new practices. The lack of knowledge about what will happen next affects such users' efforts to make innovation use more efficient for them.

Successful facilitators of LoU III users are those who are willing to do all sorts of seemingly low-level nitty-gritty tasks to help the implementor achieve short-term success in use. They offer many "how-to" tips and may publish a newsletter and establish a telephone hot line to answer mechanical-use questions as they arise.

Successful facilitators have been known to organize materials in the closet, co-plan with the teacher, run and fetch what is needed, bring in substitute materials when glitches occur, and co-teach or demonstrate teaching in the LoU III teacher's classroom. As noted in the discussion of adaptations, LoU III implementors typically make a series of changes in their use of the innovation to find a system that works for them. A knowledgeable and experienced facilitator can be a highly significant source of help—and thus can receive immediate expressions of gratitude.

Level of Use IVA Routine If the user has been given sufficient time and adequate help, LoU IVA Routine may be reached. At this level, the implementor has mastered the innovation and its use, and has established a regular way of working with it. At this level, users do not plan to make any adaptations or changes; instead use is stabilized. These users may be heard to comment, "Why should I change? My way is working fine." Thus, the LoU IVA person is making no adaptations.

The facilitator may conclude that this user needs no help, since use is established. In this case, congratulations and some celebratory symbol from the facilitator could be wise. On the other hand, a discussion with the user, or an observation to determine how this person's use aligns with the ideal variation on an IC Map (see Chapter 3), could be very informative and ultimately lead to a new set of actions, perhaps a move toward LoU IVB.

Level of Use IVB Refinement Some users begin to observe and wonder how well their use of the innovation is working for the benefit of their clients (in the case of classrooms, this would be students). Based on their reflection and assessment, they make adaptations in the innovation or in their use of it to increase benefits for their clients. These actions signify LoU IVB Refinement. The key here is making adaptations for the clients' benefit (not for the benefit of the user, as in LoU III). Note again how the factor of adaptations helps to understand and distinguish the Levels of Use.

The facilitator is typically welcomed warmly by the LoU IVB person, who is looking for new ways to make the program as successful as possible for students. Since the LoU IVB user is wondering how well the program is working, a key action of the facilitator is to suggest or to help the teacher to find assessment or evaluation tools or rubrics to check on student work. Conversation about adaptations or adjustments in the program to accommodate the assessment findings would be helpful to the LoU IVB user. Providing journal articles and examples of what other users have done will also be useful to this person.

Level of Use V Integration The LoU V Integration person, like the LoU IVB individual, makes adaptations for the benefit of clients, but the LoU V action is done in concert with one or more users. The collaboration is between users, not between a user and a resource person such as a counselor, librarian, or principal. The two or more users collegially plan and carry out adaptations in their use of the innovation that will benefit their students.

LoU V is a significant phase for the evolution of a change process and for the professional culture of the school. Change facilitators should do all that they can to nurture and facilitate its development and continuation. The facilitator's task is to make it possible for people who wish to work together to do so. Thus, seeking accommodations in the schedule to include concurrent planning periods and other logistical arrangements will be greatly appreciated by these users.

It should be noted that some users wish to work together to better manage the new program and its demands, and to increase the users' efficiency and decrease the workloads that new programs frequently demand. This can be a wise means of providing additional help and support to peers. However, this reason for working together is part of LoU III Mechanical Use, not LoU V, which entails collaborating to make adaptations in use for *client* benefits, not *user* benefits.

Level of Use VI Renewal   At Level of Use VI Renewal, the user is exploring or implementing some means to modify the innovation in major ways or to replace it altogether. The modification may constitute one very significant addition or adjustment, or multiple small adaptations that add up to significant change. In either case, the adaptation is intended to benefit clients. Again, making the adjustments is central, and it is the size or number of adaptations that places a person at this level. Curiously, persons at Level of Use VI comprise a small part (2½ percent) of the CBAM database.

Facilitators for persons at this level may applaud them and stay out of their way. However, these users may be called upon or may offer to provide additional materials or resources that will translate their adaptations into reality. For example, the LoU VI individual might be invited to provide professional development activities for and with others to share a possible new direction. Or the user may be asked to join a design team that is planning an entirely new replacement program or a revision of the current program. On the other hand, if the program is meant (through the decision of someone in authority) to be used without changes in its design, the facilitator may find him- or herself in the position of having to tactfully explain that the proposed adaptations are not in line with the expectations of the school, district, or state.

In summary, the operational definitions for each LoU are behavior-based and action-oriented. Levels of Use does not focus on attitudes or feelings; Stages of Concern does that. Because these actions can be observed, facilitators find the LoU construct and definitions useful for observing and analyzing what users are doing, for better understanding their needs, and for further facilitating implementation. Assessing LoU is critical in evaluation and research studies. Otherwise, there is no certainty that the so-called treatment group only contains users and that there really are no users in the control group.

Assessing an Individual's Level of Use

Whereas information about a person's Stages of Concern may be obtained in several ways (see Chapter 4), LoU may be assessed only through long-term observation or use of a specially designed focused interview protocol (Loucks, Newlove, & Hall, 1975). Various researchers and others have attempted to develop a paper-and-pencil measure to determine LoU, although we have consistently stated that it will not work. Measuring behaviors through self-report (as is done in assessing feelings through the Stages of Concern Questionnaire) is like trying to decipher semaphore signals by listening to a radio. In a word, using a questionnaire to rate one's behaviors and to make the distinctions across the levels is not possible.

There are two configurations of LoU interviews: (1) the LoU branching interview; and (2) the LoU focused interview. In both, the person's placement at a LoU is determined by decision points, which are the distinguishing actions or behaviors. In the descriptions above, the factor of adaptations was used as an abbreviated way to introduce each decision point. Figure 5.2 offers a fuller explication of each LoU and the decision points that are used to define them.

The LoU Branching Interview

In the one-legged interview, the facilitator visits with the user in a brief and casual way to gain a broad view of an individual's Level of Use in order to offer appropriate assistance. In a word, the outcomes of this conversation are for facilitation purposes—to make a quick assessment of a person's LoU and to do something that will facilitate further use of the innovation.

The branching interview is constructed so that the facilitator, through a series of questions, gains information about the user's innovation-related behaviors (see Figure 5.3). To gain this quickly assessed estimate of the overall LoU of the individual, the initial question is, "Are you using the innovation?" The response separates nonusers from users, and depending on the response, the "no" or "yes" branch is followed. Then the facilitator needs to ascertain which of the three types of nonusers or five types of users the individual may be. The key in the interview is to stimulate the person to descibe and provide examples of behaviors that he or she is taking in relation to the innovation. The interviewer then refers to the decision points and LoU definitions to determine the person's LoU, which provides the guidance in structuring help and assistance.

The LoU Focused Interview

For research, implementation, assessment, and evaluation studies, more rigorous and detailed data are needed. For these purposes, the prospective LoU interviewer undergoes a three-day training and certification program to prepare for using a more formalized interview protocol, to gain data on levels and categories, and to reliably rate interviews. The result of this process is a matrix constructed by the interviewer to portray a more descriptive account of the individual's behaviors (for training manual on this process, see Loucks et al., 1975). The key to this process is employing questions that are based on a set of seven categories or dimensions that compose each LoU: knowledge, acquiring information, sharing, assessing, planning, status reporting, and performing (see Figure 5.4).

Knowledge   This is the individual's practical and theoretical understanding of the change—its characteristics or elements, how to use it, its potential effects, and the advantages and disadvantages of its use. Unlike the other categories, which relate to the implementor's behavior, this cognitive dimension is not expressed as a behavior. Rather, the knowledge category reflects the degree of complexity and sophistication of one's understanding of the innovation and its use. The higher the LoU, the more complex the knowledge schema.

FIGURE 5.2   Levels of Use of the Innovation with Decision Points

Decision Point F: Begins exploring alternatives to or major modifications of the innovation presently in use

Level VI, Renewal: State in which the user re-evaluates the quality of use of the innovation, seeks major modifications of or alternatives to present innovation to achieve increased impact on clients, examines new developments in the field, and explores new goals for self and the organization

Decision Point E: Initiates changes in use of the innovation for benefit of clients based on input from and in coordination with colleagues

Level V, Integration: State in which the user is combining own efforts to use the innovation with related activities of colleagues to achieve a collective impact on clients within their common sphere of influence

Decision Point D-2: Changes use of the innovation to increase client outcomes based on formal or informal evaluation

Level IVB, Refinement: State in which the user varies use of the innovation to increase the impact on clients within his or her immediate sphere of influence. Variations in use are based on knowledge of both short- and long-term consequences for clients.

Decision Point D-1: Establishes a routine pattern of use

Level IVA, Routine: Use of the innovation is stabilized. Few if any changes in use are made. Little preparation or thought is given to improving innovation use or its consequences.

Decision Point C: Makes user-oriented changes

Level III, Mechanical Use: State in which the user focuses most efforts on the short-term, day-to-day use of the innovation, with little time for reflection. Changes in use are made more to meet user needs than the needs of clients. The user is primarily engaged in an attempt to master tasks required to use the innovation. These attempts often result in disjointed and superficial use.

Decision Point B: Makes a decision to use the innovation by establishing a time to begin

Level II, Preparation: State in which the user is preparing for first use of the innovation

Decision Point A: Takes action to learn more detailed information about the innovation

Level I, Orientation: State in which the individual has acquired or is acquiring information about the innovation and/or has explored its value orientation and what it will require

Level 0, Nonuse: State in which the individual has little or no knowledge of the innovation and no involvement with it, and is doing nothing to become involved

Users

Nonusers

From *Measuring Levels of Use of the Innovation: A Manual for Trainers, Interviewers, and Raters* (pp. 173–195) by S. F. Loucks, B. W. Newlove, and G. E. Hall, 1975: Auston: The University of Texas at Austin, Research and Development Center for Teacher Education.

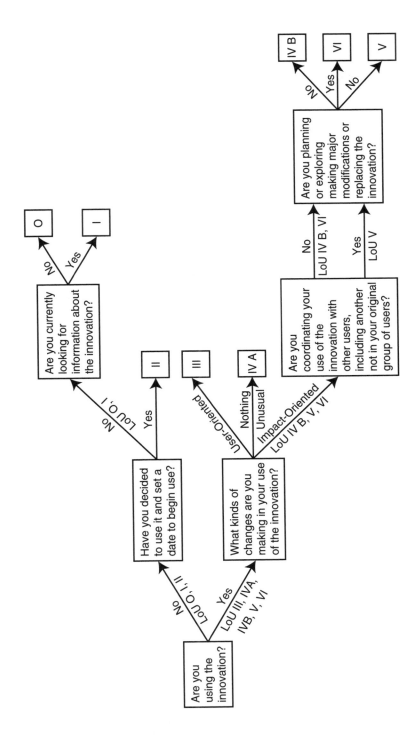

FIGURE 5.3 Format for the LoU Branching Interview

From *Measuring Levels of Use of the Innovation: A Manual for Trainers, Interviewers, and Raters* (p. 22) by S. F. Loucks, B. W. Newlove, and G. E. Hall, 1975: Austin: The University of Texas at Austin, Research and Development Center for Teacher Education.

FIGURE 5.4   Levels of Use Categories

Knowledge: That which the user knows about characteristics of the innovation, how to use it, and consequences of its use. This is cognitive knowledge related to using the innovation, not feelings or attitudes.

Acquiring Information: Solicits information about the innovation in a variety of ways, including questioning resource persons, correspondence with resource agencies, reviewing printed materials, and making visits.

Sharing: Discusses the innovation with others. Shares plans, ideas, resources, outcomes, and problems related to its use.

Assessing: Examines the potential or actual use of the innovation or some aspects of it. This can be a mental assessment or can involve actual collection and analysis of data.

Planning: Designs and outlines short- and/or long-range steps to be taken during the process of innovation adoption; i.e., aligns resources, schedules activities, meets with others to organize and/or coordinate use of the innovation.

Status Reporting: Describes personal stand at the present time in relation to use of the innovation.

Performing: Carries out the actions and activities entailed in operationalizing the innovation.

Acquiring Information   This category focuses on actions taken to seek information about the innovation through such behaviors as questioning colleagues and others, reviewing printed materials supplied by a vendor, visiting sites where the innovation is in place, or writing to request descriptive material.

Sharing   Sharing reflects what individuals tell others about their innovation use (or nonuse), including related ideas, problems, and plans. Through this report of what is shared with others, the LoU interviewer gleans information relative to what the individual is doing with the innovation.

Assessing   Mentally exploring actual or potential innovation use to determine its strengths and weaknesses is the focus of assessing. Informally or formally collecting and analyzing data about what is being done and its effects are examples of assessing. However, assessing may also be only mental reflection about use of the innovation.

Planning   Thinking ahead to design and outline short- and long-term actions to take relative to use of the innovation constitutes planning. The individual is looking beyond today's use to next steps.

Status Reporting   This category entails the individual's reporting his or her own views of overall use of the innovation. The information about the individual, derived from the interviewer's questions in this category, provides a general description of the person's LoU.

Performing   The performing category represents actual use of the innovation and what it looks like in the workplace (most frequently classrooms). In the LoU interview, specific examples of use will be rated in the performing category.

One of the interesting aspects of the LoU categories is that all, with the exception of performing, represent actions relative to innovation use that occur outside the actual moments of its delivery in the classroom. As is obvious, much activity related to using innovations occurs beyond the classroom, or use site, and significant time and activity are invested in such behavior.

How the levels and categories relate (for further explanation, see Hall & Hord, 1987) is depicted in the LoU Chart in Appendix 3. For each LoU, the category behavior that occurs is different. Description of these behaviors is found at the intersection of the horizontal row that describes a particular LoU with the vertical column that addresses each category. The trained LoU interviewer is skilled at asking questions that allow the user to describe what he or she is *doing* in relation to each category. The trained LoU interviewer can also rate the bits of information obtained in an interview in order to determine the overall LoU.

Applying Levels of Use

There are two major ways in which Levels of Use can be employed. One is in planning for and facilitating the change process; the other is in conducting evaluation and research studies. The first can be considered formative use; the latter involves the summative domain.

Facilitation of Change

Like Stages of Concern, Levels of Use provides an understanding of implementors' relationship to the innovation. However, unlike SoC, which represents affect about innovations, LoU focuses on the implementors' behaviors. Thus, the LoU concept and its measures contribute in a second way to describing change at the individual and group levels. These descriptions enable the change facilitator to understand where each person is and to determine appropriate support for furthering the change process. For facilitating purposes, the first need is for an overall estimate of the LoU of the individual, which can be obtained with a one-legged conference or an informal branching interview.

Frequently, it is desirable to obtain an estimate for a group of persons, for instance, all the kindergarten and first-grade teachers, or an academic department in a high school. This is done by interviewing each individual and aggregating the data.

This assessment is followed by provision of interventions for the group. Similarly, data could be collected from all or a sampling of individuals to assess the Levels of Use in a school or system. This may well be the case for planning. If district and even state data are desired, representative sampling could be done across the unit.

We strongly believe that each person's Level of Use and success with a change is in large measure influenced by the facilitation he or she receives. If no support and facilitating interventions are offered, many will never fully implement the innovation, and others will remain nonusers. Further, those who are at LoU III Mechanical Use need interventions that will help them move beyond this level, or they may adapt the innovation to make it easier for them to manage, or they may stop using the new practice altogether. There are, however, effective actions that change facilitators can take to assist individuals in moving up the use levels.

From a strategic perspective, assuming that all potential implementors across a system should ultimately be users, the facilitator's first challenge is to intervene in ways that support individuals in moving from LoU 0 Nonuse to LoU I Orientation. Although, hopefully, intended users would have been involved to some degree in deciding to adopt or to develop the innovation, this is frequently not the case. The facilitator, therefore, may need to begin by making people aware of the impending innovation and all expectations regarding the individual's role with it. The first objective is to stimulate people to actively seek information (Decision Point A), thus moving them to LoU I Orientation. Keep in mind, however, that each person must move through Decision Point A in order to be characterized as being at LoU I Orientation.

At LoU I Orientation and II Preparation, information is needed from the facilitator about the purposes and requirements of the change, and the time lines for implementation. This information should be general so as not to be overwhelming, yet specific enough to allow people to move to the next level. At these nonuse levels, individuals also need information about required materials and equipment—their purchase and preparation—and about how to get started. The advice should be practical, with only a moderate amount of attention to theory.

As use is inititated, most if not all first-time users of an innovation will be at LoU III Mechanical Use. Typical behaviors reflect concerted effort to find and organize materials. Effort is invested in searching for time to plan for and put new ideas into practice. These users try multiple ways of handling various parts of the innovation. There are innovation-related surprises as well as a short-term focus to planning (e.g., for the next day). During this period, then, the user typically needs help in finding, ordering, and organizing materials.

Help in finding the time for managing these logistics and for experimenting with the innovation is imperative. Facilitators who can help LoU III users do this will be greatly appreciated. "How-to" workshops to develop management skills and to provide guidance in structuring tasks are essential. Making it possible for users with common problems to meet with an experienced user to ask technical questions is another effective intervention that can be a high priority for LoU III users at this time.

If people have appropriate facilitative assistance and time, they typically move to LoU IVA Routine. They have established a way to use the innovation that they believe works for them and their students or other clients. By definition, the LoU IVA user does not experiment with the program further, makes no adaptations in the program or in her or his way of delivering it, and states that she or he plans to continue the current use. This is an especially important time to check on the user's Innovation Configuration (see Chapter 3).

If the LoU IVA user meets the expectations set forth in the goals of the change effort, one intervention here is to celebrate. Give praise and other recognition to reinforce the person's efforts. If, on the other hand, a user is using a less-than-desirable configuration of the innovation and has become stable (LoU IVA Routine) in this pattern, the facilitator needs to encourage further refinements in use. Interventions to help the user continue to change may be in order at the same time that encouragement is being provided.

LoU IVB Refinement users are typically a pleasure for facilitators. These people are searching for new materials, activities, or other refinements that will benefit the students. Importantly, they are also mentally assessing how well the innovation and their use of it are working for their students. Thus, these users welcome suggestions for assessing effectiveness and new ideas for improving varied aspects of the program or practice. Putting them in contact with others to access new information is a key intervention. Bringing others to visit them to see their ideas at work is confirming and rewarding. In addition, LoU IVB users may be potential facilitators.

If individuals are interacting with other users to coordinate their use and are making efforts to work together for their clients' benefits, they are diagnosed as LoU V Integration. Through collaboration, they are making adaptations in their use for client gains. In classroom innovations, they may be regrouping their collective students to take advantage of their interests, or reorganizing activities and/or materials to accommodate differing ability levels. The facilitator supports the LoU V users by making it possible for them to more easily coordinate their efforts (e.g., by restructuring schedules, space, etc.). Time for planning together will be of utmost importance. If the integration involves several people, training for them in shared decision-making could be relevant.

Normally, not a lot of a facilitator's time is directed to LoU VI Renewal users. In typical change processes, very few people reach this level, and those who do have typically done so by virtue of their own creative abilities and energy. Further, these users are interested in significantly modifying the innovation, which may or may not mesh with the planned goals of the change effort. These users can be a very positive force in change because they have ideas, and because their ideas are focused on improved outcomes for their clients. They could, however, be headed in a completely different direction from the one the innovation's designer intended. Their work should thus be either supported and applauded, or channeled in more productive ways that are consistent with organizational goals.

Motivation for Movement in LoU

One aspect of LoU that has been the source of interesting speculation but little research is the causes for change in LoU. Does change come about simply as a result of increasing experience with the innovation, or is it related to affective aspects of the person? What causes people to move to higher Levels of Use? Are there particular keys to understanding why people move to lower LoUs and from use to nonuse? Do certain kinds of interventions make a significant difference in movement? Although each of these questions is intriguing, there has been little research to aid in developing answers. One reason for this is the multivariate nature of the questions, which means that they would be best answered with a longitudinal design, a project few researchers are willing to undertake.

The simplest way to think about the motivational aspect of movement in LoU would be to assume a one-to-one correspondence with movement in Stages of Concern. There is an obvious correspondence between LoU and SoC. For example, task concerns correspond to the LoU III Mechanical Use, Stage 5 Collaboration concerns correspond to LoU 5 Integration. But we know that this picture is too simplistic. Using large databases from cross-sectional studies, we have been able to predict one diagnostic dimension from knowing the other only at the extremes. In other words, if a person is a nonuser, it can be predicted statistically that he or she is likely to have more intense self concerns. If the person is at the higher LoUs, it can be predicted that she or he is likely to have aroused impact concerns. However, no prediction of SoC is possible when a person is at LoU IVA Routine, which means that any SoC profile seems possible in this case.

Our preferred hypothesis about the relationship between movement in LoU and motivation is as follows. At the lower Levels of Use, the actions cause the arousal of concerns. For example, when a person attends an orientation workshop, the Stage 1 Informational and Stage 2 Personal concerns increase in intensity; use is driving concerns. At the higher levels, concerns would seem to drive LoU. A teacher who has concerns about certain students not doing well in mathematics will take action to learn about alternative approaches (LoU IVB Acquiring Information). A teacher who is developing concerns about working with a colleague, so that they can serve more students (Stage 5 Collaboration), is likely going to start talking with the colleague about what they might be able to do (LoU V Integration). All of this is speculative, but does have a great deal of attractiveness. The simple linear relationship, although initially logical in an intuitive way, is too simplistic. Human emotions and behaviors are much more complex, especially when it comes to their dynamics during times of change

Evaluation of Change

In using LoU for evaluation of implementation, the three-day formal training and certification in the rigorous LoU focused interview, data collection, and data coding are required (see Loucks et al., 1975). Such training permits the evaluator or researcher to ascertain with reliability each individual's Level of Use in each of the categories and the overall LoU. Having such a precise measure of LoU makes various interpretations possible: How effective was the implementation plan? How effectively has facilitation been conducted? How far has the change process moved? Has institutionalization been achieved?

For instance, if users are at LoU III Mechanical Use, student/client outcomes are not likely to be higher than would be found in a control group of nonusers. (Remember all those evaluation reports with no significant differences?) On the other hand, if teachers are at LoU IVB and are making changes in the innovation or in their use of it to increase student outcomes, this information is helpful in interpreting how effective the innovation may be. Whether for facilitating the change process or evaluating implementation, Levels of Use is a valuable tool.

Sidelights about LoU

Two final little items: you may have noticed that Stages of Concern uses Arabic numerals for its naming system, while Levels of Use employs Roman numerals. This is simply an effort to further differentiate the two concepts and their classifications. We are also careful to say *Stages* of Concern and *Levels* of Use, and not vice versa.

You may have wondered why Level of Use IV is the only one divided into two sections, LoU IVA and LoU IVB? The answer is one of history and pragmatics. When the initial LoU verification study was launched, there were only seven levels, 0 through VI. However, as the research team went about its explorations, the need for an additional classification became very apparent. To add this level, without having to renumber the entire database, LoU IV was split into two levels: IVA Routine and IVB Refinement.

In the Vignette that follows, we will use an individual teacher, rather than a school, as an example of LoU in a change process. And, rather than supplying analysis at the end of the Vignette, we will analyze this individual as we learn her story.

VIGNETTE

Time Series Snapshots of Hypothetical User

Students of CBAM have suggested that it is easier to understand Levels of Use if the example of a "real live person" is provided for each level. Therefore, we introduce Louise, a hypothetical language arts classroom teacher in a high school. We will trace Louise through all the Levels of Use, describing her at each one, including the decision points. But please remain aware that in reality, people do not move hierarchically from one level to the next. Sometimes an individual may skip a level, move back to a lower level, or reach a level and move no further. At other times a user may drop the innovation entirely (this is not rare, particularly at LoU III) if she or he receives no help and becomes increasingly unable to make sense of the change or to use it efficiently.

Louise, who has been in the school for four years, is considered a good teacher by the students and is respected by her peers. Her principal told her that he had heard that the state board of education was recommending that schools think about including a service project in the curriculum, and he asked Louise what she thought. Louise expressed a lack of information and interest, as she was not sure what it was all about (LoU 0 Knowledge). Further, she had just purchased a new home and had a new lawn planted, and was busily occupied with preparations for the school year that would begin shortly. She gave no attention to service learning (LoU 0 Performing), and asked the principal no questions (LoU 0 Acquiring Information).

[Overall, Louise is at LoU 0 Nonuse with regard to service learning.]

At the end of September, the gentle autumn rains had come to Louise's lawn, and to her classroom came a student from another high school in the city, who asked Louise if the class would be doing a service learning project. Louise said, "No, I don't think we'll do that this year." However, the topic came up again on Saturday, when Louise was playing tennis with some colleagues, one of whom mentioned going to an orientation session on service learning and asked Louise what she thought. She described her student's question and borrowed materials from her tennis partner's workshop to review (LoU I Acquiring Information and Performing)

[Because Louise has taken action to learn more about service learning (Decision Point A), she has moved to Level I Orientation.]

The principal supported Louise's expression of interest and encouraged her to learn more. Louise found the materials to be highly interesting (LoU I Assessing). She talked with her language arts department chair and called her language arts coordinator to find out what was available in the school and district relative to service learning (LoU I Acquiring Information). The principal suggested that Louise visit the American history teacher in the school who had begun implementing service learning.

Subsequently, she attended a second district inservice session on service learning and became quite excited about the ideas (LoU I Acquiring Information and Assessing). She shared what she was doing with her second-period junior level language arts class, whose members asked questions and expressed interest (LoU I Sharing). Louise decided that she would attend a series of three workshops. Her principal said that the school's budget would support teachers who wanted to attend the workshops that focused on the philosophy of service learning and on how to use it with high school students. As a result, Louise said that she would begin to "do" service learning with the second-period class immediately after Thanksgiving.

[Because Louise has decided to use service learning and sets a specific time to begin (Decision Point B), she is at LoU II Preparation.]

Louise attended the workshops on service learning and considered them to be quite good. She thought that the philosophy and values of service learning were well articulated and that they provided a meaningful basis for selecting the materials and choosing activities for students (LoU II Assessing). She began to collect materials and to make lesson plans for her class that would engage in service learning (LoU II Performing). Further, Louise and the other workshop participants were networking and sharing tips on how to get started, even though some people were from rural areas some distance away from the city (LoU II Sharing and Acquiring Information).

On schedule, Louise initiated service learning with her second-period class after the Thanksgiving break. Since the holiday season of giving and sharing with others was in the air, Louise had thought this might be a good time to launch service learning.

It was a good time, but it was also a maddening time. Louise had prepared all the suggested materials to teach the first activities, but was unsure about how (or with whom) to make contacts for doing service projects in the community (LoU III Knowledge). The students were excited by the plans and clamored to be quite independent in all phases of the service projects, while Louise was trying to keep up with finding and providing materials, activities, and ideas (LoU III Planning and Performing). She made a number of unproductive phone calls to community members to enlist their support and placement of projects. She commented, "Everything seems to take more time than I had anticipated" (LoU III Status Reporting). A crisis almost occurred one day when she had not prepared sufficiently for the class and a school board member stopped by.

Parents telephoned, and some came to the class, to find out what was going on, which was a mixed blessing for Louise in the midst of all that she was trying so hard to do. The parent inquiries were both useful and distracting. It took significant time to explain service learning and their children's role in it to each one, although after hearing about the projects, many parents offered their support, time, and resources. She tried to train one of the parents to make assignments for the students, but this required more of her time than was helpful, so she dropped this idea (LoU III Performing). The principal checked in regularly, providing support and some suggestions and ordering materials that were needed. Somehow Louise made it to the holiday break.

[Because Louise is using the innovation and making user-oriented changes (Decision Point C), she is at LoU III Mechanical Use.]

During the December-January break Louise reflected on her work with service learning and how disappointing her use had been (LoU III Assessing). She decided that she definitely would not expand it to other classes until she had ironed out the wrinkles, and that in the spring semester the second-period class would do only two projects and that there would be a great deal of planning (LoU III Planning). Louise would invite the class to reflect on their experience, and together they would correct their errors and discuss frustrations. She would guide them to an area of language arts curriculum that would fit well with the projects, thus integrating service learning so that it and language arts were more meaningful. More importantly, this would save her valuable classroom time (LoU III Planning). She talked this over with the langage arts coordinator, who supported her assessment and plans (LoU III Sharing).

At the end of the school year, Louise breathed a sigh of relief. She and the second-period juniors had accomplished the two projects, the second coming off more smoothly than the first (LoU III Assessing). Louise had asked the workshop leader and the history teacher to come into her classroom several times to give her pointers and ideas (LoU III Acquiring Information). This had helped a great deal. Having someone in the building who was more experienced with service learning had been especially meaningful. Louise and the students assessed the triumphs and traumas of the two spring projects, and all felt that they had made significant strides in how to do service learning successfully (LoU III Assessing). Further, the principal congratulated the students and Louise publicly on their efforts.

In the fall, Louise continued to do service learning with that year's second-period junior class, using the improved methods that she and her students had developed during their spring projects. She made no adaptations in the projects nor in her way of working with students for the fall semester (LoU IVA Performing).

[Because Louise has determined a satisfactory way to do service learning and has repeated her approach in the fall (Decision Point D-1), she is at LoU IVA Routine.]

In the following spring semester, Louise and her class did two service projects and each went well. But for the second one, after talking with her principal and carefully training and planning with the students, she gave them the opportunity to make their own contacts to initiate their projects. She felt this additional responsibility would improve the students' understanding of the community and of how to go about making arrangements in the "real world" (LoU IVB Assessing). It did indeed make the students feel very empowered and capable. This move was also applauded by the parents, who saw it as an opportunity for their children to develop poise and confidence while giving service to others.

[Because Louise has adapted her use of the innovation to increase client outcomes (Decision Point D-2), she is at LoU IVB Refinement.]

In May, the principal dropped a hint to the local newspaper's editor, a friend in the Rotary Club, who picked up on the story of Louise's students and sent a reporter to interview the class. Louise suggested that the reporter also interview the history teacher (Thomas) and his class about their service learning experiences. The discussion between the two teachers and the reporter after the interviews focused on the local railroad museum and its need for exhibits, publicity, and docents to guide tours for lower-grade children.

Later that night, Louise had an idea—in the fall, why couldn't she and Thomas organize the senior students from their classes into task forces that would explore the museum's needs and determine how to address them (LoU V Planning). The senior students, who would have experienced service learning and who could offer the content and capacity of their history and language arts courses, would be allowed to develop plans and procedures for the various parts of the project, although they would be monitored carefully by their teachers.

At the beginning of the fall semester, Louise and Thomas and their classes began to meet together during second period in the media center, where there was space to accommodate them. Louise worked in-depth with various groups of students while Thomas floated to facilitate and support the others. The two teachers did extensive planning for this team-taught, blocked cohort of students. They would frequently exchange assignments so that each played various roles with the students, keeping their work fresh and their ideas stimulating to the students (LoU V Performing). They occasionally invited the principal to actively participate in their project.

[Because Louise has initiated student-oriented change in the innovation in coordination with Thomas (Decision Point E), she is at LoU V Integration.]

Louise was quite pleased with her work with Thomas (LoU V Assessing). The history students had led the research among community "old-timers" to gain information about the early days of the railroad. The language arts students supplied leadership in designing publicity about the museum. All students developed scripts about the various exhibits and trained each other to deliver the information to younger children. They made schedules for the children's visits and assigned themselves as docents to guide the tours. Louise and Thomas were very excited about working in tandem with their students (LoU V Performance).

Then, during the Thanksgiving holiday, Thomas moved to another state, which forced Louise to consider a new dimension to service learning. Stimulated by the gift of some computers and related equipment from her uncle, during the winter holiday she began to explore how her students might use e-mail to connect with students of the other teachers in her workshop network (LoU VI Assessing).

The language arts coordinator and principal conferred with Louise about the new idea. They decided that the students from various schools who would communicate by e-mail would select a common service topic for investigation in their respective communities, and then use the technology to share information, report needs, brainstorm solutions, develop plans, critique each others' ideas, and share results of their projects.

[Because Louise has explored major modifications in how to plan for and execute service learning (Decision Point F), she is at Level VI Renewal.]

This is not the end of Louise's story, but it is quite enough for now.

1. Consider the time line of Louise's journey through Levels of Use. What reaction, if any, do you have to the pace of her movement?
2. What, if anything, should Louise's principal and/or curriculum supervisor do with her now?
3. Does Levels of Use give you a means for understanding the process of using new programs? Explain your response.

Summary

In this chapter, Levels of Use, a second diagnostic dimension of the CBAM, was introduced and described. The decision points, which differentiate the levels that include the nonusers and users of innovations, were presented as a means for precisely identifying individuals at the various levels. An additional means for illuminating the eight levels is the use of seven categories, which were also described.

As outlined in this chapter, two procedures—one that is informal, which is used for facilitation purposes, and one that is more rigorous, which is used for research and evaluation purposes—may be used to assess individuals for their Level of Use. How Levels of Use may be employed to facilitate the change process was discussed, as were abundant examples of interventions that can be applied to assist individuals and groups in their movement to higher Levels of Use.

A Vignette of a teacher's LoU as she learned about and used service learning was shared, along with rich descriptions of her use as she proceeded through her hypothesized journey. Similar to the work that a rater of LoU interviews would do, codings of the level and category were given to pieces of information and data that were revealed in the case story. While this case is purely an invention, it reflects real life and provides an intimate portrait of a user of an innovation at various Levels of Use.

We also made reference to the importance of documentiong Levels of Use in research and evaluation studies. In doing such studies, it is crucial to assess LoU in the control/comparison group as well as in the treatment group. We almost guarantee that both groups will contain a mix of users and nonusers.

Guiding Principles of Levels of Use

1. With any innovation, each person exhibits some kind of behaviors and thus can be identified as being at a certain Level of Use.
2. The decision points that operationalize the levels and the information related to categories contribute to the overall description of an individual's Level of Use.
3. It is not appropriate to assume that a first-time user will be at Level III Mechanical Use. Nor should it be assumed that a person who has used the innovation several times will not be at LoU III.
4. An interview is the only means by which to successfully and efficiently collect LoU information. A written format cannot sufficiently account for an individual's varying responses at each LoU. The only alternative to the LoU interview would be extended ethnographic fieldwork using the LoU chart as the observation and interview guide, which is what was done in the original LoU interview validity study (Hall & Loucks, 1977).
5. Informally gathered information about an individual's LoU can be used for facilitating implementation of change; more rigorously collected LoU data can be used for conducting research studies of change and for evaluating the extent of implementation.
6. The Levels of Use are presented in a logical sequence, but this is not always followed by everyone. Typically, people move sequentially from LoU 0 to LoU IVA, and then may move up, down, or stay at LoU IVA.

DISCUSSION QUESTIONS

1. Describe an experience you have had with a change wherein you can identify the different LoUs.
2. How does the factor of change discriminate each of the five levels of users?
3. Use examples to illustrate and discuss how the categories expand the descriptions of an individual's LoU.
4. What are the two major LoU applications to a change effort; how are they similar and different?
5. Think of an innovation, such as technology or problem-based learning. How could LoU be used as a diagnostic tool to plan for its implementation?
6. How might teachers' Levels of Use of a new math program be used to explain student outcome scores three years after introducing the program?

FIELDWORK ACTIVITIES

1. Interview three people (e.g., teachers) about an innovation. Use the LoU branching interview technique to estimate each individual's LoU, and then design an appropriate intervention for each. If you can't find three teachers, use classmates. Remember that they don't have to be users for you to assess their LoU.
2. Plan how Levels of Use could be employed at the school district or state level to assess implementation of a systemwide school improvement project.
3. Identify a change effort that is early in its initiation at your campus or in your workplace. Explain how you would use Levels of Use to develop and guide a three-year implementation plan.

REFERENCES

Charters, W. W., Jr., & Jones, J. E. (1973). On the risk of appraising nonevents in program evaluation. *Educational Researcher, 2*(11), 5–7.

Hall, G. E., & Hord, S. M. (1987). *Change in schools: Facilitating the process.* Albany: SUNY Press.

Hall, G. E., & Loucks, S. F. (1977). A developmental model for determining whether the treatment is actually implemented. *American Education Research Journal, 14*(3), 263–276.

Hall, G. E., Loucks, S. F., Rutherford, W. L., & Newlove, B. W. (1975). Levels of Use of the innovation: A framework for analyzing innovation adoption. *Journal of Teacher Education, 26*(1), 52–56.

Loucks, S. F., Newlove, B. W., & Hall, G. E. (1975). *Measuring Levels of Use of the innovation: A manual for trainers, interviewers, and raters.* Austin: The University of Texas at Austin, Research and Development Center for Teacher Education.

PART THREE

The Imperative for
Leadership in Change

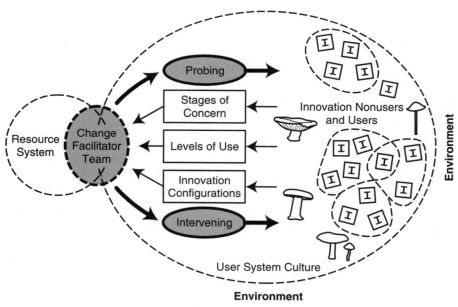

THE CONCERNS-BASED ADOPTION MODEL

While there are multiple factors associated with the success of change processes, a highly significant one is leadership. Skilled change facilitators use the CBAM diagnostic tools and techniques, described in Part Two, to effectively facilitate change processes. The key is what the facilitating leaders do with the diagnostic and other information.

Chapter 6 reports six major strategies or functional types of interventions used by facilitators for increasing the potential for success in change. These six strategies were identified from a review of the literature on change leadership, in which the CBAM research is a prominent source. These six strategies can serve facilitators as a guide for planning and acting as a change process unfolds. But just what is an intervention? The definition, the kinds and sizes of interventions, and their analysis are the focus of Chapter 6.

Research informs us that facilitators approach change in differing ways, thus, expressing different Change Facilitator Styles. The concept of style differs from behavior, a distinction that is made clear in Chapter 7. Additionally, three Change Facilitator (CF) Styles—Initiator, Manager, and Responder—are defined and differentiated. Important information in this chapter is the description of the relationship of CF Style to higher levels of implementation success.

A focus on shared or collaborative leadership and team work has become increasingly frequent in current descriptions of organizations. This is an especially important concept and *modus operandi* in schools, as administrators and teachers alike strive to accomplish all that is asked of them. Furthermore, there is a high likelihood that no one person will have the capacity to deliver all that is demanded by the complexities of change. Thus, the Change Facilitator Team approach, described in Chapter 8, is desirable.

This part of the text should not be viewed as a recipe book, for all changes occur in their unique organizational setting and require context-specific actions. Instead these chapters provide ideas about approaches for developing the change leadership team that should be considered in facilitating change in one's own organization.

CHAPTER

6

Describing What Change Facilitators Do

Interventions

I am so pleased. Our school improvement team just finished writing a grant for $50,000 that will supply resource materials and equipment for our new science program.

What can I do? My teachers have been to the fall series of three workshops and they still don't understand how to operate the Students-Plus Tutoring process. It appears that one-to-one help is now needed.

Interdisciplinary curriculum development and teacher teaming have required a significant amount of time and resources across these first three years for their support, but they are well launched in our school, and we are preparing to report to the board about our efforts.

For decades there has been a lack of understanding of and attention to the process of change. There exists generally, in the public and professional minds, an assumption that change just happens. We are reminded of two theories articulated by Chin and Benne (1969):

1. The Rational Empirical approach to change postulated that a good program or process provided to good people would find its way into their practice. (The clue here is *good* program and *good* people.)
2. The Power Coercive approach maintained that a good program or policy delivered to good people through the offices of a power or authoritarian figure would certainly ensure change in practice. (The key here is *power* and its influence.)

Even today these two approaches tend to be engaged by would-be change agents who assume that change will just happen if an attractive or needed innovation is presented (or mandated). What is typically overlooked by such would-be reformers is that most change implementors have full-time (or more!) jobs, and don't have the opportunity to carefully and methodically design a self-changing approach. There are particular difficulties if the innovation is one vastly unfamiliar to the persons who will implement it.

What we know from our own research and review of the literature on successful school change is that facilitators are needed in a major way to support implementors. The main purpose of this book is to help would-be change facilitators to understand this and to develop the insights and skills needed to address successful change. And these facilitators are very active, as has been abundantly discussed in previous chapters. Through the reviews of school change success stories, we have with certainty identified many of the actions required of facilitators. These change facilitation actions are the topic of this chapter.

FOCUS QUESTIONS

1. What do we mean by interventions?
2. Who delivers interventions?
3. To support successful change efforts, what six basic kinds of interventions are needed?
4. What additional kinds of interventions may be considered by facilitators?
5. What are the sizes of interventions that researchers and practitioners use for studying and planning change?
6. How can an individual intervention be analyzed and studied?

Intervention Definition

We have used and will continue to use the term *intervention* with great regularity in this book. We know, as stated, how significant the work of facilitators is in the process of supporting change efforts. Facilitators provide the interventions that can increase the potential for the success of change or allow it to fail. Thus, we think it is important to understand this term as we use it in this chapter. Our explanation and definition follow; please bear with us.

If a central office curriculum coordinator brings microscopes to a teacher who is implementing a new life-science curriculum, this is an intervention to support the teacher's use of the change. If a university professor coaches three principals in developing instructional leadership, this is an intervention in behalf of the principals' new roles. If a principal conducts staff development for all the faculty in cooperative learning techniques, the principal has provided an intervention to the staff. If two teachers talk about what they think of the innovation, that, too, is an intervention.

In the context of the change process, any *action* or *event* that influences the individuals involved or expected to be involved in the process is an intervention

(Hall & Hord, 1987, p. 143). Notice the use of the terms *action* or *event*. An action is deemed to be planned and focused deliberately on an individual, group, or all users or prospective users of a new program or practice (see Figure 6.1). Such an action could be sending an article about the use of math manipulatives to all primary teachers who teach mathematics. Discussion in a staff meeting about how implementation is going is another intervention.

An event, on the other hand, is something that occurs outside the deliberations and plans of the change process. Has this ever happened to your effort? Because we have observed that events do indeed influence the process of change, we have included them in our intervention definition. Events that we have observed in our work include:

A blizzard that prevented all truckers from delivering necessary equipment for a district's new astronomy program;

A fire in the intermediate service center's print shop that caused a three-week delay of materials for the high school's drug prevention pilot effort;

A learning styles consultant's accident on a mountain trail that resulted in rescheduling campus-based facilitators' preparations and planning for the project.

Whether the intervention is an action or event, its related influence may be either positive or negative. In the examples of actions above, the influence was intended to be positive, but the examples of events all suggest negative influence. This does not mean that all actions are positive, nor that all events are negative, however. A refusal to approve funding for a "how-to" workshop (action) can be negative, while a flat tire that forces teachers to carpool (event) and thereby take the opportunity to share success stories would be positive.

We have seen and recorded wide-ranging interventions—from quite simple and short-term actions to multiyear strategic plans. An example of a short-term intervention would be a school improvement team member stopping by to say hello to another teacher and then asking her if she has any needs regarding the new computer technology. Another, more complex example is a change facilitator observing an implementor and providing feedback on his use of a new instructional strategy. An

---

FIGURE 6.1   Definition of an Intervention

An Intervention is an

Action	or	Event

that is typically

Planned	or	Unplanned

and that influences individuals (either positively or negatively)
in the process of change.

intervention's simplicity or complexity may be analyzed, and this, as well as the various levels of interventions that constitute a typology of interventions that facilitators can consider in their work, are addressed later in this chapter.

Intervention Delivery

Who are the deliverers of interventions? The research and stories of successful school change are almost unanimous in identifying the principal as the primary catalyst and facilitator of site-based change. And, yet, as we will discover and discuss in Chapter 8, the principal is not alone in this endeavor. It is easy to assume that principals and superintendents, because of their positions, are change facilitators. While this is desirable, it is not always true. Even if it is the case, almost inevitably, because of the multiple roles of principals and superintendents, others share in the change facilitation (see Table 6.1).

Thus, based on our observations, we suggest that innovation-related interventions and change facilitation support and assistance may be delivered by any person who assumes the role and responsibilities of the change facilitator (whether implicitly or explicitly).

One implication is that many change process participants do not realize that they take actions that influence an individual, a group, or perhaps the entire change process. Another implication is that many people can be involved in the delivery of planned interventions. One significant result is that the burden of support and assistance to the users and nonusers is shared. This is important in view of the limited time that people in schools typically have to invest in facilitating change. Sharing the responsibilities of the facilitating role means also that the role is not necessarily positional, but may be operationally defined by what the facilitator does, which is the focus of the discussion that follows.

Six Functions of Interventions

The Southwest Educational Development Laboratory (SEDL), headquartered in Austin, Texas, is one of the federally funded regional labs committed to educational change and improvement. At the SEDL, considerable time and attention were given

TABLE 6.1   Sources of Interventions

Campus	District	Community	State
Principals	Superintendent	Parents	Policy-makers
Key teachers	Curriculum coordinators	Business	State board/
Counselors	Instructional supervisors	representatives	superintendent
Students		Legislators	

in 1990–95 to the matter of implementing planned change in the schools and districts of its region. The SEDL staff had previously spent much time and effort assisting these schools and districts in planning for their school improvement efforts. While planning activities for change seemed generally to receive useful attention by school practitioners, the issue of implementing the change seemed to fall between the cracks (a point that was made in Change Principle 2 of Chapter 1).

The SEDL staff believed that focusing on implementation was critical for the success of school change and thus improvement. In an effort to ascertain if practical materials and activities were available for schools to develop important implementation knowledge and skills, the SEDL staff conducted a national exploration. Suspicions about the lack of such materials proved correct; little was found for practitioner use. As a result, the SEDL staff undertook a broad review of the leadership and change facilitation literature to identify relevant research-based concepts and information that could support the development of effective facilitative leaders for school improvement projects. To help these busy practitioners get to the center of change facilitation work, this wide-ranging review of the literature focused on the actions and behaviors of leaders who were facilitating change (Hord, 1992), in other words, on interventions. What could be more important, the staff asked, than assisting potential facilitators in understanding the demands of the role and the interventions required?

The literature review resulted in identifying these interventions, which were organized into six types or functions (see Figure 6.2). A major source of this information came from the CBAM research, specifically the Principal/Teacher Interaction Study reported by Hord and Huling-Austin, (1986) and the conceptualization of Game Plan Components in an intervention taxonomy done by Hall and Hord (1984). These six functions were deemed necessary for making change happen, and they constituted the job description of the change facilitator. They also provided the framework for a training and development institute that was designed to enable busy educators to assist local schools and districts, as well as to prepare state departments of education staff and others to realize successful change in their respective organizations (Boyd et al., 1993). These six functions, as described below, are designed for students early in their study of the change process. Additional functions and concepts of interventions follow thereafter.

Function I: Developing, Articulating, and Communicating a Shared Vision of the Intended Change

A first step in moving toward a changed and improved future is the development of a shared dream or vision of what will be, that is, a vision of the future that increases student outcomes. The goal of increased student outcomes results from specific changes or innovations that are selected for adoption and implementation. Many change efforts fail because the participants do not share mental images or pictures of what classroom and/or school practice will look like when an identified change is implemented to a high quality. Picturing the change in operation provides the target

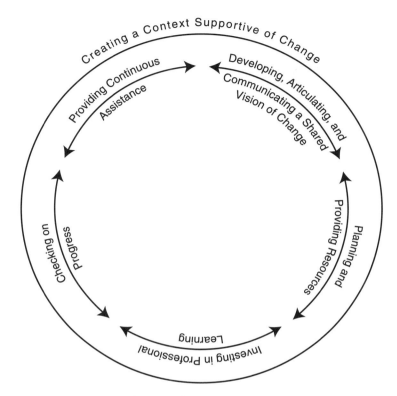

FIGURE 6.2   Six Functions of Interventions

for beginning the change journey. A part of this process can be creating an Innovation Configuration Map (IC) of the change—a useful way of defining what the
change/innovation will look like when it is actually and actively in operation in its
intended setting (see Chapter 3).

The elements of the shared vision of change must be as clearly defined as possible, and facilitators must continuously communicate this vision to enable implementors to move toward high-quality implementation. When there is a shared vision,
facilitators can be consistent in supporting individuals and groups.

Specific facilitator interventions for developing a shared change vision could
include but are not limited to engaging the school staff and community in identifying its beliefs and values regarding the purposes of the school; determining areas of
the school program in need of change and improvement; selecting solutions to
address the areas in need; collectively developing clear mental images of the solution (i.e., the vision of change) when it is in operation in the school or classrooms.

The shared vision can be communicated in multiple settings: in the media,
such as the public press and school and district newsletters; at school board and other

community meetings; at the local coffee shop; and even on the golf course. The idea is to continually remind all constituents, in various ways, of the vision and where the school is in relationship to realizing it. Related is the understanding that attention to the vision needs to be provided throughout the process of change in order to capture and capitalize on (or diminish) evolving changes in the vision.

For further material on vision and on the six functions of basic interventions, see the Additional Readings at the end of this chapter.

Function II: Planning and Providing Resources

When an initial vision for change has been established (the vision can certainly evolve and change as the school staff experiences, learns, and gains more expertise), planning for its realization is both possible and necessary. All logistical factors and resource allocations, along with policy implications, must be considered. Although it seems obvious, the planning and provision of resources represent an important means by which implementors are enabled to initiate implementation and sustain the change process. We have observed change efforts that lacked necessary resources, which forestalled the expected beginning of the change process and doomed the entire effort.

Planning is not a one-time event. Like a holiday trip, destinations sometimes change, and frequently, unexpected additions may be made for increased effectiveness and/or satisfaction. Thus, while a plan is essential for understanding where the change journey is moving, it should never be considered to be cast in concrete. Likewise, the resource requirements for a change are altered across time as implementors become more expert in the use of an innovation and as the configuration of use may make differing demands on materials. Not to be forgotten is the regular depletion of program materials and equipment and the need for updating supplies to teachers and students.

One of the most important, and most typically lacking, resources for change is time: time for planning, time for staff development, time for sharing, etc. Also important, of course, is time for facilitators to do *their* work. School administrators and facilitators would do well to find or create quality time to devote to the change effort. And, scheduling time for teachers to meet together to discuss successes and problems during implementation has proved to be valuable to change efforts.

Other specific actions of facilitators related to this function include developing policies related to the change or innovation; establishing rules and guidelines by which the implementation will be executed; staffing new roles and/or realigning existing ones; scheduling meetings and other regular and nonregular events; seeking and acquiring materials and equipment; providing space; and accessing funds needed for the new program or practice.

Function III: Investing in Professional Learning

Change means developing new understandings and doing things in new ways. If faculty are going to use new curricular programs or instructional practices, they must learn how to do that. Thus, *learning* is the basis of and the corollary to change. Formal training and other forms of staff and personal development, then, are essential to prepare implementors for the change. Such learning opportunities for the implementors should be ongoing as they develop more expertise in using the identified change. All too frequently training workshops are scheduled only at the beginning of a change process. Stages of Concern (SoC) can be used to design and shape the development and learning sessions in the preimplementation period of preparation as well as during implementation, when implementors are changing from novices to mature users of the new practices (as discussed in Chapter 4). Note also that different levels of understanding and different learning are characteristic of peoples' knowledge at each Levels of Use (LoU; see Chapter 5).

Leaders of the change effort will need to consider the following interventions, and others, in the learning and development category: scheduling training and development sessions across time as the implementors move from novice toward expert; identifying and contracting with trainers and other consultants (internal and external); providing information about the change; teaching the skills required of the innovation; developing positive attitudes about use of the new program; holding workshops; modeling and demonstrating innovation use; and clarifying misconceptions about the program or practice. At this point the training is characterized as formal; that is, it is provided as large-group instruction. Professional learning interventions at the individual or small-group level are found in Function V.

It is important that training and development are innovation related and focused on the vision of the change. When this occurs, implementors gain the information and learn the skills necessary for the new way of behaving in the classroom and school. Too often professional development has been vague and off-target. With a focus on the staff's concerns about their new program and practices, and on the vision of what the change will look like in operation, investing in professional learning will pay large dividends.

Function IV: Checking on Progress

Because change does not happen overnight, the process must be continuously assessed and monitored. Even though a clear articulation of the change has been expressed and material and human resources have been provided, the change journey is not without its bumps and detours. A significant set of facilitator interventions focuses on keeping a hand on the pulse of change. One-legged or informal interviews are an excellent way to check with individual implementors to identify needs, clarify questions, and solve problems. Not only does this enable the facilitator to assess progress, but it also signifies to the implementors that their efforts are valuable and worthy of notice and support.

Decision-makers and regulatory agencies have always known that what is measured or monitored is likely to be given attention. A change effort will be given more attention if facilitators assess its implementation.

More often than not, the change effort is lost when the leadership team, or whatever the facilitating team is called, fails to routinely check the progress of each implementor. Important checking actions include gathering data about the implementors' needs; collecting information about the knowledge and skills of the implementors; collecting feedback at the end of workshops and providing feedback on the feedback; systematically measuring, analyzing, and interpreting SoC, LoU, and IC; and talking informally with users about their progress. It is important that data collected about implementation are analyzed, carefully interpreted, and used to guide subsequent interventions.

Function V: Providing Continuous Assistance

Assisting is directly coupled to assessing, as discussed (above). When needs or problems are identified, a response is required to support implementation. Assistance may take the form of supplying additional materials, providing formal or informal learning activities, teaming with the implementor to demonstrate refinement of practice, and coaching. It makes sense to assess progress in order to identify needs and then to provide assistance to respond to the needs. This coupling of *assessing* and *assisting* is labeled *coaching, consulting*, or *follow-up*, and typically occurs with individuals or very small groups of implementors.

These are crucial behaviors by facilitators. Other assisting actions of facilitators include stopping by to greet implementors and simply asking, "How's it going?"; responding to individual's questions and confusions; encouraging individuals in their use of the innovation; assisting single and small-group implementors in problem-solving; providing follow-up and technical assistance; conducting quick conversations about the implementors' use and reinforcing what they are doing; and celebrating successes both small and large, publicly and privately.

Function VI: Creating a Context Supportive of Change

Increased attention is currently being paid to the context, climate, and/or culture of the school and how this factor influences the workplace of the professionals involved and subsequently their responses to change. For example, Boyd (1992b), in a review of the literature on context that supports or inhibits change, defined two components of context. One is the *physical*, or nonorganic aspects of an organization—its building facilities, schedules, policies, and the like. The second component is the *people* element—the beliefs and values held by the members and the norms that guide their behavior, relationships, attitudes, and so on. While the context is identified by its two parts, the parts are interactive and influence each other. For example, a small faculty in a small facility (but one with an available meeting space) will find it much easier to come together to interact and build trust than a much larger faculty spread over multiple buildings. A supportive context decreases the isolation of the staff; provides for the continuing increase of its capabilities; nurtures positive relationships among all the staff, students, and parents/community members; and urges the unceasing quest for increased effectiveness so that students benefit (for further discussion of the characteristics of a supportive context for change see Chapter 10).

In such a context the participants value change as a means for improving their effectiveness and seek changes in order to improve their practice. Boyd (1992a) reports that school leaders can take actions, such as the following, to create this context:

1. *Shaping the physical features of the context* by manipulating schedules and structures (such as faculty meetings) so that people can come together and share improvement ideas, by allocating resources to support the improvement effort, and by developing policies for enhancing staff capacity.
2. *Modeling* the behaviors and norms desired of the staff by interacting and cooperating in a significant way with all staff, by working with focus and commitment, and by being highly visible in the daily routines that they hope the staff will emulate.
3. *Teaching and coaching* by reading, studying, and subsequently sharing materials that will nurture and develop the staff's expertise, by attending professional development activities with the staff, and by attending conferences and sharing their substance with the staff.
4. *Addressing conflict* by facing it rather than avoiding it, and thus using conflict as a vehicle to resolve disputes and build unity.
5. *Selecting, rewarding, and censuring staff* by recognizing their work publicly and privately, by inviting the staff to share their efforts and experiences related to improvement goals, and by insisting that staff commit to school goals through the selection and termination processes.

In summary, these six types of basic interventions or functions, identified from the SEDL's Leadership for Change Institute (Boyd et al., 1993), have been widely used as a framework for developing the knowledge and skills that facilitators need to plan for change, monitor its progress, and evaluate its outcomes in terms of degree of classroom implementation.

Additional Kinds of Interventions

Four of the six basic intervention types discussed above—planning and providing resources (developing supportive organizational arrangements), investing in professional learning (training), checking on progress (monitoring and evaluation), and providing continuous assistance (providing consultation and reinforcement)—accounted for the majority of interventions identified in earlier CBAM studies; the original CBAM names are shown in parentheses (Hall & Hord, 1984, 1987; Hord & Huling-Austin, 1986; Hord et al., 1987). Two of the six categories of interventions—developing a shared vision of the change and creating a context for change—were identified by Hord (1992).

The CBAM studies revealed two additional Game Plan Components that are less frequently executed but quite important in change efforts: communicating externally, and disseminating information. We examine the importance of these interventions next.

Communicating Externally

An important but often neglected set of interventions are those actions taken to keep individuals and groups external to the implementation site informed about what is happening. In order to gain their support or approval, they need to be informed by the on-site participants. One of the quotes at the beginning of this chapter reports that the change effort on interdisciplinary curriculum is going well and that a report on progress will be made to the board. It is easy to understand the politically and economically astute reasons for communicating externally to such an influential group, but too often too little is done too late.

Activities related to this category of interventions include describing the change and its purpose to those outside the school, publishing a monthly newsletter, making presentations at various district and community meetings, keeping the external members of the site council and the PTO informed about progress and setbacks, informing all possible constituents about progress, and developing a campaign to gain the support of the public and other relevant groups.

Disseminating Information

Efforts to share information about the new program or practice and to let others know of its value and positive impact, with the intention of persuading them to adopt the program, are dissemination interventions. In broadcasting the virtues of the innovation, broader support and influence may be gained as well, but in this category the primary intent is to inform prospective adopters from other sites.

In order to accomplish the purpose of this category, the facilitators engage in various activities including mailing descriptive information to persons external to the school, making presentations at regional and national meetings, encouraging others to adopt the innovation by reporting its benefits, making large-group presentations about the innovation to potential adopters, providing free sample materials, and training expert colleagues to represent the innovation.

Note that it is not necessary to do disseminating interventions in order to have change success at the home site. As a matter of fact, spending too much time on disseminating, especially early in implementation, can draw needed energy and resources away from the project. Early dissemination also runs the risk of appearing premature, since everything may not have been worked out at the home site. Four or five years into a change process can be an excellent time to begin disseminating actions for at this point they can serve to reward and expand the perspectives of successful implementors while increasing visibility for all.

In the early work, the CBAM intervention classifications reported above were labeled "Game Plan Components" and were part of a system that provided for further detailed and enriched planning and analysis of a change endeavor. The additional concept of sizes or levels of interventions, identified in the intervention tax-onomy, was developed for research purposes. However, many experienced change facilitators have also found them to be instructive and useful.

Sizes of Interventions

Game Plan Components constitute one size of interventions, but we have also iden-tified other sizes of interventions which are distinguished by their relative duration and the degree to which they affect few or many people. In classifying by these two factors, policy-level interventions are identified as the most comprehensive of the interventions. Strategies, tactics, and incidents are additional interventions that can be distinguished by size (see Figure 6.3).

Policies

Since they affect the whole organization and exist typically for an extended amount of time (years), the policies of an organization must be taken into account when plan-ning for change or when studying a planned change project. Policy interventions could include contract specifications that restrict staff development to the school day. Or there may be a policy that prohibits staff development during the school day, thus requiring its scheduling for after the formal school hours, with stipends being paid to the teachers who participate. Such overarching interventions can have significant and far-reaching influence on a change process. Facilitators ignore them at their risk.

Game Plan Components

Earlier in this chapter, these interventions were referred to as "functions." This size intervention, which represents a major planning device for a change effort, is a clus-tering of behaviors into meaningful and functional groupings that provide a frame-work for the facilitator.

FIGURE 6.3   The Relative Size of Interventions

Policies: Decisions that affect the whole organization for an extended period

   Game Plan Components: Major functional groupings of interventions

      Strategies: Interventions that operationalize the Game Plan Components into actions

         Tactics: Sets of small actions that comprise the strategies

            Incidents: Brief in-time actions that focus on one or a few users or nonusers, and that may or may not add up to tactics

Strategies

These interventions make the Game Plan Components more explicit and translate them into describable actions. Strategies are long-term, and are designed to accomplish specific change process objectives and operationalize the Game Plan Components through their impact on a large number of the implementors. For example, under the Game Plan Component of monitoring and evaluation (checking progress), the strategy of one principal who was closely guiding and supporting change in his school was to collect, every Friday, samples of students' work related to the innovation. This strategy led to another strategy that became a part of the providing consultation and reinforcement (providing assistance) component, as the principal led the staff in reviewing the students' work every other week. This strategy informed the teachers about additional possibilities for students related to the innovation and reinforced and/or encouraged various teachers in their use of the innovation.

Tactics

This intervention is defined as a set of small, interrelated actions. A day-long workshop would be a tactic that is part of the strategy of designing and providing training sessions across the first year of implementation. The strategy is, in turn, part of the Game Plan Component of training.

Other examples of tactics are visiting each implementor in his or her classroom over a three-day period to solicit concerns about training sessions for the new computers and scheduling a consultant to be in the school for a week to provide technical assistance to any teacher who indicates interest.

Incidents

We have learned with certainty how significant the small and more individualized interventions known as incidents are. They are short in duration, focus typically on one or just a few implementors, and occur in informal ways. This is not to say that they are unplanned, for they are so powerful that they should be on the mind of every facilitator. It is in these little day-to-day, moment-to-moment actions (which frequently take the form of the one-legged conference described in Chapter 4) that the change effort is most frequently won or, unfortunately, lost. We and our colleagues have observed that in schools where there are significantly more incident interventions, teachers have greater implementation success due to this personalized help and support. There are many opportunities for enacting incident interventions, such as the following:

- When meeting a user or nonuser in the hallway, the facilitator can offer comments to support his or her hard work with the innovation or to increase his or her interest in learning about it

- At the staff mail box, the facilitator can share requested information with the teacher who is early into use of a new mathematics program
- Crossing the parking lot to go home, the facilitator can inquire about the innovation equipment that was sent to a teacher the day before
- In the cafeteria line, the facilitator can provide a brochure about professional development sessions

The effective facilitator uses the small interactions to provide help and assistance.

If the facilitator or policy-maker thinks only of workshops as the key interventions for a change effort, the implementors will be short-changed. In our studies of interventions, we have found a wide range of incident interventions in the Game Plan Components that provide resources, assess progress, and provide assistance. It is in these one-to-one interventions that individuals and small groups have their idiosyncratic—and vastly important—concerns attended to. It should be noted also that incidents form the building blocks that become tactics and ultimately strategies.

In a bit more detail, incidents may be further described as one of five types: isolated, simple, chain, repeated, and complex.

Isolated Incident   This singular action is distanced in time, space, and purpose from any others. It is given little time and generally is addressed to a single individual. An example is requesting a teacher to respond to a request from a parent for information on language manipulatives.

Simple Incident   While this single-action intervention is typically short and aimed at one or only a few individuals, it is linked in its purpose to other interventions. When a facilitator stops by to see the two second-grade teachers to check on their concerns about their new science curriculum, this is an example of a simple incident. Peer faculty could also provide this same intervention to their colleagues on a one-to-one basis. An innovation-related announcement about an upcoming workshop made in a staff meeting would also be a simple incident intervention.

Chain Incident   As suggested by its name, this is a series of short incidents provided to multiple targeted individuals by the same person and for the same purpose. A facilitator dropping by to remind each teacher of the afternoon's workshop in the cafeteria is an example.

Repeated Incident   Unlike the chain incident which delivers the same action to multiple audiences, the repeated incident delivers the same action to the same target multiple times. The central office's Director of School Improvement reminding the assistant principal three times to complete the implementation report for the superintendent is such a repeated incident.

Complex Incident   This incident involves a set of related incident actions that occur within a short period. An example, in the definition section of this chapter, noted a feedback conference with a teacher held following an observation. This complex intervention could also include the development of a growth plan for supporting the teacher and a number of related topics, such as scheduling a follow-up focused observation.

The sum of all these intervention sizes or levels is a comprehensive set of actions undertaken to provide nonusers and users with what they need to successfully implement any given change. But an even more specific exploration, known as the Anatomy of Interventions (Hall & Hord, 1987), may be done by researchers and facilitators to analyze a change effort.

The Anatomy of Interventions

The interventions described above address the different sizes of interventions. The internal parts of an intervention can also be analyzed in terms of codes related to each part: source, target, function, medium, flow, and location (see Figure 6.4). Such an analysis and coding of interventions across time make it possible to ascertain who is providing intervention actions to whom, for what purpose, how, and when. Thus, redundancies and gaps may be identified and corrections taken so that all persons involved receive the supportive interventions that are needed.

Source

The source of an intervention is the person who is initiating the action. Typically, this will be a facilitator who has determined the need for the intervention and designed it to respond to that need. However, the source could be any campus or district person who makes a change process–related action. Teachers, as well as persons more external to the implementation site, do initiate actions. However, in our studies, it is clear that principals and others on a leadership or school improvement team (see Chapter 8) are the most frequent sources of interventions.

FIGURE 6.4   Internal Elements of Incident Interventions

Source: Person(s) providing the action

Target: Person(s) receiving the action

Function: Purpose of the action

Medium: Means by which the intervention is delivered (telephone, face to face, etc.)

Flow: Directionality of the intervention action (one-way, interactive, etc.)

Location: Where the action took place

Target

The person who will receive the action is the target. The target may be a single individual with particular concerns or many persons (such as participants in a workshop). If hundreds of persons are targeted, the intervention will obviously be less personalized. The diagnostic dimensions—Stages of Concern, Levels of Use, Innovation Configurations—provide data useful in designing interventions that will be relevant and effective for the target.

Function

Function is the purpose of the action. Interestingly, an intervention can have multiple functions. In analyzing interventions, it is frequently difficult to identify a single purpose to any one action. On the other hand, it's quite useful for functions to be multipurposeful. For instance, it is easy to imagine that when a facilitator (particularly a principal) drops by a classroom to ask the teacher how the new instructional strategy is working, the teacher can feel supported and also somewhat pressured to be using and improving use of the strategy. The visit signals that the principal considers the new practice important (pressure) and is also interested in supplying help (support). The same intervention also provides the principal with information about how the innovation is going.

    Source, target, and function can provide the facilitator with important information about who is being attended to in a change effort, by whom, and for what purpose. Redundancies (which do not occur very often) and gaps in the provision of intervention actions may be revealed by analyzing these subparts of interventions. For research purposes, the three subparts noted above—along with medium, flow, and location—may be coded using a set of carefully defined codes and coding rules. See Hall and Hord (1987) for additional information.

    This chapter has provided increasingly finer "cuts" at analyzing interventions. The following Vignette returns to the basic six functions of interventions.

VIGNETTE

Implementing a New Car

Perhaps a simple story of the integration of a new product into everyday life will be helpful in illustrating what so frequently happens when something new is introduced to individuals.

    In 1982 Mrs. H challenged her husband's practice of securing two heavy but speedy, gas-demanding Oldsmobiles for the family by researching and purchasing a new four-door Honda Civic hatchback. This car, silver in color, had a standard transmission, heat, air conditioning, and windshield wipers, and that was it—no radio, no frills. Fortunately for Mrs. H, this car proved abundantly successful, until after thirteen years and nearly no visits to the mechanic except for the recommended periodic checkups, the Honda service technician proclaimed that, at 195,000 miles, "Silver Belle" was "terminal."

Not surprised, although she had planned to run this car to 350,000 miles (a record in effect at this dealership), Mrs. H presented herself at the Honda showroom. Now note the parallels between this personal experience of change—buying a new car—and the steps in the six basic interventions recommended for any change process:

Create a Context Supportive of Change

The Honda showroom was filled with shiny autos, festive balloons, and coffee and cookies for the potential customers. A charming and not unattractive young salesman, Jeff, offered to help Mrs. H review the auto possibilities.

Develop a Shared Vision

Jeff was quite insightful in playing to Mrs. H's concerns for information and her growing interest in a "fine, new car." He was descriptive and persuasive in developing the mental images in the prospective buyer's mind of sailing along the highways in a handsome and upscale new car.

Plan and Provide Resources

When Mrs. H decided to make a purchase, Jeff planned the process, developed a contract, and queried Mrs. H about her resources to pay for the car. Although her personal concerns erupted over the prospects of writing such a large check, Jeff assured her that she was doing the right thing, thus decreasing these concerns. Further, he asked her to give him thirty minutes when she picked up the car the next day.

Invest in Learning

When Mrs. H arrived the next day, Jeff sat behind the wheel, with Mrs. H leaning in the car window, as he recited his litany: this button does this, that one does that, the lever on the left is, this knob controls that, etc. At the conclusion, he handed Mrs. H the keys, told her to have fun, and thanked her for her business.

At this point, Mrs. H's management concerns escalated and she left the dealership parking lot with some trepidation (albeit excitement also), but successfully executed the traffic, hills, and curves to her home.

Check on Progress

To this day, nearly two years later, Mrs. H does not know how to play a tape in the car (although she keeps a supply of them ready just in case). When does she think about using the tape player? When she is sailing down the freeway, which is not a good time to refer to the user's manual. Finally realizing that this was an unacceptable situation, she brought the manual into the kitchen so that she could study it.

Provide Continuous Assistance

"You goose," Mrs. H said to herself, "this is not the appropriate place to study the car manual; you should be in the car." She was also still not clear about how to tune the radio. Further, certain buttons and thingamajigs on the dashboard were befuddling.

The lesson of this not-untrue fable is that the training in use of the car that the change facilitator/salesperson provided was perfunctory, with no hands-on experience, no practice, and no feedback. Further, he did no checking into Mrs. H's use of the car. The lack of personalized training, with the absence of checking progress, followed by no follow-up, has left Mrs. H as a very low-quality user of her car.

Mrs. H and her car provide an excellent example of what happens far too often to teachers in classrooms. They become interested in new programs after learning how they work in similar places and developing a vision of how they can contribute effectively to their work so that students benefit. Many times adequate resources are provided, although this is not always the case. Staff development in the new program/practice is provided at the beginning in very ineffective ways (as it was for Mrs. H). Almost without exception, poor training is followed by an absence of the continuous help and assistance that can assure that high quality (rather than perfunctory) use results in classrooms and contributes to students' growth, learning, and success.

1. Have you had an experience similar to Mrs. H's with a new product (such as a new computer, microwave oven, or cell telephone), when you did not receive proper support? Reflect on your experience and consider what might have been done to make your implementation of the new product more successful.

2. It would appear that sales personnel, school administrators, and others who are interested in changing their public's products or practices assume a great deal about their clients' capacity with those innovations. How could you help Jeff, the car salesperson, or a school or district administrator understand the real needs of clients for supportive and appropriate interventions?

3. Why would we use a story about purchasing a car in a chapter on interventions? How does it relate to what happens all too frequently when new programs and practices are introduced in schools and classrooms?

Summary

The concepts, strategies, and tools described in this chapter were created and designed with change facilitators in mind (whether they be school principals, district supervisors, key teachers on the campus, or others). Typically, interventions are made without prior thought. Our intent in this chapter was to focus on the concept of interventions and to introduce a number of ways that they can be considered, classified, and assessed.

It is absolutely clear that in those change processes where there are statistically significant more innovation-related incident interventions, teachers have greater implementation success. It is also clear that in schools where there is coherence in incident interventions that accumulate to form tactics and ultimately strategies, change is more successful. And, if interventions focus on LoU V Integration, there is a more collaborative culture and greater sharing of a vision. Strategies will be needed to promote collaboration if that element of culture is desired in the staff's workplace.

Interventions take time and thought. Without them, members of the organization work in isolation and innocence in terms of use of the innovation. As we admonish in our workshops, "Change facilitators, *do* something."

Guiding Principles of Interventions

1. Successful implementation of new policies, programs, processes, practices, and even new personnel does not just happen. Assuming that the announcement of such changes is sufficient is tantamount to little or no implementation, or very superficial implementation at best. Interventions both small and large make the difference.
2. While principals have been identified as change facilitators or significant suppliers of interventions, others also make many of these actions. Whoever will assume the role and responsibilities—whether they are teachers, parents, central office personnel, community members, or others—can serve in these capacities.
3. Many types of interventions must be provided to ensure the success of change efforts. Facilitators must acquaint themselves with and use their knowledge of interventions in planning, monitoring, and assisting their organization's efforts to change and improve.
4. Because change is accomplished at the individual level, facilitators will need to use diagnostic tools for shaping the interventions supplied to individuals, as well as to remember to provide groups with the array of interventions necessary to insure each implementor's success with change.
5. Interventions may also be targeted for whole system change, remembering to employ them across all the persons in the system.
6. Since *learning* new information, skills, and behaviors is at the heart of any change project, facilitators would do well to keep this basic premise in mind as they consider, design, and deliver the interventions necessary for change process success.

DISCUSSION QUESTIONS

1. What preparation relative to interventions should be provided to a person who will serve as a change facilitator? Would your prescription be different if the facilitator was based at the school, district, or state level?

2. What length of time should be allotted for implementing a new curriculum such as a constructivist-based mathematics program? What strategies should be included? Provide a rationale for your response.

3. *Little Things Mean a Lot*—how might this song title apply to the various types of interventions?

4. How might a campus-based practitioner, a state policy-maker, or a researcher employ the information on interventions in this chapter?

FIELDWORK ACTIVITIES

1. Obtain the implementation plans for two schools' change efforts. Which basic kinds of interventions are included and which are absent in each case? On this basis, compare, predict, and explain the results likely to be gained in each school.

2. Develop a plan for making a presentation to the school board using the six basic types of interventions as a framework to explain the attention and resources needed to further a change process.

3. Develop a plan of interventions to be supplied to a school whose staff will be implementing problem-based learning or some other complex innovation. Be as thorough and comprehensive as possible, identifying key strategies within each Game Plan Component and examples of relevant incidents.

REFERENCES

Boyd, V. (1992a). Creating a context for change. *Issues . . . About Change, 2*(2), 1–10.
Boyd, V. (1992b). *School context: Bridge or barrier for change.* Austin, TX: Southwest Educational Development Laboratory.
Boyd, V., Fuentes, N., Hord, S. M., Mendez-Morse, S., & Rodriguez, D. (1993). *Leadership for change.* Austin, TX: Southwest Educational Development Laboratory.
Chin, R., & Benne, K. D. (1969). General strategies for effecting changes in human systems. In W. G. Bennis, K. D. Benne, & R. Chin (Eds.), *The planning of change* (2nd ed.), pp. 32–59. New York: Holt, Rinehart & Winston.
Hall, G. E., & Hord, S. M. (1984). A framework for analyzing what change facilitators do: The Intervention Taxonomy. *Knowledge: Creation, Diffusion, Utilization, 5*(3), 275–307.
Hall, G. E., & Hord, S. M. (1987). *Change in schools: Facilitating the process.* Albany: SUNY Press.
Hord, S. M. (1992). *Facilitative leadership: The imperative for change.* Austin, TX: Southwest Educational Development Laboratory.
Hord, S. M., & Huling-Austin, L. (1986). Effective curriculum implementation: Some promising new insights. *The Elementary School Journal, 87*(1), 97–115.
Hord, S. M., Rutherford, W. L., Huling-Austin, L., & Hall, G. E. (1987). *Taking charge of change.* Alexandria, VA: ASCD.

ADDITIONAL READINGS

Developing, Articulating, and Communicating a Shared Vision

Barth, R. S. (1990). *Improving schools from within*. San Francisco: Jossey Bass.

Blumberg, A., & Greenfield, W. (1980). *The effective principal: Perspectives on school leadership*. Boston: Allyn & Bacon.

Cuban, L. (1985). Conflict and leadership in the superintendency. *Phi Delta Kappan, 67*(1), 28–30.

Fullan, M. G. (1992). Visions that blind. *Educational Leadership, 49*(5), 19–20.

Hord, S. M., & Estes, N. (1993). Superintendent selection and success. In D. S. G. Carter, T. E. Glass, & S. M. Hord (Eds.), *Selecting, preparing, and developing the school district superintendent*, (pp. 71–84). Washington, DC: The Falmer Press.

Planning and Providing Resources

Brandt, R. (1987). On leadership and student achievement: A conversation with Richard Andrews. *Educational Leadership, 45*(1), 9–16.

Louis, K. S., & Miles, M. B. (1990). *Improving the urban high school: What works and why*. New York: Teachers College Press.

Peterson, K. D., Murphy, J., & Hallinger, P. (1987). Superintendents' perceptions of the control and coordination of the technical core in effective school districts. *Educational Administration Quarterly, 23*(1), 79–95.

Investing in Professional Learning

Fullan, M. G. (1985). Change processes and strategies at the local level. *The Elementary School Journal, 85*(3), 391–422.

Hord, S. M., & Boyd, V. (1995). Staff development fuels a culture of continuous improvement. *Journal of Staff Development, 16*(1), 10–15.

Joyce, B., & Showers, B. (1980). Improving inservice training: The messages of research. *Educational Leadership, 37*(5), 379–385.

Murphy, J., Hallinger, P., & Peterson, K. D. (1985). Supervising and evaluating principals: Lessons from effective districts. *Educational Leadership, 43*(2), 78–82.

Checking on Progress

Fullan, M. G., with Stiegelbauer, S. M. (1991). *The new meaning of educational change*. New York: Teachers College Press.

Murphy, J., & Hallinger, P. (1986). The superintendent as instructional leader: Findings from effective school districts. *The Journal of Educational Administration, 24*(2), 213–231

Rutherford, W. L (1985). School principals as effective leaders. *Phi Delta Kappan, 69*(1), 31–34.

Providing Continuous Assistance

Bush, R. N. (1984). Effective staff development: Making our schools more effective. *Proceedings of Three State Conferences* (223–238). San Francisco: Far West Laboratory for Educational Research and Development.

Coleman, P., & LaRocque, L. (1990). *Struggling to be good enough: Administrative practices and school district ethos*. London: The Falmer Press.

Creating a Context Supportive of Change

Boyer, E. L. (1995). *The basic school: A community for learning*. Princeton, NJ: Carnegie Foundation for the Advancement of Teaching.

Deal, T. E., & Kennedy, A. A. (1982). *Corporate cultures*. Reading, MA: Addison-Wesley.

Deal, T. E., & Peterson, K. D. (1990). *The principal's role in shaping school culture*. Washington, DC: U.S. Department of Education.

Garmston, R., & Wellman, B. (1995). Adaptive schools in a quantum universe. *Educational Leadership, 52*(7), 6–12.

Hord, S. M. (1997). *Professional learning communities: Communities of continuous inquiry and improvement*. Austin, TX: Southwest Educational Development Laboratory.

Little, J. W. (1982). Norms of collegiality and experimentation: Workplace conditions of school success. *American Educational Research Journal, 19*(3), 325–340.

Senge, P. (1990). *The fifth discipline: The art and practice of the learning organization*. New York: Currency Doubleday.

7 Defining Change Facilitator Style

Different Approaches Produce Different Results

His attitude is so positive that it is often mistaken for expertise! You can't help but like him.

As she uses a finger to draw several loops that converge in the air, a staff person observes, "That teacher draws in things I didn't even know were out there. She always is thinking about how all the pieces can fit together."

Everything is so well organized and gets done on time. He is like a cook who follows the recipe.

Leaders and leadership are popular topics for discussion and research. There are debates about whether a certain person is a good leader and what the characteristics of effective leadership are. There are literally thousands of research studies that examine characteristics and behaviors of leaders in a never-ending quest to answer the age-old question of how leaders can make a difference. In this chapter we consider leadership in a special context—*change*. We will examine recent studies that have focused on leadership during change processes and describe how different approaches relate to implementation success. By the end of this chapter, you will have a set of rubrics to assess yourself and leaders you have known. You also will have some clues about how to work with and influence different types of leaders.

FOCUS QUESTIONS

1. Are there important variations in how different leaders facilitate change?
2. How is the concept of style different from behavior?

3. What are the key differences between the Initiator, Manager, and Responder Change Facilitator Styles?
4. Which Change Facilitator Style will be most closely correlated with higher levels of implementation success?
5. Which type of change facilitator do you like to have as a supervisor?
6. Which Change Facilitator Style do you prefer to use when you are in a leadership role?

Each of us has our favorite stories about leaders who were great to work for, the ones who respected our skills and potential, who let us take on extra responsibilities, and who helped us to grow professionally and personally. We also have stories about the leaders who did not trust us, who maintained control over the smallest details, and who would not give genuine consideration to our ideas. And then there are those leaders who are very friendly, who always had time to chat, and who verbally encouraged us to try anything, but in hindsight we can see that they never made a definite decision and that each attempt at change seemed to fall apart during implementation.

These types of experiences with leaders are typical rather than atypical. There are varied approaches to leadership, and different people lead in different ways. Further, there are patterns and similarities among those leaders who do make a difference and among those who do not make a difference. Depending on how the leader leads, the followers and the organization will have very different change process experiences, and the ultimate results of the change will differ as well.

We have identified different approaches to leadership that we call *Change Facilitator Styles*, which are defined by the use of different interventions and of different perspectives about how to approach change processes. Depending on their styles, they send different signals to their staffs and spend their time doing different things. The effects of these different Change Facilitator Styles can be observed in the amount and degree of success that the followers have in implementing and using the change.

In this chapter the concept of Change Facilitator Style and its implications for leaders will be introduced. Although the focus of our research has been on the formal heads of organizations, namely school principals, keep in mind that leadership in change efforts is not something that is done only by the designated administrator(s) at the top. *Everyone who is engaged in change has a responsibility to assist in facilitating the process.* In addition, everyone will have a particular Change Facilitator Style. In other words, although most of the research presented in this chapter was done with school principals, the findings have implications for anyone who is facilitating change.

Two sets of implications of this work on Change Facilitator Style need to be kept in mind: First, regardless of your position in an organization, you have a potential role to play in helping to facilitate the change process, and in doing this you will have your own Change Facilitator Style. (What will it be?) Second, the formally designated leaders of the change process will have their Change Facilitator Styles.

(How can you best work with each?) Everyone, whether principal or teacher, plant manager or assembly-line worker, has a potential role in facilitating the change process. Whether they knowingly assume this role and how they go about it is the main topic to be addressed in this chapter. You also will be introduced to some ways to analyze Change Facilitator Styles and to think about implications for working with others in change leadership.

The History of Research on Leaders and Leadership

Which way did they go?
How many of them were there?
I must find them!
I am their leader!

This oft-cited refrain summarizes much about leadership in general and especially as it relates to leadership in change. It is used here to introduce you to a number of important questions: What do you believe are the important characteristics of good leaders? What kind of leader do you like to work with? And how do you lead?

We can use the metaphor of a dog-sled team to introduce some of the important differences in the way that leaders lead. Some leaders are like the lead dog. They like to be at the front, checking out the view ahead and breaking trail for those behind them. Others like to lead from within the team. They often say that they are not comfortable with the visibility that comes with being at the front, while those who like the front position point out that the view is always the same for those behind. Still other leaders stay at the back of the sled, like the drivers, riding the rails of the sled, pushing the sled, and barking out commands to those on the team who are not pulling hard enough. Some leaders seem to be more like the spectators and race officials. They watch from the side while the team, sled, and driver travel by. They are ready to evaluate, and occasionally cheer, the performance of the team and driver, but do not enter the race themselves. So again, which kind of leader do you like to be with? How do you lead? Lastly, which type do you think makes the biggest difference?

The Legacy of Research on Leadership

Leaders and leadership have been the subject of study and theorizing for most of the twentieth century. In fact, so much has been written about these subjects that there are major anthologies that just summarize the history of study and examination of leaders and leadership (see, for example, Bass, 1990). Leaders have been studied to see if particular traits, such as their height, are associated with effectiveness. Many different models of leadership have been proposed, such as the important work by Fiedler (1978) suggesting that the style of effective leaders is contingency dependent. In other words, a different style of leader is needed for different situations. Others have studied specific behaviors of leaders in the hopes of identifying a critical set of needed skills and competencies (see, for example, Leithwood & Montgomery, 1982). Many have proposed models of leadership that suggest that how a leader leads needs to be considered across two dimensions: a task dimension and a people, or relationship, dimension (see, for example, Blake & Mouton, 1964). According to some, the "best" leaders are those who exhibit high levels of both task and relationship behaviors. Others advocate shifting the balance of task and relationship behaviors depending on the "maturity" of the followers (see, for example, Hersey & Blanchard, 1988).

This long and extensive legacy of research, theory, and model-building about leaders and leadership has focused primarily on business and industry contexts. Very little has been done with education organizations, and even less with leaders and leadership during change processes. One notable exception would be the fifty-year history of activity and action research related to what is called *organizational development* (OD), which has an extensive legacy of writing about models and practices with implications for schools (see, for example, Schmuck & Runkle, 1994; Miles, 1971). Unfortunately, the research findings indicate that the OD approach has not lasted in school settings (Fullan, Miles, & Taylor, 1980), although there has been a recent revival of interest in applying it in supervision processes (Hall & Shieh, 1998).

Studies of Leaders during the Change Process

Nearly all of the research and models about leaders and leadership had their beginnings in studies of individuals in leadership positions or in theorizing about what people in leadership positions should be like. By contrast, our research on leaders and leadership in change had a very different beginning. Rather than starting with an agenda to look at change leaders, we stumbled onto the need to look at leaders because of some research findings about teacher success and lack of success in implementing change.

As a research team, we were analyzing a very extensive set of data about teachers' Stages of Concern (SoC), Levels of Use (LoU), and Innovation Configuration (IC) Maps. We had just completed a two-year study of teachers' implementation of a very innovative science curriculum in a large (eighty school) suburban school district. All of the teachers had participated in carefully designed workshops that were presented by lead teachers. SoC, LoU, and IC Map data had been collected twice a year, and the district office change facilitators had devoted themselves to coaching teachers. So we expected that at the end of two years all of the teachers would be at the same point in terms of implementation. Wrong!

In the SoC, LoU, and IC Map data we found very distinct variations that appeared to represent school by school differences! We were able to sort the schools into three groups according to how the implementation data differed. To use the SoC data as an illustration, in Group A were schools that exhibited a gradual lowering of self and task concerns and an arousal of Stage 4 Consequence concerns. In Group B were schools that revealed generally flat concerns profiles that were low on all stages. In Group C were schools whose teachers had the "Big W" concerns profile. In other words, they had low Stage 1 Informational concerns, high Stage 3 Management concerns, and a serious "tailing up" on Stage 6 Refocusing concerns. These teachers were not pleased with having unresolved task concerns and had some very strong ideas about what should be done about them.

We were puzzled about how to explain these data. All the teachers had received the same district workshops and the same curriculum materials. The schools were generally alike in terms of student socioeconomic status and the like, and they all had had two years to implement the new curriculum. So we decided to present the three stacks of school data to our district change facilitator colleagues and ask how they would explain the clustering of the schools. With very little hesitation they said: "It's the principals! In the schools in Group A, the principals are very active and supportive of teachers using the new curriculum. In Group B the principals are well organized, but they don't push their teachers to go beyond the minimum. In Group C schools, the principals don't help their teachers. They talk a good game, but they don't follow through."

The outcome of these discussions with our school-based colleagues was a set of studies to document and analyze the intervention behaviors of school principals to see, if indeed, what they did as school leaders could be correlated with the extent of teacher implementation success. From these and the earlier studies of teachers engaged in change processes, the concept of Change Facilitator Style emerged. These studies did not originate with some a priori model of leadership or theories about what good leaders do. As with other CBAM studies, the work on Change Facilitator Style came out of what happens to real people living and working to implement change.

The Concept of Change Facilitator Style

Interestingly, as obvious as it is, many school district leaders, staff developers, and researchers miss the fact that *all principals are not the same*. Principals view their role and priorities differently, and they operationally define their roles differently in terms of what they actually do each day. One implication of this fact was that in studying principals as change facilitators, we needed to sample schools so that we had representatives of different ways in which principals lead change efforts. Our emerging concept of Change Facilitator Style provided the means of doing this, for we could select study schools using the descriptions of principal leadership that had been discovered in comparing schools in Groups A, B, and C.

Note that so far we have been talking about "style." For the rest of this chapter, it will be very important to understand that there is a big difference between the concept of style and the idea of leader behaviors. Style represents the overall tone and pattern of a leader's approach. Behaviors are a leader's individual, moment-to-moment actions, such as talking to a teacher in the corridor, chairing a staff meeting, writing a memo, and talking on the telephone. The overall accumulated pattern and tone of these behaviors form a person's style. As will be illustrated more clearly in Chapter 10, more effective leaders remember that each of their individual behaviors is important in and of itself as well as a sign of their overall style.

Three Change Facilitator Styles

Our studies of principals revealed that there are three distinct Change Facilitator (CF) Styles: the Initiator, the Manager, and the Responder. We know that these three do not represent all possible styles, but, they do represent three contrasting approaches that are regularly seen in change processes. In this section, each of these CF styles is described. To make the descriptions come alive, we have included some of our favorite examples and anecdotes from the studies. Formal definitions of each Change Facilitator Style are presented in Figure 7.1.

While reading these descriptions keep in mind several questions:

1. How well do these descriptions match with leaders you have experienced?
2. Which CF Style is most highly correlated with greater teacher success in implementing changes?
3. Which CF Style do you use?

Initiator Change Facilitators   Initiators have clear and strongly held visions about what their school should be like. They are motivators who are continually articulating what the school can become. When issues come up, they listen to all sides and quickly make decisions based on what they think will be best for students and what will move the school closer to their vision. Initiators set high expectations for teachers. They expect them to be engaged in teaching, supporting students, and contributing to the effort to continually improve the whole school. For example, one elementary school had a goal of children writing every week. To encourage teachers and students in this effort, one Initiator principal asked teachers to give him samples of all students' writing each week. He then displayed the samples around the school halls and common areas.

Initiators push teachers, students, parents, and personnel in the district office to support the things that will help students learn, teachers teach, and the school move forward. Sometimes they push too hard, which makes some feel pressured and uncomfortable. They also are knowledgeable about how the system operates and on occasion will work with the philosophy that it is easier to seek forgiveness than prior approval.

Initiators consciously question and analyze what *they* and others do. They reflect on what others have told them, on what issues may be emerging, and on how well tasks are being accomplished. They listen to teachers and students. They not only make decisions but consciously work to make sure that all decisions and actions move people and the school in the desired direction. They are focused on assessment, instruction, and curriculum. Initiators also have a great deal of passion. They care

FIGURE 7.1   Descriptions of Three Change Facilitator Styles

Initiators have clear, decisive long-range policies and goals that include but transcend implementation of the current innovation. They tend to have very strong beliefs about what good schools and teaching should be like and work intensely to attain this vision. Decisions are made in relation to their goals for the school and in terms of what they believe to be best for students, which is based on current knowledge of classroom practice. Initiators have strong expectations for students, teachers, and themselves. They convey and monitor these expectations through frequent contacts with teachers and clear explications of how the school is to operate and how teachers are to teach. When they feel it is in the best interest of their school, particularly the students, Initiators will seek changes in district programs or policies, or they will reinterpret them to suit the school's needs. Initiators will be adamant but not unkind; they solicit input from staff and then make decisions in terms of the goals of the school, even if some are ruffled by their directness and high expectations.

Managers represent a broad range of behaviors. They both demonstrate responsive behaviors toward situations and people, and initiate actions in support of the change effort. The variations in their behavior seem to be linked to their rapport with teachers and central office staff and to their understanding and acceptance of a particular change effort. Managers work unobtrusively to provide basic support to facilitate teachers' use of an innovation. They keep teachers informed about decisions and are sensitive to teacher needs. They will defend their teachers from what are perceived as excessive demands. When they learn that the central office wants something to happen in their school, they become very involved with their teachers in making it happen, yet they do not typically initiate attempts to move beyond the basics of what is imposed.

Responders place heavy emphasis on allowing teachers and others the opportunity to take the lead. They believe their primary role is to maintain a smoothly running school by focusing on traditional administrative tasks, by keeping teachers content, and by treating students well. They view teachers as strong professionals who are able to carry out their instructional role with little guidance. Responders emphasize the personal side of their relationships with teachers and others. Before they make decisions, they often give everyone an opportunity to have input so as to consider their feelings or to allow others to make the decision. A related characteristic is their tendency to make decisions in terms of immediate circumstances rather than longer range instructional or school goals. This seems to arise in part from their desire to please others and in part from their more limited vision of how their school and staff should change in the future.

---

deeply about their students, teachers, and the school. Their pushing, monitoring, and bending of the rules are done to support everyone in doing his or her best. They also have what we are calling strategic sense, which means that they do not lose sight of the big picture while they are doing the day-to-day activities. They anticipate what might happen and envision alternative responses that they may need to employ.

Manager Change Facilitators   Managers approach the leadership of change efforts with a different set of behaviors and emphases. They are skilled at making their school run like a well-oiled machine. The bells ring on time, everyone knows how to get supplies, schedules are planned well in advance, and the various forms are filled out correctly and processed promptly. As proposals for change are made by teachers or those outside the school, Managers do not rush in. When asked by an external facilitator or a teacher to try something different, their first response will likely be, "Well, that is an interesting idea, but my teachers are real busy right now." Managers buy time, which they use to study and learn more about the change and to consider whether they should have the school engage with it.

An important consequence of this delaying is that teachers and the school are protected to some extent. This dampening of the initiation of change also buys time for the principal and teachers to learn about the proposed change and to prepare for an efficient implementation. As a result, when changes are implemented, they tend to proceed smoothly and to acceptable levels.

Manager principals also try to do many things themselves rather than delegating to others. They arrive at school very early in the morning, stay late in the evening, and return on the weekends to do more of the tasks. They work to meet the needs of the staff and to get the jobs done. In many ways, they demand more of themselves than they do of others. They often decide, "It is easier for me to do it right the first time than to have someone else do it and then have to fix it."

Responder Change Facilitators   Responders approach leadership with a primary focus on what is happening now. They do not have many ideas about what the school should be like in the future or where education is going. Instead their attention is on others' present concerns and perceptions. Therefore, when they do one-legged conferences with teachers and others, their purpose is to discover concerns and perceptions about current topics and issues. Responders also spend time on the phone checking with other principals about their perceptions of what the assistant superintendent was talking about in the last principals' meeting "when she said. . . ." They engage in the same sort of discussions with community members and students. The pattern to their talk is chatting and listening to concerns.

Responders are most willing for others to take the lead. For example, if a teacher wants to try a different curriculum approach, the Responder principal will say, "Go ahead. You know we always like to be innovative in this school." If someone from the district office or a nearby university wants to start a new project in the school, the Responder will welcome that person as part of the overall goal of trying to keep everyone happy. As a result, many disparate projects and activities can be going on in different parts of the school.

In contrast to Initiators, Responders delay making decisions. They want to have first heard from everyone about their concerns and perceptions. When they do have to make a decision they tend to do it at or shortly after the deadline. And, the decision will be most heavily influenced by the last person who talked to them. Thus, it is possible for a teacher or someone else to influence a decision right up to the last moment.

Another part of the Responders' CF pattern is the tendency to minimize the size and significance of proposed changes. They often feel that a change proposal is not as innovative as it advocates claim. "So what's the big deal?" a Responder may say, "We have been doing most of this already; you just have a different name for it." Also, Responders tend to hire strong and independent teachers believing that, "they know more about teaching than I do. It is my job to work with the community and do the other things so that they can teach."

Discussion and Implications of Change Facilitator Style

Now that we have introduced the different Change Facilitator Styles, it is important to think about some of the implications, issues, and questions. If the style descriptors offer nothing else, they can help you think about yourself and what you think are important characteristics of leaders during change processes. The different CF Styles described here do not represent all principals, nor do most principals fit perfectly into one of these styles. However, they do appear to represent the more commonly found approaches to change leadership.

A Continuum of Change Facilitator Styles

One way to think about the relationship of one CF Style to the others is to place them on a 100-point number line (see Figure 7.2). The stereotypic Responder is positioned at point 30, the stereotypic Manager at point 60, and the Initiator at point 90. Then, by using the paragraph definitions (Figure 7.1), it is possible to envision what persons who are purely one of the three styles would be like. For example, one principal might behave somewhat like a Responder but overall tend to be more of a Manager. That person could be placed around point 50 on the number line. A leader who is developing a clearer vision about the school and is sometimes thinking of more long-term goals might be somewhere between the Manager and Initiator CF Styles, around point 75.

Other CF Styles can be imagined by envisioning what people would be like at the extreme ends of the continuum. For example, a leader that scores above 100 would be a despot that does not listen and just decrees, while a person at the 0 end would display an extremely laissez-faire approach, neither taking a position nor helping with the change. Off the chart, far to the left would be the covert saboteur who works behind the scenes to scuttle the change effort.

FIGURE 7.2   A Continuum of Change Facilitator Styles

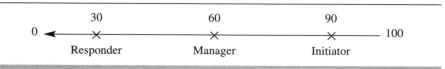

Additional Research and Support for Change Facilitator Styles

One could question whether these different CF Styles actually exist. How can we be assured that they are not just figments of the authors' imaginations? Addressing this question is one of the important purposes of research. This is also one reason we took the time in the introduction to this chapter to explain the background studies that led to the hypothesis that there are different Change Facilitator Styles. In this section, some of the related and more recent research studies are introduced.

The first research study on change facilitator styles was the Principal/Teacher Interaction (PTI) Study (Hord & Huling-Austin, 1986). In this study we used full-time ethonographers to systematically document the interventions of nine elementary school principals for an entire school year. We also assessed implementation by measuring teachers' Stages of Concern, Levels of Use, and Innovation Configurations. We found that indeed there were statistically significant differences in the quantity and quality of the principals' interventions and that they could be clustered according to the three hypothesized Change Facilitator Styles (Hall et al., 1984; Hall & Hord, 1987).

Studies by a number of other researchers in the United States have independently confirmed that principal intervention behaviors can be clustered according to these three styles (see, for example, Trohoski, 1984; Entrekin, 1991). In addition, studies have been done in Belgium (Vandenberghe, 1988) and in Australia (Schiller, 1991) with similar results. In a major test of the cross-cultural generalizability of the three Change Facilitator Styles, Shieh (1996) documented the intervention behaviors of six elementary school principals in Taiwan and observed the same differences in style and surprisingly similar anecdotal examples of perspectives and approaches to change leadership. Thus, although they certainly do not represent all possibilities, these three Change Facilitator Styles do have a basis in systematic studies in a number of settings and do offer a way to think more holistically about change leadership.

Research Relating Change Facilitator Style to Implementation Success

The relationship between principal Change Facilitator Style and teacher success in implementation has been studied also. For the PTI study, the CBAM diagnostic dimensions of SoC, LoU, and IC provided very useful benchmarks, or mileposts, for assessing the degree of implementation of the innovation. Teachers who moved to higher Levels of Use of more sophisticated configurations, with reduction of self and task concerns and arousal of impact concerns, would be considered as having had more implementation success. Their degree of implementation success could be compared with the intervention behaviors of their principals and the principals' Change Facilitator Style. In most of the studies cited above, this comparison was made. In the original PTI Study a correlation of .74 was found between Change Facilitator Style and teacher implementation success. In the other studies (for example, Schiller, 1991; Vandenberghe, 1988; and Shieh, 1996), similar patterns have been observed.

The general finding was that teachers with Initiator principals have the highest levels of implementation success. Teachers with Manager principals are successful too, but not to the same extent as teachers in Initiator schools. Teachers with Responder principals are rated a distant third in terms of implementation success. One way to summarize these findings is to suggest that the Initiator principals "make it happen." They have the vision, passion, and push to help things move in the desired direction. They make decisions quickly and there is consistency. Manager principals "help it happen." They see that things are well organized. They protect their teachers, but when implementation becomes an objective, it is accomplished efficiently. However, unlike the Initiators, they do not have the excitement and energy to keep doing more.

The conditions in schools led by Responder principals are quite different. These leaders "let it happen." Yes, they do listen to perceptions and concerns, but they never resolve issues with certainty. They continue to be open to new input and as a result do not bring closure, or else will hear another piece of information and change their minds. They are statistically significantly less active in terms of the number of change-related interventions they make. The result for teachers is less implementation success and a tendency to have "Big W" SoC profiles (see Figure 4.4). Shieh (1996) observed that in the first months of implementation teachers in Responder schools tend to use more of the less desirable variations of the innovation, whereas teachers in initiator schools used more of the desirable variations.

Metaphors for Change Facilitator Styles

Metaphors can be a useful way to summarize a great deal of information and ideas. A metaphor that should help in thinking about the totality of each CF Style is that of a game.

The Initiator is a chess player. Just as chess has many pieces, each with its own rules for being moved, the Initiator sees the differences in the school's people and activities. And just as good chess players use strategies and anticipate many moves ahead, Initiators are not only engaged in doing the day-to-day activities of change leadership but are constantly thinking about what needs to be done next. Most importantly, Initiators have several strategies in mind in anticipation of possible scenarios that could unfold.

Manager leaders play a board game too, but it is a simpler one—checkers. There are different pieces and rules of movement, but the view of the organization is less complicated. With checkers there are tactics rather than strategies, prediction is simpler, and winning is less complex. Still, in checkers, as in the manager style, there is a sustained purpose to the actions.

The game metaphor for Responders is that of flipping coins. Each flip of the coin is an act that is independent of the one that came before and the one that will follow. To a surprising degree, this is the case for the intervention behaviors of Responders. Each action tends to be taken independently. Much less consideration is given to stringing together such actions as individual one-legged conferences, faculty meetings, announcements, and notes to teachers. For example, teachers may be told at the beginning of the school year that they are responsible for maintaining the materials closet, but the Responder principal never checks to see if they are doing the task. Interventions do not accumulate to make tactics and strategies or to develop coherent themes that teachers can see.

Underlying Dimensions of Change Facilitator Style

In more recent research we have been examining some of the underlying dimensions of Change Facilitator Style. For this work we have developed the Change Facilitator Style Questionnaire (CFSQ) that asks teachers how they view the intervention actions of their principal (Hall & George, 1988, 1999; Vandenberghe, 1988). Through this work we have identified six underlying dimensions of change Facilitator Style, each of which can be rated separately. Different combinations of these dimensions then describe different Change Facilitator Styles. The six dimensions of CF Style are defined in Appendix 4.

Three examples of principal profiles, identified by the CFSQ, are presented in Figure 7.3; each represents the norm group for one of the styles. Profile interpretation is guided by the six scale definitions that are presented in Appendix 4.

Teachers see Initiator principals as being high on social/informal, formal/meaningful, administrative efficiency, and vision and planning dimensions. This profile fits with what would be expected from the earlier descriptions of Initiators, with the possible exception of being high on the social/informal scale. This research finding brought home an important point: Initiators have many one-legged conferences that not only are related to use of the change/innovation (formal/meaningful), but also deal with personal and general topics of discussion (social/informal). In other words, Initiators talk with teachers about how the change process is going and find time for social chat too.

The CFSQ profile for Manager principals is relatively flat and at the midlevel of each scale. Teachers see Manager principals as doing about the same amount of intervening relative to each of the six CFSQ scales.

Teachers view Responder principals as being high on the dimensions of trust in others and day-to-day. These findings are consistent with the Change Facilitator Style descriptions presented earlier in this chapter. Responders tend not to focus on making the school run efficiently nor on engaging in long-term vision and planning. What is particularly interesting about this profile is the low score on social/informal. Based on our description of the Responder style, one would expect that a Responder would be rated highly on informal, nontask-related talk and chat, but this was not the finding for these principals.

Changing Change Facilitator Style

Figure 7.4 is a CF Style profile of a very talented Initiator elementary school principal. At the time of our study, she had been the principal at this school for nearly ten

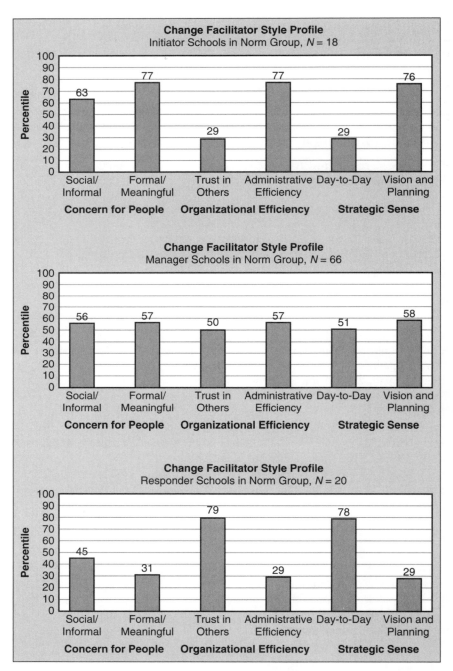

FIGURE 7.3   Stereotypical Change Facilitator Style Profiles for Stereotypical Initiator, Manager, and Responder Styles

years. She and her school have received a number of significant state and national awards. This school has developed well and is continually doing new and exciting things for children. As would be expected in a school led by an Initiator, in the past the teachers had rated this principal very high on vision and planning. They had seen her as having some focus on the day-to-day and administrative efficiency dimensions, which Initiators consider to be the foundation upon which they are able to lead change processes. She had had a high score on formal/meaningful, which we would expect as well, since Initiator change facilitators spend a lot of time in one-on-one interactions that are directly related to teacher use of the change. The social/informal scale of this principal's CFSQ profile was what would be predicted too, since Initiators spend time informally and personally with their staffs. That was her CFSQ profile in the past.

The accompanying CF profile (Figure 7.4) shows that leaders can change their style. However, the CF Style change described here did not occur until the principal had been in the school a number of years. It is not easy to change one's style. It is easier to consciously work on adjusting one's behaviors so that they fit each situation. In other words, change facilitators are not likely to change their style, but they most certainly should do different things depending on the current SoC, LoU, and IC of their clients.

The important as well as interesting points in this profile, which are not characteristics of all Initiators, are the very high score on trust in others and the low vision and planning score. When we asked the principal about these changes, she pointed out that she had been at the school long enough so that she was not doing as much leading by herself. Instead she now was trying to develop and empower her teachers to do the leading for various projects and tasks. She has teachers doing more presentations around the state, and she is pushing her teachers to lead more within the school. As a result of this shift in her style, her teachers now rate her much higher on the trust in others scale and low on vision and planning.

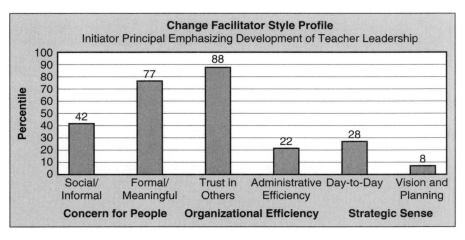

FIGURE 7.4   **Change Facilitator Style for an Initiator Principal Emphasizing Development of Teacher Leadership**

Change Facilitator Style as a Significant Factor in Change

Change Facilitator Style is an important factor in determining change process success. Another major theme in this book has been how the actions of change facilitators accumulate to form the larger patterns of interventions that we call tactics and strategies (see Chapter 6).

Of course, the three CF Styles of Initiator, Manager, and Responder do not represent all the possibilities but rather certain basic types that differ in a number of important ways. The concepts and distinctions of Change Facilitator Style can have various applications, some of which have been suggested above; others are summarized below.

Change Facilitator Style as a Heuristic

The concept of Change Facilitator Style can serve as a heuristic, or a device that helps us think about what we should do in leading change processes. Using the CFS concepts we can ask ourselves questions such as:

1. What kind of Change Facilitator Style do I want to have?
2. In the successful change processes that I have been a part of, what was the Change Facilitator Style of the leader?
3. When I interview for a new position, what characteristics will I look for in my new supervisor?

Working with Different Change Facilitator Styles

CF Styles also offer clues about why and how to be more influential with different leaders. Each leader by definition will be emphasizing particular aspects of the change process and elements of use of the innovation. They consider different factors when making decisions, and the amount of time that they need to make decisions varies considerably. Teachers and others who have determined the leader's style will have more influence. They also will be more accurate in predicting what the leader will decide. For example, when teachers would like their principal to make a decision in a particular direction, what they say to influence the decision-making and when and how they say it, will need to be adjusted to fit the principal's CF Style.

Whatever the issue to be resolved, Initiators will want to have reasons and evidence that explain how the decision will affect student success and advance the school. They will expect teachers to have well-developed ideas and clear descriptions, supported by facts. Timing is important, since Initiators tend to think far ahead. They like to be able to anticipate what will work as well as what might go wrong. Providing them with information early in the process is key. Once they have heard what is being suggested, they may need to consult with others, but will make a decision fairly quickly.

In contrast, Responders will be less interested in hearing specifics and more likely to encourage "going ahead" without careful thought or fully understanding all that may follow. In their effort to be encouraging, they frequently will agree to two or more initiatives that overlap and may actually compete. In other words, do not count on continuity of support and follow-through. One piece of good news is that Responders will allow and even encourage an array of change initiatives. Don't forget, however, that if what is being asked involves a major decision or may create controversy, Responders are very slow to agree. They will want plenty of time for talk, which may seem like a way to avoid making a decision. A good approach when dealing with a Responder is to begin with casual social chat and then raise the general topic. An important side strategy would be to regularly and continually monitor other related decisions that the Responder is making.

When making a request or a suggestion to Manager leaders, remember that they will want to hear about the time, logistic, and cost implications of the issue. The structuring of work and scheduling are important considerations for them. Be prepared to know what will be needed and have suggestions about how your ideas can be managed. Managers can decide quite quickly if what is being asked is in line with initiatives that are already up and running. However, an entirely new proposal is likely to run into the dampening effect, which results from a combination of Managers' desire to protect and maintain stability, and their need to study and ponder.

The Relationship of Change Facilitator Style to Other Factors

The possible relationships between CF Style and other characteristics of leaders have not been studied, although many hypotheses can be offered. For example, there appear to be connections between CF Style and aspects of personality. Some forms of intelligence and creativity may be at play as well. However, there have been no empirical studies of these issues, nor of the Stages of Concern of leaders with different Change Facilitator Styles. One hypothesis would be that Initiators move more rapidly from self to task to impact concerns during a change process. Another would be that Responders rarely have high impact concerns. In testing any of these hypotheses, it must be remembered that change in Stages of Concern will, at least in part, be related to the context. What happens to people's concerns, even for leaders, is to some degree dependent on what is going on with others above and below them in the same organizational context.

Changes in Change Facilitator Style

For the most part, Change Facilitator Styles do not change quickly. From all that we know, a person's CF Style is quite stable. It does not change from day to day or from innovation to innovation. Of course, there will be changes in behaviors, the intervention actions that are taken moment to moment and day to day. The priority that a leader gives to different innovations can vary, as can the leader's actions, but the person's overall Change Facilitator Style will remain constant. This assertion of only limited short-term change in style contradicts the position of a number of current leadership experts. For example, various workshops are offered to help leaders analyze and change their "style." The clear implication is that workshop participants will learn, in these two- or three-day sessions, how to change their overall approach to leadership. In other words, they will learn how to change their style. Our research and experience suggest that only in times of major changes in context can leaders quickly change their overall style. Even then, we see more cases of context shifts, when the leader has been unable to adapt his or her style to the sudden changes, than we have of successful short-term change to match the new realities. One quick way to test our position on the limited capability of leaders to change their style is to look at political leaders to see whether their styles change. Think about recent American presidents, each of whom was associated with an overall style, which the press made stereotypical in many ways. Can you think of times when these presidents broke away from their preferred/dominant style? What happened?

The Relationship of Change Facilitator Style to Organizational Variables

Change Facilitator Style can be related to organizational climate and organizational culture. It seems reasonable to expect that there would be relationships between the Change Facilitator Style of the principal and the climate and culture of the school. How teachers feel about their school and their perceptions of what counts should be a reflection of the style of the leader. In a few of the early studies, estimates of organizational climate were found to be related to the principals' Change Facilitator Style. The general trend was that organizational climate was more positive in schools with Manager and Initiator principals than with Responder principals. Recent studies of Belgian schools (Staessens, 1993) have clearly documented that the organizational culture is much more positive and professional in schools with principals whose style more closely resembles the Initiator. Again, the organizational culture in schools with Responder principals seems to be much less healthy and professional.

VIGNETTE
Principal Succession

One of the interesting applications of the work in Change Facilitator Style is its use in envisioning different scenarios in which change can occur in a school principal. This analysis could be done from one or more perspectives. For example, if you have accepted the position of principal, you should be interested in finding out about the Change Facilitator Style of your predecessor. You could also be interested in this analysis if you are a teacher in a school that is going through a turnover in principals, or if you are on the interview committee or in the district office with an assignment to advise on the selection of a new principal for a particular school. In any of these cases, having an understanding of CF Style concepts would be helpful. They can be used to understand the kind of leader the school needs next and to anticipate what the problems will be in the transition. Let's imagine what some of the transitions could be like. To do this we will use a combination of real cases and hypothetical examples.

Frequently, an Initiator principal is hired to replace a Responder. Consider the setting that the newly assigned Initiator will enter. To begin, Responder-led schools are characterized by the "Big W" concerns profile (see Figure 4.4). Teachers are not happy about their continually high Stage 3 Management concerns and their "tailing up" on Stage 6 indicates that they have some very strong ideas about how things ought to be. Remember too that a Responder principal does not make clear and final decisions. We also know that in a Responder school a small clique of teachers will have more control over what happens and a large number of teachers will have little say in what occurs. In addition, each teacher tends to be strong and independent, because the Responders attitude is, "I hire strong teachers who know more about teaching than I do." The result is that the teachers rarely agree on anything, ranging from which texts to use to where to place the coffee pot.

Administrators in the district office are delighted that a well-known Initiator principal has agreed to take over this school and "turn it around." This principal is known for having a strong focus on student success, and she insists that all the teachers work toward the betterment of the school: "My expectation is that they should lead, follow, or get the hell out of the way."

Given your understanding of Change Facilitator Style, what do you predict will happen in this situation? Will the transition go smoothly? What kinds of issues will be problematic? Will students be more or less successful? And what will the district office administrators do as the scenario unfolds?

In our case files are a number of examples of a transition from Responder to Initiator Style. One of the opening steps for Initiators is to study closely the achievement data of students and the records of the teachers. The Initiator arrives with a set of key themes, such as "treat students as you want to be treated," that she emphasizes repeatedly.

In our case study of the previous Responder principal, there was an unequal distribution of resources, with certain teachers getting more and some getting little. The newly arrived Initiator principal expects that resources will be distributed evenly and that there will be no favoritism. She also presses for teachers to use certain teaching practices and curriculum materials. All of the new principal's actions are intended to move things in the direction of her vision.

The reactions of teachers are aligned with how their influence has been affected and the degree of change that is expected of them. The clique of teachers that had more influence with the Responder principal are unhappy with the changes. In fact, some of them are complaining to the district administrators, and some even go directly to the school board. When asked, teachers who were not part of the influential clique but who are now being treated fairly express appreciation for the new principal, but they do not express their satisfaction to the district administrators or school board.

Typically, the administrators in the district office start to worry when they hear that things are not going well at the school. In this case, as with a number of similar transitions that we have observed, the district administrators maintained a hands-off stance, leaving the Initiator principal to sink or swim, on his or her own. One district administrator observed, "Well, I don't know if Teresa is going to make it." Ironically this was the same administrator that placed Teresa in this situation. Rather than moving to address the concerns of the complaining teachers or to overtly encourage and support the new principal, the district administrators merely listened to the reports from the school. This Vignette does have a happy ending. Two years later Teresa was acclaimed for having turned the school around.

Obviously there is more to this case that could be told. The purpose here was to briefly introduce the strategy of using Change Facilitator Style concepts to examine transitions in school principals. In thinking about these transitions, it is important to consider the CF Style of the departing as well as the incoming principal. It is also necessary to understand what the school has been like and what the new principal will expect it to become. Remember too that teachers, parents, district office administrators, and students may perceive and consider aspects of the principals' CF Style differently.

1. What do you remember about a change in leadership at a school or other organization that you have seen? Was there a clear change in leadership style? How did the leaders differ in what they considered to be important? How did your role/work change as the style of the leader changed?
2. What is the Change Facilitator Style of your current principal/leader? Describe some of the things that you have learned to do to work effectively with this person. How do you think your role/work would change if your principal/leader had a different CF Style?

Summary

In this chapter, we have focused on characteristics of those who lead change processes. Three Change Facilitator Styles have been proposed and confirmed through studies that documented the moment-to-moment and day-to-day intervention behaviors of principals. We have drawn on the research to help illustrate and explain these different approaches to change leadership. One important point that was made early in this chapter was that *everyone* who is part of a change process has the opportunity, and some responsibility, to help lead. We also pointed out that attention must be given to distinguishing between facilitators' individual actions or behaviors and their overall style. As we will discuss in Chapter 9, the very same action by leaders with different Change Facilitator Styles will be perceived and interpreted very differently by their followers. In other words, often what counts is not what you do but how others interpret what you do.

The style of change leadership makes a major difference in the implementation success of the followers. There are many implications of being able to distinguish the different Change Facilitator Styles, including their use by the followers, who need to work with leaders with different styles, as is illustrated in the Vignette, and by the leaders themselves, who may want to analyze and reflect on their approach to change facilitation. In conclusion, it is crucial to remember that, since principals and other leaders, like students and teachers, are different, we should not treat them as if they were all the same.

Guiding Principles of Change Facilitator Styles

1. Change Facilitator Style is the overall pattern that is derived from accumulated observations of individual leader behaviors. CF Style provides the context for understanding and interpreting the moment-to-moment actions of a change leader.
2. Initiators focus on doing what will be best in the long term for students and the school, rather than primarily on making people happy in the short term.
3. Schools with Manager leaders attain implementation success. However, there is little effort to move beyond the acceptable minimums.
4. Responders ask about concerns but are less active in attempting to resolve them and in facilitating change. They just tend to keep checking on how people are feeling about issues in general.
5. Influencing leaders with different CF Styles requires customized approaches. Responders are most interested in staff feelings, Managers focus most on administrative and organizational efficiency, while Initiators want to hear the facts and reasons about how student success will be effected.
6. Change Facilitator Styles do not change quickly. Individual behavior will change from setting to setting, and each action will be interpreted in terms of the overall style. But a change in one's style, if it occurs at all, appears to be caused only by a major change in circumstances or the passage of time.

DISCUSSION QUESTIONS

1. Develop and describe another Change Facilitator Style, one that is different from the Initiator, Manager, and Responder styles described in this chapter. What are characteristic behaviors of this style, and what would be its effects?

2. In small groups, use specific examples of behavior to discuss and analyze the Change Facilitator Style of a leader such as a principal, district superintendent, college president, dean, or department chair. Using the number line in Figure 7.2, first estimate his or her style. Then use examples of specific behaviors and actions as well as the more general description of overall style to place this person at a specific point on the continuum presented in Figure 7.2. How does this match your estimate?

3. Develop a brief description of your own Change Facilitator Style. Describe your behaviors during one change effort. In hindsight, what style were you using? What do you now know that you could have done differently?

4. Develop a chart or summary figure that identifies and describes actions and approaches that you should and should not take to positively influence (i.e., to get along with) supervisors each of whom uses one of the three Change Facilitator Styles.

5. One of the heuristic applications of Change Facilitator Styles is to apply them to various succession scenarios. For example, what happens when a Responder follows an Initiator, or when a Responder follows a Responder? A number of succession patterns are possible. Pick one and predict what would happen in the organization with the professional staff, support staff, and change initiatives. Would change occur more quickly, more slowly, or at the same pace? Would the same change initiatives continue? How long would it take for effects of the new leader's style to be detected?

FIELDWORK ACTIVITIES

1. Ask two people to describe how they work to facilitate change. One of the people you interview should have a formal administrative position and be a designated leader. The other person should be one of the so-called followers. When interviewing the follower, keep in mind that at first the person is likely to say that he or she has no leadership role. But delve further by asking how he or she participates in planning meetings or helps other people who are engaged with the change process. All of these actions are change facilitating (or inhibiting) too.

2. Ask an experienced educator (e.g., a teacher or professor) who has worked for a number of administrators to describe what it was like to interact with people with different styles. Develop a report on the person's feelings and perceptions when he or she was engaged in change. You also should ask about the times when change was more and less successful.

3. One of the themes in this chapter has been that a critical factor in change process success is the Change Facilitator Style of the leader. If you were to interview prospective leaders of a change effort, what kinds of questions would you ask? Develop a list of the questions and explain how you would expect the answers to differ depending on the person's Change Facilitator Style. You could also use this activity when you are being interviewed for a new position. After all, the leadership style of your supervisor will make a difference in how successful you can be.

REFERENCES

Bass, B. M. (1990). *Stogdill's handbook of leadership: A survey of theory, research, and managerial applications* (3rd ed.). New York: The Free Press.

Blake, R. R., & Mouton, J. S. (1964). *The managerial grid.* Houston: Gulf.

Entrekin, K. M. (1991). *Principal Change Facilitator Styles and the implementation of consultation-based prereferral child study teams.* Unpublished doctoral dissertation, Temple University, Philadelphia.

Fiedler, F. E. (1978). The contingency model and the dynamics of the leadership process. In L. Berkowitz (Ed.), *Advances in experimental and social psychology* (pp. 59–112). New York: Academic Press.

Fullan, M., Miles, M. B., & Taylor, G. (1980). Organization development in schools: The state of the art. *Review of Educational Research, 50*(1), 121–183.

Hall, G. E., & George, A. A. (1988). *Development of a framework and measure for assessing principal change facilitator style.* Paper presented at the annual meeting of the American Educational Research Association, New Orleans. (ERIC Document Reproduction Service No. ED 336 401).

Hall, G. E., & George, A. A. (1999). The impact of principal Change Facilitator Style on school and classroom culture. In H. J. Freiberg (Ed.), *School climate: Measuring, improving, and sustaining healthy learning environments.* Philadelphia: Falmer Press.

Hall, G. E., & Hord, S. M. (1987). *Change in schools: Facilitating the process.* Albany: SUNY Press.

Hall, G. E., Hord, S. M., & Griffin, T. H. (1980). *Implementation at the school building level: The development and analysis of nine mini-case studies* (Report No. 3098). Austin: The University of Texas at Austin, Research and Development Center for Teacher Education. (ERIC Document Reproduction Service No. ED 207 170).

Hall, G. E., Rutherford, W. L., & Griffin, T. H. (1982). *Three Change Facilitator Styles: Some indicators and a proposed framework.* Austin: The University of Texas at Austin, Research and Development Center for Teacher Education. (ERIC Document Reproduction Service No. ED 220 961).

Hall, G. E., Rutherford, W. L., Hord, S. M., & Huling, L. L. (1984). Effects of three principal styles on school improvement. *Educational Leadership, 41*(5), 22–29.

Hall, G. E., & Shieh, W. H. (1998). Organizational development and supervision: Relationships past, present, and needed. In G. R. Firth & E. F. Pajak (Eds.), *Handbook of research on supervision* (pp. 842–865). New York: Macmillan.

Hersey, P., & Blanchard, K. H. (1988). *Management of organizational behavior: Utilizing human resources.* Englewood Cliffs, NJ: Prentice Hall.

Hord, S. M., & Huling-Austin, L. (1986). Effective curriculum implementation: Some promising new insights. *The Elementary School Journal, 87*(1), 97–115.

Hougen, M. C. (1984). *High school principals: An analysis of their approach to facilitating implementation of microcomputers.* Unpublished doctoral dissertation, The University of Texas at Austin.

Leithwood, K. A., & Montgomery, D. J. (1982). The role of the elementary school principal in program improvement. *Review of Educational Research, 52*(3), 309–339.

Miles, M. B. (Ed.). (1971). *Innovation in education.* New York: Columbia University.

Schiller, J. (1991). Implementing computer education: The role of the primary principal. *Australian Journal of Educational Technology, 7*(1) 48–69.

Schmuck, R. A., & Runkle, P. J. (1994). *The handbook of organization development in schools and colleges* (4th ed.). Prospect Heights, IL: Waveland Press.

Shieh, W. H. (1996). *Environmental factors, principals' Change Facilitator Style, and implementation of the cooperative learning project in selected schools in Taiwan.* Unpublished doctoral dissertation, University of Northern Colorado, Greeley.

Staessens, K. (1993). Identification and description of professional culture in innovating schools. *Qualitative Studies in Education, 6*(2), 111–128.

Trohoski, C. G. (1984). *Principals' interventions in the implementation of a school health program.* Unpublished doctoral dissertation, University of Pennsylvania, Philadelphia.

Vandenberghe, R. (1988). *Development of a questionnaire for assessing principal Change Facilitator Style.* Paper presented at the annual meeting of the American Educational Research Association, New Orleans. (ERIC Document Reproduction Service No. ED 297 463).

8 Expanding Views of Change Leadership

The Change Facilitator Team

Working with my principal has been very interesting. We meet once a week to plan what I am going to do. Then both of us go about meeting with teachers and seeing what we can do to help them to incorporate the use of manipulative materials into their lessons.

—Lead teacher

You know, schools really are different. When I go to some schools, the principal is there to greet me and has a list of questions and teachers that I should visit. In some other schools, even when I call in advance to schedule my visit, the teachers don't get the word that I am coming and the principal seems surprised to see me.

—District office curriculum coordinator

They all have really helped me. Having Alan (lead teacher) available half-time has really made a difference for me. I always know where to find him, and he knows all these little tricks that have helped me plan and to organize each lesson. Our principal has made it clear that doing this is important, and she is in all our classrooms every week. Then, of course, Leslie from the university has been here a lot, and she presents the workshops too.

—Teacher engaged in implementing an innovative approach to teaching mathematics

Leading and facilitating change processes is a big job. It takes time and requires specialized knowledge and skill. Facilitating change is frustrating at times and very satisfying at other times. No matter how small the change, it entails work that is additional to everyone's regular responsibilities. However, if no one comes forth to lead and facilitate a change effort, in the end little will be accomplished. Some teachers may try to make the innovation work in their classrooms, but, as most people discover, it is extremely difficult to sustain a change process without ongoing support from the top.

The importance of having a formal leader, such as the school principal or district superintendent, serve as the key change facilitator (CF) was made in Chapter 7. We also described there how the style of that change facilitator has been shown to make a significant difference in the degree of success teachers have with implementing change. In this chapter, the major theme is that principals/superintendents don't do it alone. There are a number of other change facilitator roles, each of which can be very important to overall change process success.

FOCUS QUESTIONS

1. Who else besides the key administrator can have a change facilitator role?
2. Do Second Change Facilitators have to perform their role full-time?
3. Does a site need the involvement of change facilitators from outside the organization?
4. What do we know about how change facilitators work together as a team?
5. What difference does the Change Facilitator Style of the administrator make in how the team of change facilitators works?
6. Does the principal/superintendent have to be the primary change facilitator?

The formal leader needs to be the *First Change Facilitator*. However, instead of facilitating change singlehandedly, in more successful change efforts the First Change Facilitator works with a second and sometimes a third facilitator. In combination they comprise a *Change Facilitator Team*, whose dynamics and degrees of effectiveness vary depending on the members. Each of the CF roles, the dynamics of the interworkings of the team, and the effect of Change Facilitator Style are examined in this chapter. Here again, examples from real organizations and findings from research will be used to illustrate the concepts and to emphasize important understandings about change.

The Leader Doesn't Do It Alone: The Case for a Second Change Facilitator

A story from one of our research studies is fun to tell here. When we launched the first major study of principals as change facilitators, each research team member was assigned to document any and all of the innovation-related interventions made by one of nine principals. After all of us had returned from our first site visit, each one could not wait to tell the others that "in my school someone else [besides the principal] is making a lot of interventions!" Our study plan had naively assumed that most of the change-related interventions would be made by the principal. What we discovered was that, regardless of the CF Style of the principal, there was another person in each of the schools who was making a large number of innovation-related interventions.

The Second Change Facilitator Role

This other person who was making many change-related interventions in some cases was the assistant principal, but more often was a teacher who had a special assignment in the school, part of which was to help with implementation. In one school it was the Title/Chapter I pull-out teacher. In others it was a master teacher who had been given some released time to help other teachers implement the innovation. Elsewhere it was the department chair or team leader who had extra interest in and specialized expertise related to the change.

We now call this person the *Second Change Facilitator*, or *consigliere*. A consigliere is an advisor or trusted colleague of the formal leader. We know that in nearly every school there will be a second person who has special responsibility to help facilitate implementation. The Second CF works with the principal to assist teachers individually as they have concerns and seek assistance, and to monitor how the change process is going. Frequently Second CFs have a special role or assignment that grants them time to be available for and to work with other teachers relative to implementation of the change. Sometimes it is an informal role whereby other teachers recognize that this individual is a useful resource and seek him or her. Often it is a person who has been in the building longer, is more experienced, is recognized as being an expert, and is creditable with fellow teachers. In the diffusion change perspective (Rogers, 1995), such a person is called an *opinion leader,* an individual whom others trust and turn to for advice and information about the innovation and the change process.

Being a Second Change Facilitator Is Only Part of the Job   Ironically, although Second CFs have added responsibilities, they typically receive no extra credit or pay. They seem to perform in this function as a form of volunteer professional service and don't expect special recognition or status. However, if schools had teacher career ladders (Ebmeier & Hart, 1992), the Second Change Facilitator would definitely be paid on a higher rung.

When different innovations are being implemented in a school, a different person usually serves as the Second CF for each innovation. For example, the Second CF for the literacy initiative could be an experienced teacher who loves reading and literature, while the Second CF for the technology plan may be the chair of the business department, who has been a computer buff "way back to the Apple II days."

First and Second Change Facilitators Partnerships   The Second CF works not only with teachers but also with the First CF, a part of the role that gave rise to the use of the term *consigliere*. In many ways, the Second CF is an informal advisor and assistant to the First CF; both need to be cognizant of what the other is doing and to be able to trust each other. They need to share information about what teachers are doing and to jointly analyze their successes, concerns, and needs. Although the First and Second CF understand that there is a hierarchical relationship between them in a supervisory sense, they approach the change facilitation job as a partnership. (One implication of this is that when we are training principals and superintendents in CBAM concepts, we ask that their consiglieres be present too.)

Formalized Examples of Second Change Facilitator Roles

There are notable exceptions to the generalization that the Second CF role is informal and unrecognized. In some schools and districts, special assignments and even full-time roles have been established to support and facilitate implementation of specific innovations and/or change processes in general; two such examples are presented here. These examples also illustrate how structures and roles can be realigned to support and facilitate ongoing change processes.

Mathematics Teachers as Second Change Facilitators The U.S. Department of Defense has its own school system for the children of the military. This system is composed of school districts that are located all around the world. As one would expect, there is a continuing expectation for these districts and their schools to change in order to be up-to-date.

One of the curriculum changes that this system has been grappling with recently is how to teach mathematics. Teachers and administrators are being asked to make changes that are consistent with the standards of the National Council for the Teaching of Mathematics, which, among other things, expect teachers not only to be using many manipulative materials but to be teaching in ways that focus on helping students to develop their own mathematical understandings, instead of having the teacher present sets of operational rules that all students are to memorize.

In the Hessen School District (outside of Frankfurt, Germany), the superintendent (who is an Initiator) implemented a special form of the Second Change Facilitator role (Johnson, 2000). She recruited three classroom teachers, who were well known as skilled mathematics teachers, to work full-time for two years across the district to facilitate all teachers' implementation of the new approach to teaching mathematics. Each of these math coordinators works with five schools. Their job includes being in classrooms to coach teachers, doing model lessons, developing and presenting topical workshops, and constructing an Innovation Configuration (IC) Map of mathematics teaching. (A component of their IC Map was presented as Figure 3.4.)

The Hessen district superintendent is very actively involved too. On a day-to-day basis, she talks with the mathematics coordinators, principals, and teachers about how the new approach is working. She is thus functioning as the First Change Facilitator and the math coordinators are serving as the Second Change Facilitators for this districtwide change initiative. Because the superintendent is certified to do Levels of Use (LoU) interviews, she did her share of teacher LoU interviews during the implementation assessment study. In this case the unit of change is the district, and all schools are being supported and facilitated at the school and classroom levels by the First and Second Change Facilitators.

Building Resource Teachers as Second Change Facilitators

Douglas County is a rapidly growing school district in Colorado that has many new teachers each year (25 percent in four years). The district is constantly building new schools in an attempt to keep up with the growth. It also is engaged in implementing many major curriculum and education reform initiatives. For example, in addition to the regular curriculum changes initiated by the district, the state has mandated implementation of standards, and the district has implemented a performance pay plan for teachers, administrators, and classified employees. There is obviously a lot of change going on in this district.

However, this district has very visionary leadership, strong support from the teachers' union, stability and wisdom on the school board, and community interest and active support. As a result, there is a pattern of constantly looking forward, not only in terms of the kinds of changes that are needed but also about how best to facilitate the change process. One result has been the creation of a new change facilitator role, the Building Resource Teacher (BRT).

The establishment of this new role began when the district leadership opened to discussion and examination the traditional way of supporting curriculum change and mentoring new teachers. In the past, mentor teachers had been assigned to new teachers, and Teachers on Special Assignments (TOSAs) had been placed in the district office to lead curriculum change. As a result of extensive dialogue, however, the district did away with the traditional roles and pooled the resources to create a new full-time position for every school, a Building Resource Teacher.

The BRTs are master teachers who have a full-time job in each school that deals with developing staff, mentoring new teachers, providing instructional leadership, coaching all teachers, and facilitating all changes. BRTs cannot dispense discipline, serve as building administrator when the principal is out, or have students permanently assigned to them. Their job is to help the teachers grow and the school develop its professional culture.

BRTs are full-time Second Change Facilitators. Their role is to work with all teachers to prepare for, train in, and ultimately to use effectively the innovations that are adopted by the school district. BRTs work closely with their principals and assistant principals, but they are not administrators. They serve as one leg of the three-legged "leadership stool," with the principal and assistant principal functioning as the other two. But, unlike the others, BRTS do not evaluate or hire teachers. Instead, their job is to work full-time with teacher change and development, and to do this in conjunction with what the principal and other school and district leaders have envisioned.

The Third Change Facilitator Role

In larger schools especially secondary schools, a third person sometimes makes a noticeable number of change-related interventions. This person does not typically have assigned time in which to perform this role but nonetheless is active in facilitating the change schoolwide. Being momentarily short on creativity, we simply named these people *Third Change Facilitators.*

We know less about Third CFs, especially about who they are and how they work in secondary schools. In general, they are highly respected teachers who have a great deal of recognized expertise related to the change/innovation, but they typically refuse to be released from teaching to help other teachers. They are most willing to help when called upon and when they are not teaching, but they do not want to serve in the more formal Second CF role. Still, their expertise is such that they are called upon frequently not only by teachers but also by the First and Second CF.

In secondary schools, the Third CF is often the chair of the department most affected by a change. Other times, the Third CF is a lead teacher with substantive or technical expertise that is needed to make the change work. Although our understanding of how this role operates is quite limited, it seems to be a site-based function and one that it is less formalized. But how Third CFs are selected and exactly what they do have not been studied.

No School Is an Island: The External Change Facilitator Role

Frequently, schools are implicitly told that they can (and should) do everything by themselves. Such innovations as site-based management and the downsizing of the district central office imply that schools need little if any external assistance and support. However, schools, like other organizations, cannot have all of the necessary expertise, perspectives, and resources internally to effectively operate and continually improve. One of the key reasons that school staffs are tired is the heavy burden they assume by accepting and attempting to accomplish everything themselves. They face a large quantity of tasks and changes that are mandated, demanded, and requested by those outside the school.

In all of our studies, we have observed that site-based change is most successful when the school is not expected (or allowed) to go it alone. There always is a need for important contributions from a number of *External Change Facilitators* (XCFs), whose offices are located in places outside the school, such as the district office, colleges, intermediate units, and regional labs.

External Change Facilitators serve the local site in a number of critical ways. For example, they are a source of expert knowledge about the innovation. In some cases, they are its developers; others will have been trained by the developers and/or have been expert users of the innovation.

Another important function of XCFs is to serve as liaisons between the implementing site and external organizations such as the district central office, the school board, and others that are working toward the same change process ends. The External Change Facilitators may learn about something that is going on at one site and be able to share this information with another site. They also can keep both the change facilitators at the site and administrators at the district level informed about what the other is doing and needs.

Note that here again we have referred to the local site as a school, although the same function and dynamics operate if the adopting unit is a school district or another larger system. All have an important set of role functions to be performed by external facilitators.

In addition to serving as a liaison and source of innovation expertise, XCFs can function as coaches and mentors to the site-based change facilitators. In many ways and for most of the time, being a change facilitator is a lonely job. There are few people with whom change facilitators can talk about their work, either because there are confidentiality issues to consider or because not many people have expertise in facilitating change. External CFs thus become very useful to the internal CFs as a sounding board and source of ideas about how a difficult change process issue might be addressed. Visits by and conversations with XCFs also can provide the internal CFs with the opportunity to reflect on how the change process is going and to look at the overall picture. Keep in mind that it is very easy for change facilitators to become so engrossed in the day-to-day actions and events that they fail to pull back and monitor the larger patterns. External Change Facilitators can facilitate this reflection process by making the time available and serving as catalysts.

Another important role for XCFs is to provide independent assessments of how the change process is going and to offer recommendations for how it can be facilitated further. By conducting formal implementation assessments, external facilitators can collect data through questionnaires, interviews, and observations. The analyses of these data are then reported to the on-site change facilitators to help them in planning and facilitating the next steps. An important part of doing implementation assessments is suggestions and recommendations about how best to further facilitate the change process. As external CFs the implementation assessors may have detected particular trends and patterns and have a responsibility to offer suggestions from their perspective about what might be done next.

Change Facilitator Role Functions

Given the number of Change Facilitator Roles, one should expect that what each facilitator does will differ in some important ways. Indeed that is the case. Some functions and activities are given more or less emphasis by each role. A partial summary of these CF functions is presented in Figure 8.1.

FIGURE 8.1   Relative Importance of the Key Functions for Each Change Facilitator Role (in Decreasing Order)

First Change Facilitator
- **** Sanctioning
- **** Keeping priorities straight
- *** Providing continued backup
- *** Providing resources
- ** Monitoring
- ** Reinforcing
- ** Pushing
- ** Telling others
- ** Approving adaptations
- * Providing technical coaching

Second Change Facilitator
- *** Reinforcing
- *** Providing technical coaching
- *** Monitoring
- *** Following up
- ** Sanctioning
- ** Providing resources
- ** Training
- * Pushing
- * Telling others
- * Approving adaptations

Third Change Facilitator
- * Providing technical coaching
- * Reinforcing
- * Modeling

External Change Facilitator
- ** Serving as liaison
- * Providing resources
- * Offering expert knowledge about the innovation
- * Functioning as a workshop trainer for innovation nonusers and users and site change facilitators
- * Coaching and mentoring First and Second Change Facilitators
- * Conducting implementation assessments and evaluation studies

* The more stars the more important.

Figure 8.1 shows that sanctioning is the most important function for the First CF. Others can encourage, but only the First CF can truly anoint a particular innovation or change process as being important. How the First CF goes about sanctioning is crucial too. Simply saying at the beginning of the year that use of the innovation is important does not accomplish the sanctioning function. Sanctioning an effort is a continuing activity that includes not only formal statements but also less visible behaviors, such as arranging schedules so that those who are most engaged with the innovation have time to plan and providing supplemental resources to support the change.

The same type of activity analysis can be done for each of the other CF role functions. Each function needs to continue across time. How the activity is done is important too. If each change facilitator does his or her part across time, change processes can be very successful and unfold with a minimum of stress and strain.

Change Facilitator Teams

With all of these different change facilitators, with different roles and responsibilities, and ways of working, you would think that someone would have given careful thought to what each does and how they all interrelate. No such luck! Very little conceptual research has addressed the roles and effects of all of these change facilitators in combination. Sadly, it also appears that site and system administrators have failed to grasp the significance of understanding and managing the various change facilitators as a team.

We first proposed the *Change Facilitator Team* concept in the mid-1980s, following our discovery of the Second CF role. We had observed that the Second CF role differed in key ways, depending on the CF Style of the principal. We also had seen various XCFs coming and going. Unfortunately, other than for some initial work done by Wim Wijlic in the Netherlands, there seems to have been no study of the roles and effects of external CFs. Still, they are a critical part of the Change Facilitator Team, which will be described in more detail following the descriptions of the dynamics and functions of CF Teams.

Working as a Change Facilitator Team

In the first half of this chapter we introduced and described the roles and functions of the First, Second, Third, and External Change Facilitators independently. Here we will examine how these different change facilitators operate as a Change Facilitator Team. There should be a deliberate effort to coordinate and communicate the work of the various CFs, instead of having each function in isolation. People and the change process are affected not only by how the individual change facilitators function but also by what the CF Team does (and doesn't do).

Change Facilitator Team Functions

The ideal CF Team has a number of shared responsibilities and functions, which are summarized in Figure 8.2. Note that these items are *shared*. The most effective Change Facilitator Teams share in accomplishing everything rather than delegating functions to individuals.

Although all of the CF Team functions are important, frequently one or more is neglected. Therefore, we recommend that CF Teams keep a copy of the list presented in Figure 8.2 and regularly use it to review what they have been doing and to plan future interventions. Each of the functions summarizes a key area of skill and responsibility for each CF as well as for the CF Team.

Sanctioning and Providing Continued Backup   One of the most obvious functions of change facilitators is to sanction the change *and* the efforts to implement it. As was emphasized in Chapter 4, letting teachers know that implementing the change is important and that they will be supported is critical in preventing the arousal of and/or resolving Stage 2 Personal concerns. We all want to know that our leaders are supportive of what we are doing.

FIGURE 8.2 Change Facilitator Team Functions*

Sanctioning	Training
Providing continued back up	Reinforcing
Providing resources	Pushing
Providing technical coaching	Telling others
Monitoring	Approving adaptations
Following up	

*A CF Team can be rated in terms of the extent to which each of these functions is addressed by using the following scale:

(0)	(1)	(2)	(3)	(5)	(6)
Never	Almost never	Seldom	Some of the time	Most of the time	All of the time

The CF Team's sanctioning must also be continuous. Simply announcing at the beginning of a change process that the innovation is important will not accomplish successful implementation. Since change is a process (not an event), there needs to be continuing support as the process unfolds. A key responsibility of all CF Team members is to continuously let the implementors know that the change/innovation is important, that their efforts to implement it are valued, and that there will be continuing backup and support.

Providing Resources Organization leaders do not always provide the necessary resources to support implementation. We have seen change efforts where even required equipment and materials were not forthcoming. We are not talking about delayed delivery but the complete lack of planning and budgeting for equipment and materials. All too frequently, we are amazed to observe that other types of basic resources, such as training, are not provided. To use a nonschool example, we know of an insurance company that implemented a new, state-of-the-art computer system but did not train agents, support persons, marketing, or accounting in what it entailed or how to use it! Three years later, the executives had to hire an outside auditing firm to determine if the company was solvent. They had a three-year accumulation of mechanical Level of Use (LoU) problems and no way of knowing the condition of the company because personnel were not trained in using the new system.

Addressing the function of providing resources does not mean that the CF Team is responsible for seeing that every little item is made available. However, the team should have a plan in place in advance of implementation that outlines which resources are necessary and how they will be provided. In forming this plan, the CF Team, as appropriate, needs to ask the implementors as well as the policy-makers to assist in providing resources. As the change process unfolds, the team needs to keep checking to see if and when additional resources are needed. For example, one day we observed an Initiator principal holding a one-legged conference in the teachers' lounge, while one teacher told another that she only had one microscope although the lesson required that she have five. The principal made no comment at the time, but the next morning five microscopes were lined up on the teacher's desk.

Providing Technical Coaching   That prospective users of innovations need to learn new skills and develop specialized knowledge is obvious. Referring to the Levels of Use in Appendix 3 will help CF Team members determine which knowledge and skill elements to emphasize and when. The change process can move faster and with less stress when the "how-to's" are answered as needed and when the development of the necessary knowledge and skills are addressed by the change facilitators. The underlying assumption in this CF Team function is that at least some of the members have sufficient technical knowledge about use of the innovation and about how to facilitate change to respond to the concerns and questions of individuals as the process unfolds. When this situation does not exist, change processes slow and members of the CF Team lose credibility with the implementors. For example, if the Second Change Facilitator is well regarded as a teacher, his or her coaching suggestions and ideas about how to address the special needs of particular students will be respected. On the other hand, if the Second CF doesn't know any more about how to use the innovation than the implementors, he or she will have to make extra effort to be able to provide the needed technical coaching.

Monitoring and Following Up   The CF Team members need to regularly share with each other what they are observing about how the change process is going and what they have been doing. When this happens, each member can follow up on what the others have done. As a result, the team will deliver consistent messages and follow through on what others have initiated. This significantly reduces the possibility of the arousal of Stage 2 Personal concerns and "tailing up" on Stage 6 Refocusing concerns, since people are hearing the same messages from each member of the CF Team and having their questions answered as they are formed.

Training   Formal training is another important function of the CF Team. It is vital that the necessary initial training workshops are planned and do occur. Furthermore, training must not be viewed only as a front-end need. Most education innovations are much more complex and sophisticated than educators and policy-makers assume. It is not easy to move from one form of teaching to another. With most of today's education innovations, the CF Team needs to conceive of training in terms of at least two phases. The first phase includes the initial start-up (LoU II Preparation) and first-year implementation (LoU III Mechanical Use) training needs. The second involves training for advanced (LoU IVB Refinement and above) and more comprehensive configurations (IC Map *a* and *b* variations). Findings from our studies suggest that the advanced training workshops should be ready for the third year of implementation. They may not be needed until the fourth year, but often more expert teachers are ready for advanced training in the third year.

Reinforcing   A natural consequence of change facilitators' intervention efforts is reinforcement of the perception that use of the change is important. There also will be reinforcement of whatever the users (and nonusers) are currently doing, unless there is a direct suggestion that they should be doing something differently. CF Team members need to remember that there are these two ways in which their interventions are reinforcing.

Pushing The idea of pushing may be uncomfortable to some, yet it is an important function of the CF Team. There are many times in a change process when there is a need for the facilitators to push. Some teachers are naturally hesitant to try new approaches. Some may be hearing an undercurrent of questioning of whether the change is going to last. Other folks are just wedded to the old way. In these instances, the CF Team needs to make it clear that moving toward the innovation is necessary. Pushing can sometimes involve such gentle nudging as setting a date to begin or starting a lesson and then having the teacher finish it. In other instances the push needs to be more direct, as when an area superintendent told a Responder principal whose teachers were not moving very quickly: "You are making a career decision in relation to whether the teachers in this school use the new science curriculum."

Telling Others Frequently teachers, administrators, and change facilitators assume that everyone will know how hard they are working and how well the change is going without their having to say anything. We regularly hear educators saying something like: "Oh, I couldn't send a note to the superintendent about what we are doing. It would be bragging." However, these same educators want the superintendent to actively support what they are doing. But how is the superintendent or anyone else going to know what is going on if you don't tell them? Therefore, a very important CF Team function is to tell others about how the change process is unfolding. Of course, this sharing of information needs to be appropriate to the audience. For example, the CF Team would not tell the media all that is going wrong, while the superintendent should be told about what is problematic as well as what is going well. In summary, change facilitators need to work at keeping the different stakeholders informed and up-to-date about how the change process is going. The CF Team should not wait until there is a problem to communicate. Establish the bridges and networks in advance, and work to maintain them as the change process continues.

Approving Adaptations This CF Team Function is an interesting one, especially in this time. Since the early 1980s it has not been politically correct to suggest that there are "best" ways to use an innovation, or in other words, that fidelity of implementation should be encouraged or directed. The implication has been that the top should not mandate exactly what should be done and by inference that each teacher should be left on his or her own to decide how much and to what extent all of the components of an innovation will be used. To suggest that the leaders of change processes have a responsibility to determine the range of adaptations that will be permitted/encouraged has been seen as heresy by many.

However, if the goal is change process success, then questions related to adaptation have to be addressed by the CF Team. In any change process, there will be some users who closely follow the developer's intents and specifications. There also will be others who will make small and even large changes in the innovation. As we explained in Chapter 3, mapping these different configurations is an important planning, diagnostic, and evaluative activity. Having an IC Map is an important change facilitating tool. The CF Team will be confronted with varying degrees of alignment with and adaptation of the change/innovation. If the team allows for great variation in what teachers do under the label of the change, a greater range of configuration variations will be implemented. Along with this increase in range will come less stability and certainty about what the change process goals and outcomes can be.

The CF Team needs to have clear dialogue about this function, which presents major implications for their day-to-day roles and for the ultimate outcomes of the change process effort. As was discussed in Chapter 3, there are major implications of whichever approach is selected, whether it be high fidelity, mutual adaptation, or complete teacher choice. Regardless of the approach, it is the messages of the CF Team facilitators, given through their interventions, that approve the range and types of adaptations that are implemented.

Change Facilitator Team Dynamics and Principal Change Facilitator Style

Whenever two or more people are working together, consideration should be given to the dynamics of their interrelationships. The dynamics among CF Team members should be examined for at least two reasons. First, how they relate to each other directly affects the other participants in the change process and its ultimate success. Second, the different change facilitators need to consider their own role and relationships in order to be most effective within the CF Team. An important additional implication of our studies of CF Team dynamics is that the CF Style of the First Change Facilitator changes the overall dynamics and interrelationships of the whole team.

Elements of Change Facilitator Team Dynamics

Ten positive elements of CF Team dynamics are listed in Figure 8.3. The working of the CF Team and the interrelationships among the facilitators can be analyzed using each of these elements. In other words, as we have observed more and less effective CF Teams, we have been able to explain the differences using these aspects. For

---

FIGURE 8.3   Positive Elements of Change Facilitator Team Dynamics

1. Role differentiation	6. Continuity
2. Goal clarity	7. Collegiality
3. Open planning	8. Combining of effort
4. Accuracy of information transfer	9. Positive attitude
5. Continual interaction	10. Complementarity

example, in terms of Element 1 (role differentiation), one CF Team was composed of all principals with similar backgrounds, knowledge levels, and skills in using the innovation and change process expertise. By contrast, in another district the CF Team consisted of three principals (one from each level), the director of staff development, and a lead teacher from each level, all with different perspectives and areas of expertise. Change processes will be more successful when such variations are represented on the CF Team.

We have found similar results when assessing CF Team effectiveness using the other elements of team dynamics. CF Teams are most effective when there is: (1) clear understanding and agreement about the goals of the change process effort; (2) open planning involving all facilitators; (3) clarity and accuracy in communication; (4) constant interaction among members; (5) continuity in purpose and direction; (6) collegiality among members; (7) combining of individual efforts; (8) positive and enthusiastic attitudes toward the work and relationships; and (9) complementarity of facilitation efforts that supports the efforts of the members of the team and of the Team as a whole.

Different Change Facilitator Styles Mean Different Change Facilitator Team Dynamics

In Chapter 7 we proposed that leaders such as school principals and district superintendents facilitate the change process by using different Change Facilitator Styles. Three CF Styles that have been documented to be highly correlated with the degree of teacher success in implementing educational innovations were described. Here we examine the affect that the Change Facilitator Style of the First CF has on the CF Team dynamics. In short, the style of the leader of the CF Team determines the team dynamics.

As was explained in Chapter 7, our studies of principals' Change Facilitator Style showed how the many small, moment-to-moment interventions that are made shape the larger intervention patterns that comprise tactics and strategies. With these data it has been possible to quantify the interventions made not only by the principal but also by other members of the CF Team (e.g., the Second, Third, and External CFs). We also have fieldnotes that document how the CF Teams in different schools went about their tasks and how they were perceived. Rather than discussing all of the data analyses and statistical findings from these studies, which can be found in the research reports (Hall & Hord, 1987; Hall, 1992), we have prepared a summary graphic of how the CF Team dynamics vary by CF Style of the principal (Figure 8.4).

Initiator Change Facilitator Teams Are Collegial   In Figure 8.4, the relative size of the puzzlelike pieces is intended to reflect the relative amount of intervention activity that is characteristic of each change facilitator. In the Initiator CF Team, both the First and the Second Change Facilitator do a large number of interventions, and each does about the same amount. The External CF does not do as much, but all that is done is complementary to what the internal CFs are doing.

As Figure 8.4 also shows, when the First Change Facilitator is an Initiator, all of the positive elements of CF Team dynamics are in place and operating. Yes, the Initiator is in charge and has evaluation authority over the Second CF and other internal members of the team. However, the Initiator-led CF Team works in a collegial way; all members are "in the loop." Each knows what he or she is to do as well as what the other members have done, are doing, and will be doing. Like the other team members the Initiator coaches, attends training workshops, and helps monitor.

Manager Change Facilitator Teams Are Supervised   In Chapter 7, we pointed out that Manager leaders try to do a lot of the leading themselves. The effects of this CF Style on CF Team dynamics are reflected in Figure 8.4. The Manager First Change Facilitator directs the work and efforts of the Team. In this situation, the Second CF makes somewhat fewer interventions than the First CF. The External CF does approximately the same amount of interventions as with the Initiator-led CF Team, although there are some qualitative variations.

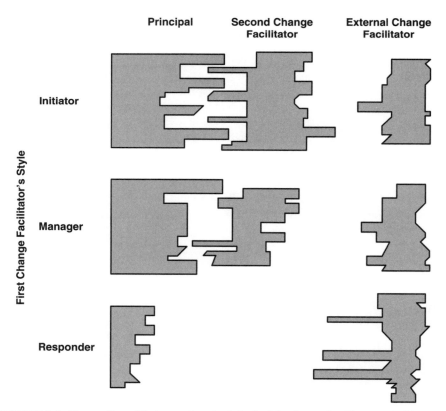

FIGURE 8.4   Proportion of Intervention Activity by Members of a Change Facilitator Team as Related to the Change Facilitator Style of the Principal

The big difference between the Initiator and Manager teams, however, is in how the CF Style of the First CF affects CF Team dynamics. Instead of working in collegial and complementary ways, the Manager supervises and directs the activity of the Second CF and others. While the Initiator CF would lead by saying, "I plan to do this; what are you going to do?" the Manager would say: "I have some time Friday morning at 9:00, when I will meet with you to plan what you are going to do next week. Then I can meet with you the following Thursday afternoon to review how it went." The focus of both is on facilitating the change process, but the dynamics are different in tone and emphasis. The Manager is controlling and differentiating roles, while the Initiator is promoting collegiality, open exchange, and sharing of all tasks.

Responder Change Facilitator Teams Are Less Active   Figure 8.4. represents what we and our colleagues have observed repeatedly: statistically significantly fewer interventions are made by Responder-led CF Team; the Manager CF makes the most interventions as an individual; and the Initiator-led team makes the most interventions as a team.

The absence of a "puzzle piece" in Figure 8.4 representing the number of interventions made by the Second CF is not an accidental omission. In the Responder CF Team, someone has been designated as the Second CF, but typically this person is not empowered and supported in the role. He or she may have been given the title when the decision was made to implement the innovation, but the follow-up by the Responder leader is not there. The Second CF may not have been supported to go to the training workshops, or may not be released from teaching or other duties in order to perform the role. Further, the Responder CF does not keep track of what the Second CF needs or is doing. We have frequently heard something like the following from Responder Change Facilitators: "I couldn't check up on what she [the Second CF] is doing. She would think that I did not trust her." In other words, here the CF Team dynamics are based on the assumption that a role assigned is a role implemented. Facilitating the change process is treated as a job that is delegated and relegated to an individual, rather than a responsibility that is shared by the entire team.

The Role of the External Change Facilitator in a Responder Change Facilitator Team

Just as the roles of the First and Second CFs are different when the First CF is a Responder, the External CF role changes too, as the XCF makes fewer interventions and the character of those interventions changes. In the Initiator- and Manager-led CF Teams, the External CF intervenes in ways that support and complement what the site-based facilitators are doing. Typically the XCF also adds specialized change-related expertise that the other members of the CF Team do not have. Most of the time the External CF's interventions are directly targeted toward increasing use of the innovation.

The focus of External CF interventions in the Responder-led CF Team is altogether different, for here the Responder is significantly more often the *target* of the interventions. Our favorite example of this, from the Principal/Teacher Interaction Study, was the following telephone call that the External CF made to the Responder principal (RP):

XCF: Hello, George, this is Mary.

RP: Hey, how are you doing? Did you go to the game over the weekend?

XCF: No, George, I did not go to the game.

RP: That's too bad. It was a good one.

XCF: George, the reason I am calling is that I have had a call from some of your teachers, and they say they don't know when the training workshop will be! Did you distribute the teacher handout?

RP: What handout?

XCF: The handout that I mailed to all of the schools telling the teachers when and where the workshop will be.

RP: We didn't get them.

This exchange is a classic example that had serious costs to a change process. The schools in the study with Initiators and Managers as First Change Facilitators received the handout and distributed them to teachers, but this had not been done in the Responder school. One consequence was that teachers were late in receiving information that was supportive of their use of the innovation, which is one of the functions of the CF Team. Another cost was that the usefulness of the External CF was diminished since she had to spend time dealing with what the First CF did not accomplish, which meant less direct support by the XCF was given to the front-line users (and nonusers) of the innovation.

VIGNETTE
Variations in the Impact of Second Change Facilitators

On a Saturday morning in November, the Building Resource Teachers from two schools happened to meet at the local coffee shop. Both had attended the same week-long, districtwide School Improvement Process (SIP) workshop last June. Both schools had identified integration of technology as their top goal for this school year.

Georgia Nelson (GN):   *Hi, Rick! How have you been?*

Rick Garcia (RG):   *Hi, Georgia! I have been well.*

GN: *So have I. Most of our kids returned to school this fall really wanting to learn. I don't know why, but it sure has made things go better.*

RG: *Come to think of it, so have ours.*

GN: *How's it going with your plans to use integrated technology?*

RG: *Well, it could be better. Russ [his principal] told the teachers at the opening faculty meeting that we would be moving ahead with technology and that I would be the point person.*

GN: *That sounds good.*

RG: *Yes, that was good. But he mentioned it in the midst of a list of other things that our school needs to do this year. You know—test scores, parents' night, membership on the social committee, and the band's raffle.*

GN: *Oh. Dr. Irving [her principal] set aside a whole hour during our first faculty meeting so that I could have teachers complete an open-ended concerns statement and I could remind them of what we had agreed to last spring when we were putting together our SIP Plan.*

You know, at first Dr. Irving was not real keen on this integrated technology push. She thought that it would take time away from her focus on using manipulative materials and having all teachers develop constructivist teaching strategies. I really had to work on getting her to see that there was no conflict, and that instead using technology could really help with these other goals.

Now, she is always asking teachers what they need and how they are doing with integrating technology into their teaching. She has made teachers' integrated use of technology my top priority, and has given me more time to work with teachers on this.

RG: *Wow! I wish that I had that kind of backup. Russ hasn't mentioned anything about technology since the first faculty meeting. We don't have all of the technology in place yet, and there has been no opportunity for me to meet and work with teachers. I have to do what I can before and after school.*

GN: *That's too bad. You and I had the same plans and ideas last June at the SIP training week. Dr. Irving has really gotten on board this fall. She checks with me every week to see how it is going and what she can do to help.*

RG: *I know that Russ is interested. He is always interested in innovative things. It's just that I can't seem to get any time or support to work with teachers. I know that many are interested.*

GN: *Well, Dr. Irving has told the teachers that she expects all of them to be integrating technology and that she will be focusing on it when she does her evaluation classroom observation cycles.*

As this story reflects, principals with different Change Facilitator Styles provide varied types and degrees of support not only to teachers but also to Second Change Facilitators. Although both schools started the school year with the same priority objective in their SIP plans, the amount of progress toward implementation is dramatically different by November!

1. Which Change Facilitator Style would you use to describe the two principals (Dr. Irving and Russ)?
2. If you had your choice, which principal would you want to work for?
   Why, and why not?
3. Second Change Facilitators have to work with principals with different
   CF Styles. If you were Georgia, what would you be able to do and need to
   do to be effective? If you were Rick, what would you be able to do and need
   to do?

Summary

In this chapter we have examined different aspects of Change Facilitator Teams. We
began by reporting on our discovery of the Second Change Facilitator, or consigliere.
We described various ways in which the Second CF role can be accomplished and their
different impact on teacher success in change. Then we introduced the roles of the Third
and External Change Facilitators. The high-priority functions for each role were also
discussed. In the last half of this chapter, we examined the functions and dynamics of
Change Facilitator Teams. We concluded with descriptions of how CF Team dynamics and functions differ depending on the Change Facilitator Style of the First CF. A
number of related points and concepts should be addressed, and several need further
research. Some of these will be proposed as Discussion Questions and suggested
Fieldwork Activities. Finally, we ask that you keep in mind the necessity of having a
Change Facilitator Team and that you reflect on the difference you can make in its
success. As a German research colleague, Ewi Hameyer, once said, "Good models of
change are never brought about by soloists." The Guiding Principles below summarize key aspects of CF team dynamics and functioning.

Guiding Principles of Change Facilitator Teams

1. The Second Change Facilitator role is critical to change success. The First CF cannot accomplish everything alone. Ideally, the Second CF will do as many facilitating actions as the First CF. They also should work in complementary ways.
2. Leadership for change is a team effort. The most typical site-based CF Team
   consists of the principal as the First Change Facilitator; a lead teacher, assistant
   principal, or department chair as the Second CF; and a respected teacher as the
   Third CF. The complete CF Team also will have one or more External Change
   Facilitators.
3. The dynamics of the CF Team vary according to the style of the First CF. There
   is a complementarity and combining of effort with the Initiator-led CF Team. In
   the Manager-led CF Team, there is more of a supervisor/subordinate relationship between the First and Second CFs. Typically, the Second CF on the
   Responder-led CF Team is left more or less on his or her own, with little support or coordination.

4. The most facilitating interventions occur in the schools with an Initiator principal, while the fewest interventions are done by the Responder-led CF Team.
5. External Change Facilitators are important for supporting and augmenting the on-site CF Team. There are many potential sources of External CFs, including district office staff, college faculty, textbook publishers, and curriculum developers.

DISCUSSION QUESTIONS

1. Think about Change Facilitator Teams that you have been a part of or that have influenced your use of a change. Who were the members? How did the CF Team function, and what were its dynamics?

2. If you have been a Second Change Facilitator, describe what the experience was/is like for you. If you have not been in such a position, describe the characteristics and interventions of a Second CF you know.

3. Under what conditions would it be important to have a Third CF. Are there times when it would not be useful?

4. Why do you think the External CF role is often unappreciated by teachers and administrators? How important has it been to have an External CF in change efforts in which you have participated?

5. This chapter was written with the explicit assumption that the First CF is the principal, superintendent, or other line administrator. What do you think happens in change processes where the First CF is *not* the top organizational administrator?

FIELDWORK ACTIVITIES

1. Pick a site that is engaged in a major effort, and develop an analysis of its Change Facilitator Team. Who are the First, Second, and External CFs? Is there a Third CF? What are the CF Team dynamics? How well are they addressing the different CF Team functions?

2. Ask an External CF to describe how he or she works in general. Then inquire about how his or her approach varies with different site-based CF Teams. Without asking directly, see if this person describes working differently in ways that are related to the Change Facilitator Style of the First CF.

REFERENCES

Ebmeier, H., & Hart, A. W. (1992). The effects of a career-ladder program on school organizational process. *Educational Evaluation and Policy Analysis, 14*(3), 261–281.

Hall, G. E. (1992). Characteristics of change facilitator teams: Keys to implementation success. *Educational Research and Perspectives, 19*(1), 95–110.

Hall, G. E., & Hord, S. M. (1987). *Change in schools: Facilitating the process.* Albany: SUNY Press.

Johnson, M. H. (2000). A district-wide agenda to improve teaching and learning in mathematics. *Journal of Classroom Interaction, 35*(1), 1–7.

Rogers, E. M. (1995). *Diffusion of innovations* (4th ed.). New York: The Free Press.

PART FOUR

Constructing and Understanding the Different Realities of Change

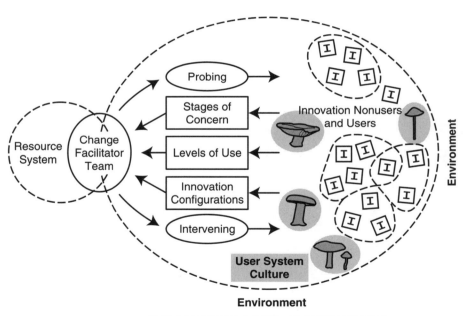

THE CONCERNS-BASED ADOPTION MODEL

Based on a rich research and practice base, there is much that can be predicted and planned for facilitating a change process, although the best laid plans of even experienced facilitators frequently go astray. However, if we look more systemically, and organically, we can increase the potential for change success. This we do, in Part Four, by examining how additional factors in the system can influence the outcomes of change processes.

For example, in Chapter 9 "mushrooms" are described and noted as nutritious or poisonous. Mushrooms spring from the understanding that the change process is influenced not only by what the facilitators do, but by how the participants perceive and interpret what is done. Interpretations made by individuals can vary widely, as can the interpretations constructed socially by groups of individuals These singular and collective interpretations frequently contribute to unintended effects, thus influencing the change process in significant ways.

The culture of an organization, a pervasive systemic factor, is an amalgamation of the values and beliefs of the organization, the attitudes and relationships that develop as people work together within a set of values, and the norms of behavior that evolve from the group's values and beliefs. For example, if a school's professional staff values successful learning for students and believe they can influence that learning, this value and belief can drive the staff to consistently changing to increase their own effectiveness. This condition can produce a culture wherein the staff is ready for or seeking change rather than being reluctant or resistant to it. Such a factor can have profound effects on whether, and the rate and degree to which, a staff will move in a change process. Chapter 10 explores culture factors.

In the final chapter of the book, we put all the pieces together. In Part One, in the first chapter we provided principles about change that have guided our study of the change process and our work in field-based change efforts. The second chapter shared a brief history of the perspectives taken by other change researchers and theorists. Part Two presented the three diagnostic tools of the CBAM, and Part Three suggested actions and approaches that change facilitators can take to make their efforts successful. In those sections of the book, we moved from whole to parts and now, as a *finale*, back to the whole.

Integrating the concepts and the wealth of additional information, including the tools and techniques presented in the larger body of the book, is the objective of Chapter 11, where all three of the CBAM diagnostic tools are used simultaneously to provide a rich discussion of two cases where the change to a new approach to teaching mathematics was the focus of study.

On a different note, this chapter also presents the commentaries of various national and international researchers and evaluators who both promote and critique the use of the CBAM in their work. These statements provide valuable issues for consideration when studying the process of change.

Finally, we ask our readers to send us your cases of change, both successful and not so successful, to help us as we continue to study the process of change in order to unravel its complications and complexities, and to learn how to make it ever more successful for all those in organizations that seek to increase their effectiveness for clients' benefits.

9 Constructing Understanding of Change

Intervention Mushrooms

District A: *Following the restructuring and downsizing of the district central office, the superintendent announces that it's all done and that everyone should get to work and do what is best for the district. The typical employee response is, "Why should I believe you now?"*

District B: *Teacher from School R: "I was so surprised last week, when my principal stopped me in the hallway to ask about what I was doing with the new computers. He never asks me anything about what I am doing in the classroom. I wonder what he was after?" Teacher from School I: "I don't see anything unusual about that. My principal is always stopping by and asking me about what I am doing. Sometimes he makes really interesting suggestions." Teacher from School M: "My principal stops by sometimes, but she only wants to see if I have enough supplies."*

District C: *First teacher: "Wasn't that neat—what the superintendent said in her talk with our school faculty? She really cares about us and what we teach our students." Second teacher: "Yes, it is the same points that she made at the districtwide meeting in the beginning of year. Best teaching practices and student success are important priorities for her." Third teacher: "Yes, it is so great to be in this school district."*

The principal point that will be made repeatedly in this chapter is that it is not what you do that counts, but how other people perceive and interpret what you do. As the above quotes illustrate, participants in a change process develop a wide range of impressions and interpretations about what the change effort is about and what different change facilitators intend. Just because the leaders of a change effort are well intentioned does not mean that the participants will see it that way. Each participant individually, and each group of participants collectively, will construct their own understandings about what was intended and what it all means.

FOCUS QUESTIONS

1. How is the interpretivist perspective different from the more traditional behaviorist perspective?
2. In the CBAM approach to change, what is a mushroom? Are mushrooms nutritious or poisonous?
3. What kinds of perceptions and interpretations of change will an individual develop at different Stages of Concern?
4. How will an individual's perception and interpretation of an intervention vary depending on the Change Facilitator Style of the intervenor?
5. What kinds of mushrooms develop through group construction of understanding of change processes and events?
6. How is group construction of understanding affected by different Change Facilitator Styles and Stages of Concern?

Fortunately, the concepts and principles about change that have been introduced in the preceding chapters can be used to better understand the different interpretations that people may develop about a change effort. The earlier concepts, such as Stages of Concern and Change Facilitator Style, can be used also to predict the types of interpretations that are likely to be constructed. Additionally, these same concepts can be used to more effectively plan interventions and facilitate the change process using the new understandings that will be developed in this chapter. In other words, all of the CBAM concepts introduced in the preceding chapters remain very relevant, and can be applied in new and interesting ways when combined with the latest findings from research and change facilitation practices. The key in this chapter will be to make a shift in thinking about and using the concepts introduced earlier. Here the various CBAM concepts will be used to explain and predict the interpretations and meanings people construct about the change process as they experience it. After reviewing the manuscript for this chapter, Carolee Hayes, formerly the Director of Staff Development for the Douglas County School District in Colorado, observed:

> This chapter represents a major shift in the book. Up to this point, the authors have taken a fairly left-brained approach to making sense of change. In this chapter, the reader will

sense a shift to considering the uncontrollable, unpredictable factors in change and is drawn into a process of integrating the controllable, predictable factors with those that are controlled only by individual and shared interpretations.

Introducing Mushrooms: A Unique Form of Intervention

In previous chapters a great deal of attention was given to discussing the different forms, sizes, and functions of interventions. In all of those descriptions and analyses, there was an assumption that change facilitators *initiated* the interventions. In this chapter, we will describe a different form of change process intervention, for which change facilitators are not the source and, in fact, over which they have little control. This new category of interventions is called *mushrooms* (see Figure 9.1).

The metaphor of mushrooms is particularly salient for describing this special class of interventions. Just as mushroom plants can be nutritious or poisonous, so can mushroom interventions. Some help advance the change process, while others erode it. Just as mushroom plants come in many colors and shapes, mushroom interventions in a change process may take different forms. There may be none, one, or a great variety. Just as mushroom plants grow in the dark and are fed manure, mushroom interventions grow in the shadows of a change process and are fed by the actions of the change facilitators and other participants. Just as it takes an expert to identify and pick the good mushroom plants, some change facilitators are much more skilled than others at detecting and sorting mushroom interventions, taking

FIGURE 9.1   Intervention Mushrooms

advantage of the positive mushrooms, and discouraging the growth of poisonous ones.

Two Ways of Knowing: Objectivist and Interpretivist

Before explaining the concept of intervention mushrooms further, it will be useful to review briefly two research traditions that have been very influential during the last three decades. Each of these traditions has made significant contributions to our understanding of the change process. As is true in most fields, there has been a history of disagreement and competition between proponents of each of these traditions. Interestingly, each can be complementary of the other. In this chapter, these two research traditions will be used in combination to better explain and illustrate the concept and dynamics of mushrooms.

The Objectivist Perspective of Change   From the 1960s to late in the 1980s, the dominant way of thinking about learning was labeled *behaviorism*. The focus in this approach was on observable behaviors. For example, classroom teachers were expected to describe student learning in terms of what the students could *do*, not what they "understood." Curriculum developers and teachers were trained and required to write behavioral objectives. The design of the research was influenced by the behaviorist perspective as well. Researchers focused on describing and counting the observable behaviors of teachers, such as the quantity of questions asked and the frequency of giving management directions. All were admonished to never ever use the word "understand," because one cannot see "understanding." Instead, they were to deal only with what could be observed.

Since the primary emphasis in behaviorist research and practice was on being absolutely objective about what one did, the term *objectivist* was applied to this approach. The goal was to remove the biases and perspectives of the observers (e.g., teachers and researchers) by describing events in terms of cold, hard facts, or in other words, objective descriptions of observed behaviors.

The Interpretivist Perspective of Change   As Kuhn (1970) so eloquently proposed, there comes a time in the study of any field of science when the established way of thinking and working (i.e., the established paradigm) is challenged by a new model (i.e., a competing paradigm). When the first paradigm fails to predict some aspects of a phenomenon, a new, competing paradigm is proposed. Such a revolution in organization and in education research and theory has been represented by the recent movement toward *constructivism*, which emphasizes how the learner develops, or "constructs," his or her own "understanding," or "interpretation," of reality. *Interpretivists* strive to analyze how understanding is developed by studying the way people interpret and give meaning to events (e.g., by examining the quotes like those at the beginning of this chapter). Rather than simply dealing with observable behaviors the interpretivist paradigm stresses unearthing and describing the interpretations and meaning that people attach to an action, event, or concept.

Intervention Mushrooms Are Constructed

So what does this discussion of paradigms, behaviorism and interpretivism mean? Combining elements of the objectivist and interpretivist paradigms is very useful for explaining a very important but little understood component of change process dynamics—intervention mushrooms. To be sure, change processes are affected by the behaviors, or interventions, of the change facilitators. But there is also another class of interventions that grow out of the participant's interpretations of what the actions of the change facilitators and others mean.

There are observable behaviors associated with mushrooms. For example, a teacher complains about having to go to a workshop. Both the teacher's complaint and the workshop are observable and describable change process–related actions, or interventions. Holding the workshop is a change facilitator–initiated intervention. But what about the teacher's complaint? It fits the definition of an intervention in that it is an action or event that can influence the change process. However, it is different in a number of ways. Depending on how the complaint was stated and what the teacher does next, the complaint could be forgotten or start to grow into a mushroom. If nothing more is heard, then the teacher's complaint disappears as an isolated incident. However, as is illustrated in Figure 9.2, if the teacher complains repeatedly and with increasing animation, a mushroom intervention is born.

We contend that most mushrooms can be anticipated. For example, to determine if the workshop complaint will grow into a mushroom, we first need to understand more about the interpretation that the teacher has given to the announcement that there will be a workshop. A number of plausible interpretations can be imagined. For example, does the teacher see the workshop as useless in terms of content because she already knows the subject? Or is there a scheduling conflict because the teacher is committed to making an exploratory visit to a site where the innovation is in use? Or is she concerned that her lack of knowledge might be exposed and that she could be embarrassed? Depending on the reason for the teacher's complaint, not

FIGURE 9.2   Initial Growth of an Intervention Mushroom

Action 1:	In a hallway conversation with Teacher B, Teacher X complains about having to attend a workshop.
Action 2:	In the lunchroom, Teacher X complains to a friendly colleague (Teacher W), who does not want to attend the workshop either.
Action 3:	In the parking lot, Teachers X and W again complain and plan to talk to their department chair.
Action 4:	The next day during planning period, Teacher X catches the department chair and complains about having to attend the workshop.
Action 5:	The department chair talks with the principal about the complaint.

wanting to attend the workshop could have very different implications for that teacher, other teachers, and the success of the change process. This is where the interpretivist perspective is key to understanding the change process. Carolee Hayes has summarized nicely:

> The metaphor of mushrooms provides an image of fungi creeping into a system without any nurturing or intention on the part of the leadership. That is a powerful image, one which all leaders have experienced when best efforts become interpreted as something otherwise. It reminds us that being right or well intentioned is only one perception of a situation.

Four Aspects of Intervention Mushrooms

There are four features of mushroom interventions that can assist in understanding their origination and growth. Two of these features are considerations from the interpretivist and objectivist perspectives that were discussed above. First, the interpretivist component of mushrooms addresses the *interpretations* that an individual or a group constructs about the meaning and intention of a change facilitator's interventions, the innovation, and the change process in general. Second, the objectivist component of mushrooms addresses the *behaviors*, or the statements and actions, that emanate from the constructed interpretations.

Two other important features of mushrooms are *potential effects* and *individual* or *group construction*. First, as with mushroom plants, intervention mushrooms can be either nutritious or poisonous for a change process. Some mushrooms, such as growing enthusiasm of teachers that the change is working, are positive and help move the process ahead. However, poisonous mushrooms, such as a growing number of teacher complaints about the quality of the materials, negatively affect the change process. The fourth feature emphasizes the point that mushroom interventions can be constructed by single individuals or by a group. Each person involved in a change process will, at least to some extent, have developed his or her own interpretations of events and intentions. Some interpretations will be discussed with others, and through these discussions a shared interpretation will be developed.

Two additional brief examples of mushroom construction will further illustrate these features. The first example is at the individual level, where the seed for a potential mushroom is planted as an individual develops his or her own interpretation of what a particular action or event means. For example, something as simple as the superintendent's statement at a school board meeting that a curriculum director from the district office will be reporting on a new initiative at the next meeting could trigger either the growth of an enormous mushroom or no reaction at all. A principal who had heard the superintendent's comment could develop an "educated guess," based on extrapolations from past experience, that a big change is coming. The principal's interpretation is his or her own (i.e., an individual construction) until he or she says to another principal, "Guess what I heard at the board meeting last night?" Then group construction begins. There is a high probability that this mushroom will grow quickly: the superintendent has another big change coming.

The Life Cycle of Intervention Mushrooms

Mushrooms are constructed out of the interpretations that each person gives to the actions and events in a change process. People look for ways to make sense of and to explain what is happening to them and around them. Efforts to make sense and explain increase during a time of change. Each participant develops his or her own interpretation and understanding based on past experiences as well as on the themes and patterns that are characteristic of his or her organization. For example, if the principal always runs a staff meeting in a certain way, the staff comes to expect that this is the regular pattern. But if one day the principal changes the way the meeting is run, it may be seen as a sign of something. At first, what the "something" is will be uncertain. If the principal explains why the change occurred, this additional intervention will alter the teachers' growing interpretations. If no explanation is offered as the meeting unfolds, each staff member will begin to develop his or her own explanation, or hypothesis, about what the change means.

The Birth of a Mushroom

Regardless of whether the principal explains the reason for the change or each staff member develops his or her own explanation, some staff may exchange interpretations following the meeting. Then there will be gradual development of a shared interpretation of what the change means. This group development of a shared understanding is often called *social construction.*

The shared interpretation becomes the *constructed theme* of the mushroom. In the example here, which is mapped in Table 9.1, one teacher thinks that the principal just forgot to do the usual routine. Another teacher thinks that the principal is using some new techniques that she picked up at a principals' conference last week. Two others believe that the change means that the principal is looking for a new job and is practicing a different leadership style. No one knows for sure what the principal is doing, but all have an individual interpretation to share and advocate. Arising out of the discussions is a *first consensus* that the principal is looking for another job: "She has been here for five years; it's time." A mushroom is born.

The Growth of a Mushroom

In the following two days, one teacher overhears the principal say to the assistant principal that she really is ready for a change. The teacher did not hear all of the conversation, but is certain about what she did hear. Another teacher, who had been at the administration building to pick up a book, hears that there is an opening for a principal "downtown." Both of these individual events are shared and interpreted by all as

TABLE 9.1   Mapping a Mushroom Intervention

Sequence of Events	Actions	Participant Interpretations	Change Facilitator's Isolated Responses	Accumulated Effect(s)
0	Principal changes meeting process.	Some notice, some don't, some are surprised.	Principal explains the change	None observed
1	Teachers talk with each other about the change.	Some see it as no big deal; some think it means something.	—	Some energy going into examination of what the change means
2	More teacher dialogue occurs.	"The principal is looking."	—	More energy going into con-structing shared interpretation
3	Superintendent makes an unannounced visit.	"The principal is being checked out."	—	Increasing talk and distraction
4	Principal says to the secretary, "I am ready for a change."	"The principal *is* looking/ leaving!"	—	More support for the mushroom and less work activity
5	Principal closes the door to take phone call.	"The principal has a call about the new position."	—	More support for the mushroom and less attention to teaching and learning

		Constructed Theme	Change Facilitator's Responses to the Total Mushroom	Accumulated Effect(s)
		"The principal is leaving."	None	Time and energy being drawn away from teaching and leaning

177

further confirmation of "the-principal-is-looking" mushroom. The mushroom is growing and beginning to take on a life of its own.

The Maturity of a Mushroom

Over the next several weeks, other actions and events occur that, if the mushroom did not exist, either would not have been noticed or would have been interpreted differently. However, with a rapidly growing mushroom, many otherwise innocuous actions are interpreted as support for the mushroom theme and contribute to its continued and quick expansion. For example, the superintendent's unannounced visit to the school and closed-door meeting with the principal further feed "the-principal-is-looking" mushroom. Teachers begin comparing the frequency of principal visits to the lounge with memories of her past behavior; "She is not in the lounge as much now." Something as simple as the principal closing the door to take a phone call adds further support to the mushroom. Events and actions, many of which may in fact have nothing in common, are thus interpreted as being part of an overall theme and pattern, or mushroom. As can be seen in this very simple example, it is quite easy for a mushroom to get started and for its growth not only to be assisted, but also to race ahead without any of the change facilitators being aware that it is happening.

Keys to the Construction
of Intervention Mushrooms

There are several ways to analyze mushrooms. Some of the techniques can be used to anticipate the growth of new ones, while other approaches can help to explain those that already exist. Most of the CBAM concepts introduced in earlier chapters are very powerful tools for understanding the different ways that mushrooms can start as well as the dynamics of their growth. Here, the concepts of Levels of Use, Stages of Concern, and Change Facilitator Styles will be used to illustrate how mushrooms are constructed, and why they turn out to be nutritious or poisonous.

Levels of Use as a Rubric for Developing
Understanding of Mushrooms

Levels of Use (LoU) was introduced in Chapter 5 as a way to describe and understand a person's gradual development of skills and expertise in using a change/innovation. In that chapter, Levels of Use was described in purely objectivist terminology. Very strong emphasis was placed on the fact that Levels of Use is a behavioral diagnostic dimension. Further, LoU was defined in operational terms, and the Levels of Use chart (see Appendix 3) is composed of behavioral descriptions and indicators that are characteristic of each level. The method of assessing LoU is a special focused interview procedure that is based purely on soliciting and coding examples of the interviewee's innovation-related behaviors. Obviously development of the Levels of Use concept and its measurement relied heavily on the objectivist research tradition.

Levels of Use from a Constructivist Perspective   Levels of Use can also be viewed and described in a constructivist tradition. Notice in particular the knowledge category in the operational definitions of Levels of Use in Appendix 3. If cognitive theory were applied to the LoU descriptions, the knowledge column of this table would be seen as presenting snapshots of gradually increasing sophistication and complexity of "understanding" about how to use the innovation. Each knowledge level represents a major step in the transition from nonuser to novice to expert. At the lowest levels, the schemas are very simplistic and incomplete. As one moves to higher Levels of Use they become more complex and multifaceted. In other words, although the early development and studies of LoU were based in the behaviorist paradigm, LoU can be explained in terms of the constructivist paradigm as well.

LoU-Based Mushrooms   LoU can be a very useful tool for predicting and understanding mushrooms. First of all, the types of mushrooms that an individual constructs will be different depending on the person's level of understanding (i.e. his or her knowledge rating). As obvious as this may seem, we frequently fail to recognize that there could be a number of potential mushrooms growing in relation to a person's level of knowledge and understanding about what the innovation is and how it can be used. For example, a person at LoU I Orientation may have such limited knowledge that even when the innovation is described in minute detail, he or she cannot make the link back to how the change would work in his or her situation. As a result, the person might reject the innovation because it is perceived as being too complex, confusing, and unrelated to the immediate problem/need.

This episode could be the beginning step in the growth of a poisonous mushroom. The mushroom could disappear if the next facilitator intervention helps the person develop a clearer connection between his or her current understanding of the innovation and his or her needs. However, if the subsequent interventions are also detailed and intricate, they could reinforce the developing perception that this innovation is too complex and not relevant. Then an individual mushroom of resistance to the innovation could begin growing.

The same intervention of providing minute detail about the innovation could easily lead to growth of a positive mushroom for a person who is at LoU IVB Refinement. He or she already has a full understanding of how the innovation works in the classroom and how it can be fine-tuned for special needs. If this person were to meet and plan with another LoU IVB individual, they both develop an interest in taking something new back to their classrooms. If these decisions were to happen several times and with several other teachers, a positive mushroom related to collegiality and collaboration could begin growing. In this case, there would be clear indication of movement toward LoU V Integration.

Stages of Concern as a Source of Mushrooms

Stages of Concerns (SoC) are a powerful catalyst for the development of mushrooms. The perceptions and feelings that one has in relation to a change process are constantly in flux, and there is a high sensitivity to everything related to the instability of change. Therefore it is important not only to be assessing SoC for use in planning interventions, but also to use SoC assessments to recognize developing mushrooms and to anticipate the potential for others to grow. Here again, the mushrooms that are constructed can be either nutritious or poisonous, and can be limited to one individual or shared by a group.

Personal Concerns: A Significant Source of Negative Mushrooms   Stage 2 Personal concerns represent a particularly sensitive time for individuals and groups. When personal concerns are high, the antennae are up and looking for anything and everything that might represent a threat to the person, real or imagined. By definition the person with high personal concerns is interpreting actions and events chiefly in terms of what they mean for him or her. They are not as concerned about what the change might mean for students or others; the concerns are centered on implications for themselves. Note that the real intentions of the change facilitator are not at issue here, but rather how someone with high Stage 2 Personal concerns *interprets* actions and events.

Persons with high Stage 2 concerns can easily interpret whatever occurs as an attempt to undercut or attack them. If this happens only once, there is no mushroom. However, if over a few days or weeks there are several events that are seen by the person as suspicious, a poisonous individual mushroom of insecurity and resentment will start to germinate: "The principal doesn't care what *I* think. He has his mind made up already." "I can't do this. I am just going to close my door and hope that nobody will see that I am not doing it." "You know the superintendent is all politics. She doesn't care at all about kids."

When two or more individuals who are growing such "insecurity mushrooms" talk to each other, the social construction process works overtime. "You are right. The superintendent doesn't care at all what we think, or how hard we have to work." "Why, the last time we did this, do you remember how she went on and on about this being such a good thing? It turned out to be an absolute disaster." At this point the individual insecurity mushrooms have combined into one that is shared and is ready for rapid growth through continued group construction. If a Stages of Concern profile were made, it would show high Stage 2 Personal concerns as well as a "tailing up" on Stage 6 Refocusing concerns. With this sort of concerns profile, the "here-we-go-again,-I-don't-buy-this-one-either" mushroom can grow faster and taller than Jack's beanstalk.

Intervening on Insecurity Mushrooms   There are many wrong ways for leaders to respond to the insecurity mushroom. One very risky approach would be to say such things as, "This really is different," or "Trust me. It will work well." "Trust-Me" interventions usually accelerate the rate of growth of this already rapidly expanding poisonous mushroom: "Sure. I should trust her. She doesn't have to do it. What does she know?" Another intervention that must only be used if carefully thought out is to put something in writing. Persons who have high personal concerns and are cultivating a shared insecurity mushroom will be able to come up with interpretations of a written document that were never intended, or even imagined, by the author. No matter how well a document is written, it can be perceived by those with high Stage 2 Personal concerns as further proof of the theme of the negative mushroom. "See, I told you so. She has no interest in what we think. She already has made the decision."

One potentially effective intervention would be to talk individually with people with high Stage 2 concerns and present a positive, straightforward stance of interest in and support for them, with reassurances that the change process will work out well. It is especially important for the leaders of the change process to constantly and continually act positively with such individuals. They also need to carefully monitor their own statements and actions for any that could be interpreted as negative or in some way doubting the chances of success. Those with supertuned personal concerns antennae will pick up on any hints of doubt or uncertainty within the leaders.

Impact Concerns: A Significant Source of Positive Mushrooms   Frequently overlooked in change processes are those people with various forms of impact concerns, who have some combination of high concerns at Stages 4 Consequence, 5 Collaboration, and 6 Refocusing. All are concerned about the impact of the change on clients, especially students. Impact-concerned people are positive and enthusiastic, and talk to each other about the strengths and successes they are experiencing in using the innovation. These are the people who naturally grow positive mushrooms within themselves and through dialogue with others.

The research and concepts related to organizational culture, such as those that will be introduced in Chapter 10, are important to keep in mind in relation to the growth of positive mushrooms, which are more easily recognized in such a culture. Positive norms are positive mushrooms. By talking to each other about teaching and student learning, teachers are growing a positive mushroom related to teacher collegiality and a shared focus on students. Interestingly, positive mushrooms such as this are quickly claimed by the change facilitators: "I know that we are collegial in this school. I have been doing a number of things to help this happen." From a practical point of view, who gets credit for positive mushrooms is of little consequence. However, researchers as well as change facilitators need to understand when and how positive mushrooms develop, since by definition, mushrooms are not knowingly created by change facilitators. All mushrooms begin their growth "in the dark"; it is the more finely attuned change facilitator who detects the beginning of a positive mushroom and actively intervenes to nurture its further growth.

Intervening on Positive Mushrooms   A frequently observed problem is that change facilitators spend little or no time attending to positive mushrooms. In fact they often fail to see their constructed themes. They may react to individual state-ments of enthusiasm, but are slow to see the whole theme. More deliberate effort needs to be given to recognizing and supporting the impact-concerned people and the positive mushrooms that they generate. Facilitators tend to be compulsive about addressing the persons with Self and Task concerns while failing to realize that the Impact concerns are a key source of supportive interventions.

Frequently, all that is needed is to take the time to offer a compliment or a word of encouragement. Visiting a classroom and observing the innovation in use can be very supportive of the further growth of positive mushrooms generated by Impact concerns. Another effective approach is to point out the existence of the positive mushroom. Once it has been identified, claim it as a strategy that all can nourish.

Change Facilitator Style and Mushrooms

Another frame to use in examining the growth of mushrooms is the Change Facilita-tor Style (CF) of school principals. In the literature there has been a long-running debate about the relationship of leader behaviors to style and whether a leader can easily change his or her style. Our studies and those of our colleagues, as summarized in Chapter 7, lead us to conclude that leaders cannot easily or automatically change their overall style. Ideally, they will adapt or adjust their behaviors from situation to situation, but they do not readily change their overall style. Therefore, one source of continuity and predictability in schools is the CF Style of the principal. Whether he or she is an Initiator, Manager, Responder, or something else, that style represents a pattern within which individual actions can be understood.

One of the generalized patterns that participants in a change process construct is a description of the style of the various leaders. Teachers interpret the individual actions of the leaders within a constructed context of their overall style. As one vet-eran teacher said to a first-year teacher after the principal had growled at her: "Oh, don't worry about that. That is the way he always is. He doesn't mean anything by it." The principal had made a comment that by itself could be interpreted as demean-ing of the new teacher. However, when it was interpreted by the veteran in the con-text of that principal's style, the meaning was mollified. *Once again, it isn't only what you do, it is how others interpret what you do.*

Different Change Facilitator Styles Have Different Meanings   An interesting example of the importance of understanding style is how the same action can have very different meanings depending on who does it. In other words, the same action done by principals with different Change Facilitator Styles will have very different meanings for their teachers.

Consider a simple change facilitator action, a one-legged interview in the hall-way, as the principal stops and says to a teacher, "How's it going with your use of the new computers?" This is a simple incident intervention that could be coded, using the objectivist paradigm outlined in Chapter 6, by source (the principal), target (a teacher), location (the hallway), and so forth. If a number of these types of interventions were recorded, a quantitative analysis could be done and different principals could be compared in terms of the frequencies of occurrence of different types of interventions and the difference that these made on teacher success in implementation. This is exactly what was done in the original Principal/Teacher Interaction Study and the subsequent studies that confirmed the three different Change Facilitator Styles. This work was described in depth in Chapters 6–8.

An analysis of the same one-legged-interview using the interpretivist paradigm would be different. Instead of coding and counting the parts of the action, the analysis would focus on the interpretation of the action that a teacher constructs. In other words, what does the intervention mean to the teacher who receives it? Our hypothesis is that it will depend on the Change Facilitator Style of the principal.

An Initiator principal meets a teacher in the hallway and asks, "How's it going with your use of the new computers?" What goes through the mind of the teacher? First, the teacher will place this individual action in the context of the CF Style of the principal. Given that this is an Initiator principal, the teacher will know that the principal is expecting several things of the teacher, including: (1) the teacher's use of the computers; (2) descriptive information about what is happening with students; (3) the identification of any need or problem. Further, the teacher knows that if something needs to be done to support the teacher, the principal will see that it is done. Based on this interpretation, the teacher goes ahead and describes some "neat" things that are happening with students, which leads to a short dialogue and ends with a commitment by the principal to stop by to see the sixth-period class in action.

If a Manager principal met a teacher in the hallway and asked, "How's it going with your use of the new computers?," the teacher's interpretive processing would differ. The teacher would understand that this principal is interested in knowing whether (1) there are any logistical or mechanical problems; (2) the schedule is working; and (3) there are enough supplies. Of course the principal is interested also in how the students are doing, in a general sense. So the teacher responds that having some additional chairs or printer cartridges would help. The dialogue continues with discussion of the need for additional rules about student uses of computers outside of class.

Interpretation of the same opening statement from a Responder principal would differ from that of either the Initiator or Manager principals. If a Responder principal stopped the teacher and asked, "How's it going with your use of the new computers?," the teacher's first reaction would be to mask surprise and to try to recover from the shock of being asked at all, since the normal style of the Responder principal is to chat in general about school topics or about some current issue in the community or in professional sports, not about what was going on in the classroom. The typical response of the teacher would be to offer some generalities such as, "Things are going well," and see what the principal says next.

The point here, as throughout this chapter, is not to present intricate depictions of principals' and teachers' actions and interpretations. Instead, the purpose is to use brief anecdotes to illustrate the mushroom concept and to ask you to shift the way that you think about an important aspect of the change process. Rather than thinking solely in terms of what the change facilitator does, consideration needs to be given to the interpretations that the participants ascribe to the actions. Again, it is not only what you do, but the meaning that others assign to what you do that counts. Further, there are both individual and group-constructed interpretations, as well as interpretations of isolated events and of perceived patterns drawn across a number of events and experiences, all of which can result in nutritious and/or poisonous mushrooms.

Mushroom Detection by Change Facilitator Style   Mushrooms may not be created knowingly, but once they occur, they can be maintained knowingly. As we stated at the beginning of this chapter, mushrooms tend to grow in the dark. Still, their presence may be detected at any point in their growth, and intervention can occur. The positive mushrooms need to be nurtured and the poisonous killed. Interestingly, Initiator leaders seem to detect positive mushrooms almost as soon as they are born. The Initiators then support and nourish their further growth. For example, they will offer encouragement to individuals. They will link the impact-concerned people with some of those with task and self concerns. They will provide extra resources or offer a special award to keep a positive mushroom growing. They may make a special point to acknowledge a positive mushroom in a faculty meeting, and attempt to recruit others to do things that contribute to its development. On the other hand, Initiators are telepathic about sensing the emergence of poisonous mushrooms and quick to take actions to kill them, neutralize their toxicity, or turn them into nutritious mushrooms.

By contrast, Responder leaders do not see mushrooms. Also, there seem to be very few positive mushrooms growing in their schools, while negative mushrooms are thriving. Further, Responders tend not to see the overall mushroom pattern and theme, which means that when they do react, they tend to respond to some of the individual actions of the mushroom instead of its constructed theme. The result is a lot of flitting around from complaint to complaint as a number of actions are taken that may contribute to the growth of existing negative mushrooms and even foster the development of new ones.

Dealing with a Growing Mushroom

Don't forget that mushrooms can be nutritious as well as poisonous to a change process. For example, teachers excitedly and continuously chatting with other teachers about the helpful things that parents are doing in classrooms is a positive mushroom that should be nurtured. Taking advantage of positive mushrooms should be a straightforward process, assuming that the different individual actions are seen in the context of the larger pattern of the mushrooms. Unfortunately, in our research studies we have regularly observed leaders and change facilitators who did not see these patterns. Instead, many react to the individual actions as if each were occurring in isolation. They do not see that there is a theme of accumulating actions that *together* are affecting the change process.

It is critical for change facilitators to become skilled in mushroom detection. They must continually be looking for positive themes arising out of individual actions and strive to support their further growth. On the other side, they must be constantly tuned to the potential for negative mushrooms, growing in the dark, at the edges of the change process. When a negative mushroom is detected, effort needs to be directed toward destroying its constructed theme, rather than responding to each individual action independently. The mushroom needs to be recognized and dealt with in its totality. Targeting individual actions in isolation will only lead to more rapid growth of poisonous mushrooms. Unfortunately, as we pointed out above, many leaders do not see the overall pattern of individual actions that aggregate to make a mushroom. In these situations, the change process does not advance as well, and there is an increased likelihood that teachers will develop a "tailing up" on Stage 6 Refocusing concerns, which leads to negative mushrooms being created.

Evergreen Mushrooms

Some mushrooms simply will not go away. No matter what is tried, they just keep coming back. We call them "evergreen" mushrooms. One example of an evergreen mushroom that we have experienced several times is the "two-against-one" mushroom that grows in offices staffed by three secretaries. Due to the intensity of the work and the extensive time in the same work environment, on occasion two of the secretaries become upset with the third. The two start having whispered conversations and leave the third out. After a while, work tasks are dropped or a key piece of information is not communicated. In an attempt to stop the growth of the mushroom, the leader talks to each secretary individually and asks what can be done to resolve the issue. This seems to take care of the problem. The three return to working as a team.

However, within months, two of the secretaries will be at odds with the third. It is a different two, but the same scenario starts to unfold. This time all three are taken out to lunch, and the problem is talked through. Perhaps some tasks are restructured or schedules are changed. However, no matter what interventions we have tried, in time this evergreen mushroom returns.

There are many other evergreen mushrooms that could be discussed, such as the annual panic over creating improvement plans, the trauma surrounding yearly evaluations, and the disbelief over administering standardized achievement tests to all students the week before vacation. These examples won't be mapped out here, but the key point is to remember that part of the wisdom of leading and facilitating change is in recognizing when something is not likely to go away. There are some parts of the change is process, such as evergreen mushrooms, that need to be understood and then worked around.

VIGNETTE

Growing a Nutritious Mushroom

Poisonous mushrooms are easy to find. We all have experienced them, and in many cases have helped to grow them. Nutritious mushrooms are less well understood and rarely celebrated. There is something about the compulsive nature of educators that makes them overlook or discount the positive aspects of their work. Therefore, we decided to present a short story about one nutritious mushroom.

This nutritious mushroom, which we shall call "enthusiasm for teaching and learning science," grew in one elementary school as a new science curriculum was being implemented. This innovation contained the usual elements: manipulative materials, living organisms, cooperative groups, no textbook, and field trips. All teachers had been given released days to participate in a series of all-day training workshops. The workshops had been designed to be concerns-based by regularly assessing Stages of Concern and adjusting each day's sessions accordingly.

Across the district, teachers in most schools were implementing the new approach and had the predictable array of Stage 3 Management concerns, such as, "The daphnia are dying," and "The crickets escaped!" In a few schools there were negative mushrooms about all the work, the mess, and the uncontrollable students.

In one school, however, we found no negative mushrooms. In reviewing our data, it was clear that the principal in this school was an Initiator. He was very supportive of the new approach to teaching science. He advocated for the new curriculum and did the little things that signaled he was willing to help. For example, when he overheard a teacher in the lounge expressing concerns about not having enough microscopes for a particular lesson, without saying anything he found the microscopes and placed them on the teacher's desk. He made sure teachers attended the training workshops. He visited classrooms when science was being taught.

Teachers were discovering that their students liked the new approach and were asking to have science classes everyday. Parents began commenting about their children's enthusiasm for science. The district office science coordinators too were pleased with how implementation was progressing in this school. We researchers were intrigued that the SoCQ profiles were low on Stage 1 Informational, Stage 2 Personal, and Stage 3 Management concerns. Further, there was an arousal of Stage 4 Consequence concerns. All of these actions and indicators document the spontaneous birth and growth of the nutritious mushroom. Everyone talked positively about what was occurring around use of the new approach.

When we pointed out this nutritious mushroom to the principal, he said that it had been part of his plan along. As the researchers, however, we had a different hypothesis: as positive actions began to occur, the principal reinforced and nurtured their expression and sharing. He also was making every effort to reduce the occurrence of actions that could lead to the growth of any poisonous mushrooms. In summary, either way in which the construction of this nutritious mushroom is diagrammed, the clear consequence was dynamic and positive schoolwide implementation success.

1. What do you see as the key actions that contributed to the construction of this nutritious mushroom? Were all of the actions needed?
2. What type of action would lead to the death of this mushroom? How long would it take to kill it?
3. In this case, the principal claimed that the nutritious mushroom had been part of his plan from the very beginning. Do you think this was true?
4. What was the principal's role in the continued growth of this nutritious mushroom? How did the teachers contribute? Did the students also have a role?

Summary

The success of any change effort is dependent not only on what the change facilitators do, but also on how the participants individually and collectively interpret and understand these actions and events. All participants in a change process are looking for ways to explain and simplify what is happening. The individual and social construction of mushrooms serves as a very useful strategy for doing this. Whether the resultant mushrooms are poisonous or nutritious depends on the Change Facilitator Styles and the Stages of Concern of all participants. An instructive example of a nutritious mushroom is described in the vignette. Success in facilitating change also depends heavily on one's ability to detect mushrooms early in their genesis. More successful change facilitators are skilled at early detection. They are quick to see the overall pattern and themes of both positive and negative mushrooms, and then take actions that are aimed at their totality, rather than just some of the individual actions. Review the Guiding Principles for reminders of how to recognize and attempt to influence the growth of mushroom interventions.

In the ideal setting, the most effective change facilitators are both objectivist and interpretivist. They observe behaviors, and they assess SoC and LoU. They use these diagnostic data to anticipate likely interpretations that could be made, and they listen for individual and social construction of meaning. They check for understanding and map the overall pattern of each mushroom. By keeping the big picture in mind, they are better able to respond to individual actions and events as they unfold. With this approach, mushrooms grow for a shorter period in the dark, and more of them can be put to positive use as the change process continues to unfold.

Guiding Principles of Mushroom Interventions

1. Mushrooms grow out of individual interpretations of actions and events as a change process unfolds.
2. A mushroom may be constructed by an individual or by a group.
3. A critical aspect of understanding a mushroom is to be able to see the overall pattern of actions that have contributed to growth of its constructed theme.
4. Mushrooms may be nutritious or poisonous to a change process.
5. In most cases, intervening in response to individual actions will not kill a poisonous mushroom but instead will contribute to its further growth.
6. Contrary to what one might predict, both positive and negative mushrooms can be constructed by people at each Stage of Concern.
7. An important change facilitator skill is to keep one's antennae tuned for actions that could be the beginning of negative and positive mushrooms.
8. Think about what you and others do to contribute to the growth of mushrooms, especially the poisonous ones. Keep in mind how others may interpret your actions.
9. To sustain or kill a mushroom, interventions must be aimed at its constructed theme, not each isolated action. There are times when individual concerns may have to go unaddressed in order to control the mushroom.
10. Sometimes an effective intervention is to point out the constructed theme of a mushroom and give it a name. Then it can be a target of action by many of the participants in the change process.

REFERENCE

Kuhn, T. S. (1970). *The structure of scientific revolutions*. Chicago: University of Chicago Press.

DISCUSSION QUESTIONS

1. Describe and analyze a nutritious mushroom that you have seen in your organization. What name would you give it? What was done to sustain it?
2. Describe and analyze a poisonous mushroom that you have seen in your organization. What name would you give it? What was done to kill it? What was done to sustain it?
3. What are some critical means of detecting mushrooms? What skills will help change facilitators detect nutritious and poisonous mushrooms?
4. What are important ideas to keep in mind when intervening on positive and negative mushrooms?
5. For each Stage of Concern, predict likely positive and negative mushrooms for a school staff that has high concerns at that stage.
6. Describe experiences you have had or observed about the construction of mushrooms with leaders using different Change Facilitator Styles. Did they react to individual incidents or to the totality of mushrooms?

FIELDWORK ACTIVITIES

1. Interview a change facilitator about the degree to which he or she is sensitive to and watches for overall patterns in a change process. See if this person can describe examples of positive and negative mushrooms he or she has experienced. What did he or she do to support or discourage the growth of particular mushrooms? As was done in Table 9.1, develop a map for one of these mushrooms to share in class. Estimate the person's Change Facilitator Style and consider whether that style is related to his or her perception and handling of mushrooms.

2. Follow the national news for several weeks; you are bound to find mushrooms growing. For example, a politician may make one small comment that the media magnifies, such as President Clinton's "I didn't inhale" statement. The media may have taken the idea out of context, or it may have been an innocent statement that begins to grow. When the politician attempts to respond in order to kill the mushroom, the response only leads to its further growth. Identify the theme and map the growth of such a mushroom. Give it a name. Then consider what you would recommend that person do if you were an advisor?

CHAPTER

10 Considering a Set of Organizational Factors

Culture

Some organizations defend themselves superbly even against their employees with regulations, guidelines, time clocks, and policies and procedures for every eventuality.
—Wheatley, 1992, p. 16

Leave the individual suspended in glorious, but terrifying, isolation.
—Bellah & Madsen, 1985, p. 6; cited in Wheatley, 1992, p. 30

[Learning organizations are] organizations where people continually expand their capacity to create the results they truly desire, where new and expansive patterns of thinking are nurtured, where collective aspiration is set free, and where people are continually learning how to learn together.
—Senge, 1990, p. 3

In the previous chapters we have reported about the change process in schools and how it can be facilitated successfully. These insights have come from the disciplined research that we and others have done, from stories of successful school change efforts, and from our own experiences acting as change agents to schools and districts. We have briefly examined some of the initiatives and innovations, what some would call "passing fancies," that have paraded through districts in high hopes of improving schools. We have looked at school leaders, their roles and styles, and how they create teams to manage the change process. In addition we have investigated tools and techniques that can assist leaders in diagnosing how the change effort is progressing.

We have learned a great deal, especially in the 1970s and 1980s, that increased understanding about school change and what needed to be done to facilitate its success. Almost always in the reports of these decades, the "hero principal" was the key to success. The efforts of these energetic, enthusiastic people, committed to the increase of student outcomes, warrant continued acknowledgment, applause, and celebration.

However, the emergence of the leadership team, in cooperation with the principal, expanded the personnel who could support implementors in their change endeavors. This development was noted and studied in the 1980s (see Chapter 8). In the 1990s, organization theorists and those concerned with increasing the quality and productivity of private or corporate businesses, and of public (educational) organizations have turned attention to (1) expanding leadership beyond the leadership team; and (2) understanding the workplace culture and its influence on the individuals involved in the organization. The quotations at the beginning of this chapter refer to this influence.

This chapter, therefore, looks at a new dimension—the school organization's culture embedded in its context—and how it interacts with the individuals engaged in the organization's work. We know that institutions, or organizations, do not change; individuals do. We know also that, while the individuals change the organization, the organization also has a profound influence on its people.

Organizational culture has been a subject of corporate world inquiry for a long time, and while schools have been likewise interested, educators have given real attention to this area only fairly recently. Despite the mandates in the last decades from state and district levels for schools to develop a climate that supports school improvement, little change in climate has occurred, due partly to lack of understanding about what such a climate might look like and about how to achieve such a climate even if one knew what its characteristics might be.

We, the authors, have lived and worked in a "learning organization" of the type that Senge (1990) has described; we have observed and studied a few schools that have the cultural attributes of a learning organization; and we profoundly believe that schools must develop this kind of context if real and continuous change and improvement are to occur. We see this as the educational challenge for the immediate future—and it is our own personal challenge as researchers and improvers.

FOCUS QUESTIONS

1. How does organizational culture influence the process of change in schools?
2. What is valued in a culture that is conducive to change?
3. How would the professionals, and all staff, interact in such a context?
4. What would a school be like where the focus is on the professional development of all, and the norm is continuous improvement in teaching and learning?
5. How would the change process work in the learning organization culture?

Emphasis on the Individual

The primary focus of the Concerns-Based Adoption Model, which many of these chapters have addressed, is the individual and the individual's needs for understanding and support in the process of change. The model has been widely appreciated by practitioners and policy-makers who believe that it promotes a humane approach to change in its consideration of individuals' concerns and their adoption and development of the use of new practices. The strategies articulated in the model, and required of leaders for successful change, are those needed to guide and support individuals in their implementation efforts.

Other models have parallels to the CBAM's focus on individuals and their concerns. For instance, Bridges's (1980, 1991) work in the corporate sector describes the change process as three transition phases. The first of these is *endings*, where the individual may experience a sense of loss or grief over what must be left behind; the second is a *neutral zone*, that is "nowhere between two somewheres" (Bridges, 1991, p. 35), as the individual feels emptiness, a sense of chaos, disorientation, and disorder, and is trying to sort out personal meaning relative to the change. The third phase, of genuine *new beginnings*, follows, as individuals are developing a step-by-step plan to take them to a new place they only partially understand.

Similarly, Scott and Jaffe (1989) propose four phases of transition through change: (1) *denial*, as people focus on the past and the way things were, and deny the need or desirability for a change; (2) *resistance*, as individuals consider their position and how the change will affect them personally (fear and uncertainty are not uncommon in this phase); (3) *exploration*, as people think futuristically about the possibilities a change can bring, but are uncertain about how things will work (another word for this phase is "chaos"); and (4) *commitment*, as people develop a clearer focus of the change and its goals, and devise a plan to reach them.

These models from Bridges and Scott and Jaffe appear to concentrate mainly on the preimplementation period of the change process. Fullan's (1991) research and writing on change, however, cover all stages. One of Fullan's images, the "implementation dip" (Fullan & Miles, 1992, p. 749), has been graphically portrayed by Busick and Inos (1992), and addresses the implementation phase (see Figure 10.1). This is the period where a change has been designed and developed by implementors at the school or district level and introduced to colleagues, or perhaps has been transferred from a vendor or another setting and introduced. As individuals struggle to make the change "work," they go through the valley, or dip, of difficulties before they reach the top and emerge at a higher level, which is an improved status.

These concepts seem to resonate, at least in part, with Stages of Concern. Stage 0 Awareness indicates that people are giving no attention to the change, since they do not expect it to affect them, or they are not informed about it. Stage 1 Information reflects an interest in learning about the change. Stage 2 Personal, which focuses on how the change will affect the individual, is described in the same language as *endings* (Bridges) and *denial* and *resistance* (Scott & Jaffe). Stage 3 Management seems quite synonymous with the *neutral zone* (Bridges), the *explo-*

ration phase (Scott & Jaffe), and the *dip* (Fullan), as people have difficulties making meaning of the change. Operationalizing the changes seems to characterize Stages 1, 2, and 3. However, as illustrated in Figure 10.1, following the dip, we add the higher impact Stages of Concern.

What is clear from these several perspectives depicting people in change is that individuals may suffer to some degree during change—experiencing anger, uncertainty, disorientation, and various other forms of stress and trauma.

As do Bridges, Scott, Jaffe, and Fullan, we recommend actions that the organization's leadership should take to respond to peoples' change anxiety or concerns at each of the above-mentioned phases and stages. That, clearly, has been the focus of this book. We have observed that the organization's typical response to people and the process of change is to assume the "Tarzan leap" (Scott & Jaffe, 1989), that people move from the beginning to the end of the phases or stages very quickly. This reaction, however, is not acceptable as we have tried to show through our discussion of peoples' needs and the leaders who attend to needs.

However, there is another dimension of school and organizational change that has been given attention by the writers noted above and that warrants our attention: the *context* in which the school as an organization operates. One part of that context

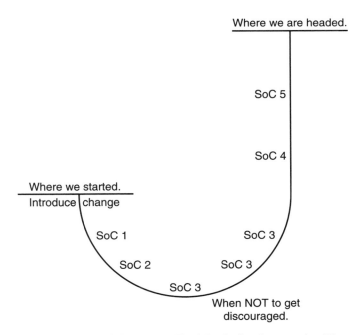

FIGURE 10.1 Using Stages of Concern to Explain the Implementation Dip

From *Synthesis of the Research on Educational Change: Implementation Phase* by K. U. Busick, and R. H. Inos, 1992, Honolulu: Pacific Regional Educational Laboratory. Adapted by permission.

is the school's own unique organizational environment that it has created, and the other is the larger context of district and state in which the school is nested. We will address the local school context.

Context? Climate? Culture?

One of the keys to success in facilitating change in organizational settings is the type of climate or culture that is developed. There is confusion and inconsistency about the use of the terms *context*, *climate*, and *culture*, which a look at the leadership literature will illustrate. At times the terms seem to be used interchangeably. Other authors use only one term, but there seems to be inconsistent definition of what is meant. Part of these conceptual and semantic problems was articulated by James and Jones (1974) in their analysis of the research on organizational climate, where they concluded that it is important to distinguish three different concepts of climate:

1. *Situational variables*: The objectively observable features of an organization such as number of staff, building features, budgets, and policies
2. *Psychological climate*: The individual's perceptions of aspects of the organization that can be measured using statistically reliable questionnaires
3. *Organizational climate*: The aggregation of the individuals' perceptions

More recently, many authors have been using the terms *culture* and *context*. In some cases, *culture* as a word seems to be interchangeable with the terms *climate* and *context*, while in other cases some important distinctions are made. For our purposes, it is not critical to delve in depth into the issues and problems with the differentiation of these terms. However, it is important to offer the caution that there are some meaningful differences in the terms that those interested in change processes should be aware of.

To simplify and clarify, we offer the following definitions:

1. *Climate* is the individuals' perceptions of a work setting in terms of a priori established concepts that can be measured empirically.
2. *Culture* is the individually and socially constructed values, norms, and beliefs about an organization and how it should behave that can be measured only by observation of the setting using qualitative methods.
3. *Context* (as defined in Boyd's [1992b] more recent review of the corporate and school literature) is comprised of (a) culture (as defined above) and (b) ecological factors (as defined in James and Jones's discussion of situational variables above).

Boyd points out that the culture (people or human factors) and the situational variables (physical or structural factor) interact to make up the context, and that these two sets of variables are difficult to separate in terms of their individual and collective effects in a setting during the change process. Nonetheless, these concepts are important for understanding change in organizational settings, and each is illustrated in this chapter. What may at first appear to be a semantic difference can in fact offer very important and useful additions to the change facilitator's portfolio of knowledge, skill, and understandings.

Attention on the School Organization

Obviously, organizational productivity is affected by its individual staff member's productivity. Currently, organizations are encouraged to remain open to the creative talents of its members and to innovation and improvement to best serve their clients. This is assessed to be true for schools as well as the corporate sector. Therefore, whether in the corporate sector or in schools, attending to the staff's work-related needs is imperative. Those studying workplace cultures of both schools and business have an important message for school improvers.

Senge (1990) was not the first to study and write about this issue. Argyris (1982), Deal and Kennedy (1982), Likert (1967), McGregor (1960), Schein (1985), and others have analyzed and commented (sometimes profusely) about the organizational culture of corporations and how people in particular settings can work more effectively. In addition, Deal and Peterson (1990), Boyd (1992b), and Boyd and Hord (1994) have identified the factors that describe school organizational cultures that support the current, and likely the future, unprecedented demands on schools to change.

Senge's (1990), thinking about work in the corporate setting, reported in *The Fifth Discipline*, has captured the attention of educational leaders who are struggling to persuade schools to become interested in change and improvement. Senge, looking to the work of Argyris (1982), identified the factors that individuals and the organization collectively need to become a "learning organization." Five disciplines, or ways of thinking and interacting in the organization, represent these factors. The first is *systems thinking,* a consideration of the whole system that also recognizes the parts and their patterns and interrelationships. The systems approach makes it possible to structure interrelationships more effectively. This discipline integrates the other four, fusing them into a coherent body.

Building a shared vision, the second discipline, is the construction of compelling images shared by the organization's members and focused on what the organization wants to create. These shared pictures of the future foster genuine commitment. *Personal mastery*, the third discipline, is the practice of continually clarifying and making personal vision more precise, identifying what each individual wants in his or her personal participation in the organization. Senge believes that unless all personal visions are included, there can be no shared vision.

The fourth discipline, the use of *mental models*, involves separating what has truly been observed from the assumptions and generalizations that people make based on their observations. Here individuals reveal their assumptions for all to examine. The final discipline, *team learning*, is the activity of coming together to dialogue and discuss in order to learn with and from each other. Developing team learning skills involves each individual balancing his or her own goals and advocacy to achieve collaborative decision-making that serves the well-being of all. This description of the interactive, collegial, vision- and decision-sharing "learning organization" can be found in the educational setting (Boyd & Hord, 1994)—and it is this new and infrequently found school culture that commands our attention and challenges our action.

Boyd (1992a), reviewing a wide range of the literature on organizational context in the public and private sectors, identified seventeen indicators that describe an educational context conducive to change. These seventeen factors were clustered into four functional groupings by Boyd and Hord (1994): (1) reducing isolation; (2) increasing staff capacity; (3) providing a caring, productive environment; and (4) promoting increased quality. How the seventeen indicators relate to the functional groupings is portrayed below in Figure 10.2.

FIGURE 10.2   Indicators of a Context Conducive to Change

Reducing isolation
  Schedules and structures that reduce isolation
  Policies that foster collaboration
  Policies that provide effective communication
  Collegial relationships among teachers
  A sense of community in the school

Increasing staff capacity
  Policies that provide greater autonomy
  Policies that provide staff development
  Availability of resources
  Norm of involvement in decision-making

Providing a Caring, Productive Environment
  Positive teacher attitudes toward schooling, students, and change
  Students' heightened interest and engagement with learning
  Positive, caring student-teacher-administrator relationships
  Supportive community attitudes
  Parents and community members as partners and allies

Promoting increased quality
  Norm of continuous critical inquiry
  Norm of continuous improvement
  Widely shared vision or sense of purpose

These factors were found actively operating in the Driscoll Square School, which was being studied by the Leadership for Change (LFC) Project of the Southwest Educational Development Laboratory (Hord, 1992, 1993). The LFC staff were interested in understanding how schools and their leaders go about the work of school change. The Driscoll School strongly exemplified the descriptors of Senge's "learning organization" and Boyd's seventeen indicators of a context conducive to school change. The Driscoll School can be characterized as a *professional learning community* (PLC) (Boyd & Hord, 1994) which is one whose professional staff meets regularly and frequently to reflect on and inquire into its practices, and to learn together and take action on their learning for the benefit of students. The brief picture of this school's culture and other elements of its context presented in the Vignette (see pp. 201–202) is illuminating.

The Professional Learning
Community Context

Rosenholz (1989) first brought teachers' workplace factors into the discussion of teaching quality by maintaining that teachers who felt supported in their own ongoing learning and classroom practice were more committed and effective than those who were not supported. Such support was manifested as teachers worked together, sharing their craft and wisdom, learning from each other, and collaborating on problems and issues of concern to them. This support increased teacher efficacy, which meant that they gave more attention to students' needs and adopted new classroom behaviors more readily.

Darling-Hammond (1996), Lieberman (1995), Little (1982), McLaughlin and Talbert (1993) agreed with Rosenholz, and have been increasingly clear and insistent about the need to provide teachers with a context that supports their professional endeavors and nurtures their collaborative efforts. Their research has revealed the influence of the workplace culture on teachers' practice and, consequently, on outcomes for students. Darling-Hammond observed that workplaces that are supportive of teachers are few and far between, and that attention must be focused on rethinking the organizational arrangements of the work setting.

Typically, schoolwide change efforts have been short-term and lacking in participation by the entire staff. Encouraging the staff's motivation to change so that improvement in the school is ongoing has been a formidable challenge to school change leaders. If the context of the school affects teachers' ability and inclination to change, what does the research tell us about such school settings? In a review of the research on this topic, Hord (1997) identified the five dimensions of these professional learning communities as follows: (1) shared values and vision; (2) collective learning and application; (3) supportive and shared leadership; (4) supportive conditions; and (5) shared personal practice (see Figure 10.3).

FIGURE 10.3   Dimensions of Professional Learning Communities

Shared values and vision: The staff's unswerving commitment to students' learning, which is referenced for the staff's work

Collective learning and application: The application of the learning to solutions that address students' needs

Supportive and shared leadership: Jointly held power and authority that involve the staff in decision-making

Supportive conditions: Physical and human capacities that promote collaborative organizational arrangement

Shared personal practice: Feedback and assistance from peers that support individual and community improvement

Shared Values and Vision

In the schools where the professional staff—administrators and teachers—are organized in learning communities, they share an undeviating focus on student learning. The staff assume that students are academically able and create visions of the learning environment that will enable each student to realize his or her potential. In this community, each individual member is responsible for his/her own actions, but the common good is uppermost. The relationships of the individuals are described as caring, and they are encouraged by open communication and trust. The vision of the PLC maintains a focus on quality, in the work of the staff and the students.

Collective Learning and Application

In the PLC, people from across the organization work together collaboratively and continually. This approach is grounded in reflective dialogue in which the staff have conversations about students, learning, and teaching, citing related issues and concerns. The reflection is accompanied by inquiry that forces debate among staff about what is important and provides them with opportunities for learning from and with each other. As a result of these learning conversations and interactions, decisions are made collectively, and new ideas and information are used in problem-solving. The collective learning and widely shared decision-making are in turn applied to action and new practice, thus expanding the repertoire of all. Such schools where staff are sharing, learning, and acting on their learning are also labeled problem-solving schools, or centers of inquiry and improvement.

Supportive and Shared Leadership

If a school staff is working collaboratively and making decisions, the role of the principal remains a highly significant one, with the principal participating with the staff as a learner and contributing democratically to decision-making. This new relationship leads to a collegial leadership in which all staff are growing and playing on the same team. Three factors are required of principals whose school staffs are operating as PLCs: a need to share authority, the ability to facilitate the work of the staff, and the capacity to participate without dominating.

Supportive Conditions

Supportive conditions provide the infrastructure and basic requirements of the when, where, and how the staff can collectively come together as a whole to learn, make decisions, do creative problem-solving and implement new practices—actions that are characteristic of the PLC. Two types of conditions are necessary: physical or structural conditions (James and Jones's situational variables), and the human qualities or capacities of the people involved. Examples of each type are provided below.

Physical Conditions   These factors include the time to meet and interact, the size of the school and proximity of the staff to each other, communication procedures, and resources. Schedules and structures that reduce isolation of the staff are important so that they can come together. Policies that foster collaboration and provide for staff development should be in place. Time is a vital resource and the hardest to find. This factor is bedeviling and currently being explored so that more creative ways may be found to create time for staff to meet and do collaborative work.

People Capacities   Positive teacher attitudes toward students, schooling, and change are found among staff in PLC arrangements. Staff's heightened interest in continuous learning and norms of critical inquiry and improvement are routinely in place. Staff's openness to feedback, which typically assumes trust among the individuals involved, must be developed for the PLC to operate optimally.

Shared Personal Practice

In the PLC, teachers visit each other's classrooms to review their teaching behavior. This practice is in the spirit of peers supporting peers. In these visits, teachers observe, script notes, and discuss observations after the visit. Making time for these activities is difficult, but the process contributes to the individual's and the community's improvement. Mutual trust and respect are imperative. The staff must develop trust and caring relationships with each other. These relationships develop through both professional problem-solving activities and social interactions of the staff. As a result, the staff finds support for each other's triumphs and troubles.

In terms of the change process, when a school staff works collaboratively in a PLC, the outcomes for the staff are significant, as reported by Hord (1997) in the literature review. Not only do teachers express more satisfaction and higher morale (school climate factors), but they make teaching adaptations for students, and these changes are done more quickly than in traditional schools. In such a context, teachers make a commitment to making significant and lasting changes, and they are more likely to undertake fundamental, systemic change.

Leadership in a Professional Learning Community

Although Hargreaves (1997) doesn't use the term "professional learning community," he suggests that "the central task in creating cultures of educational change is to develop more collaborative working relationships between principals and teachers and among teachers themselves" (p. 2). School personnel are being asked, many of them for the first time, Schmoker (1997) states, to be "thinking contributors who can generate solutions to emergent problems and obstacles. This is something new . . . [to be] brought together—regularly—to be asked for their suggestions, to develop real solutions to the most pressing concerns students face" (p. 143).

Collegial learning provides a means for enabling the culture of educational change. Thus, in their recent study of change, Caine and Caine (1997) quote a teacher as saying that "actively processing in a social context is increasing my learning" (p. 197). And, in a poetic form, Wheatley and Kellner-Rogers (1996) exclaim "that life leaps forward when it can share its learning" (p. 34). By supporting individual members, organizational learning can offer a very promising avenue to more successful change processes.

In schools where the staff exemplify the learning organization, the CBAM precepts and operating principles still apply, but in a more broadly shared way. The principal is not "the sage on stage," as some have suggested, but "the guide on the side." The requirement to understand and consider implementor's concerns and evolving use of new practices does not diminish. And the leadership actions and strategies necessary to support implementation remain *de rigueur*. It is how the leadership role plays out that differs.

In the learning organization context, all the staff share the leadership role, although the nominal leader remains the point person. Ultimate responsibility must not be abandoned, and the positional leader (principal, superintendent, etc.) assumes and maintains this responsibility—but operationally in a less visible and more democratic way. Everyone contributes ideas for change, and everyone contributes to the interventions needed for high-quality implementation discussed in Chapter 6:

- Developing a shared vision
- Planning and providing resources
- Investing in professional learning
- Checking on progress
- Providing continuous assistance

With the sharing of tasks, the obligation of any one individual is lessened— and strengthened. Each individual has the opportunity to be involved in a highly active, committed way. Over time the opportunities are accepted, and expectations and norms are established for continuing this kind of behavior. The staff value their role of involvement as decision-makers and facilitators of improvement. They experience a new dimension of their efficacy as professionals. In this way, the entire staff develop facilitating leadership that supports change.

VIGNETTE
The Driscoll Square School Difference

The Driscoll Square School, an elementary school built in 1923, is located in a large city on the fringe of the downtown industrial area. Like many schools in older urban cities, its population decreased as more and more people moved to the suburbs. Because of the decline in enrollment, the school was slated to be closed. However, a few tenacious parents prevailed, and it was saved—but as an open enrollment school, which meant that it had to generate an enrollment large enough to be kept open.

A new principal brought the vision of a child-centered school and shared authority for those working with the children. The formerly ill-maintained school soon sparkled with children's art, music, singing, and dance. Each day now starts with Morning Meeting, when all children and staff meet in the basement to celebrate children's birthdays and accomplishments: a first-grader reading his first primer aloud to the audience; third-graders demonstrating a Native American dance; and, fifth- and sixth-graders modeling how peer mediation helps to solve disagreements without fisticuffs.

Another regular event is Faculty Study, where all faculty meet on Thursdays, getting together as a total group some weeks and as grade groups on others. This two-hour block of time was gained by extending the instructional day four days a week and abbreviating it on Thursday, an arrangement that was reached after much lobbying and the signing of documents that declared that no teacher was coerced into accepting this agreement. These structures and schedules form the basis of the school's "learning community" in which all individuals refer to themselves as "family." They proclaim that the "Driscoll Difference" represents their essence. And what does this essence—their philosophy, values, and beliefs about children—look like operationally?

Analysis

Morning Meeting has established a feeling that "we are all together in this enterprise," meaning that all adults and all children are involved. Further, since all teachers "own" all children, no teacher hesitates to take whatever kind of action seems appropriate with any of the children. Most of the faculty eat lunch in one room, where they share interests, concerns, and congratulations about all the children and themselves. Because the school is crowded, there was some consideration of using this area for a classroom. But after much soul-searching, the faculty determined that their program and ways of operating would not be able to continue as effectively without this common meeting space.

Faculty Study makes it possible for the entire staff to be in one place at one time on a regular basis, with enough time to study and learn together, identify and solve problems, consider issues, and stay together on any and all matters. This has resulted in the development of the following important cultural norms:

1. A widely held vision of what the school should be
2. Broadly based decision-making across the faculty that includes a management team that energetically represents the teachers' views
3. Widely distributed and inclusive leadership wherein everyone takes responsibility to bring new ideas, help each other implement the ideas, and share the leadership function, so that they operate differently from an organization with a "hero leader"
4. A pervasive attachment to critical inquiry that challenges faculty to regularly say to themselves:
   - What are we doing for our children?
   - Is there a better way?
   - Let's try it! (This is an expression of Little's [1982] "norms of collegiality and experimentation.")
5. A norm of continuous, seamless improvement

In this culture, there is no fear about introducing and implementing change. Change is valued and sought as a means of achieving improved effectivess; change and improvement are introduced by everyone and are a way of life. However, adoption and implementation are not done frivolously. Much thought and study are given to changes and whether their implementation will support and/or enhance the school's mission.

1. Do you know of a school that exemplifies the kind of culture described at Driscoll? How did this culture develop at the school?
2. What is the role of the principal and/or key teachers in the development and operation of a school that acts as collegially as Driscoll does?
3. Discuss the advantages and disadvantages, in terms of change process, for schools that operate as Driscoll does.

Summary

There is wide agreement that the professional culture described in this chapter—one with an efficacious and caring staff, whose *heart* and *mind* are focused on children—is what is needed in schools today. However, there is a prior need for rigorous research studies that will lead to understanding about the contribution of the professional learning community or learning organization to the successful planning and implementation of change efforts. As an organizational arrangement in schools, does the PLC provide the most desirable context for the efficient, high-quality implementation of change? Does it support staff in moving more quickly to resolve lower Stages of Concern and then to progress to higher stages? Does the collaborative nature of the individuals in this arrangement aid staff in their growth and development to higher Levels of Use? Just what interventions do staff provide to their peers in their collective endeavors to change and increase their effectiveness? What configurations of the PLC might be discovered in such studies, and to what effect?

Joyce and his colleagues Wolf and Calhoun (1993) contend that the design and operation of the organization, rather than the staffs, have been the major problem in improving schools. This idea can be inferred from our description of the professional learning community as a preferred arrangement. Further, they maintain that changing the organization will result in increased creativity and vitality of teachers and students. The challenge then is to create organizational settings (the school) that honor all individuals (children and adults) in a caring, productive environment that invites and sustains a continuous quest for improvement:

> *We are beginning to look at the strong emotions that are part of being human, rather than . . . believing that we can confine workers into narrow roles, as though they were cogs in the machinery of production. . . . We are focusing on the deep longings we have for community, meaning, dignity, and love in our organizational lives* (Wheatley, 1992, p. 12)

Guiding Principles of Organizational Culture

1. Organizations adopt change; individuals implement change.
2. The organizational culture influences the work of individuals.
3. Organizations must value and support individuals in change efforts.
4. There are identifiable factors that describe the context of learning organizations.
5. Leadership for change facilitation is shared among all participants of a professional learning community.
6. The unceasing quest for increased effectiveness drives the professional learning community.

DISCUSSION QUESTIONS

1. What difference would it make to a school's change efforts if the school's culture were that of a professional community?

2. Describe key characteristics of the leadership for facilitating change in the learning organization school.

3. What functions does a context that supports change play? Explain why these functions are important.

FIELDWORK ACTIVITIES

1. Identify a school that appears to be developing a professional learning community culture. Make an instrument of the seventeen Boyd and Hord (1994) indicators by adding rating scales to each one. Administer the instrument to the school's leadership or management team. Lead a discussion with them of their results, focusing on where the school is strong and where attention is needed.

2. Find a school that has become a professional learning community. Interview longtime and new staff to solicit: (a) current descriptions of the school; (b) descriptions of what the school was like before it changed; and (c) explanations of how it became a professional learning community.

3. Find a school that is amenable to becoming a professional learning community. Use interviews with several staff members to describe their vision of such an organization. Conduct a meeting with the school improvement council to plan strategies for re-creating the school as a learning organization.

REFERENCES

Argyris, C. (1982). *Reasoning, learning, and action: Individual and organizational.* San Francisco: Jossey-Bass.

Bellah, R. N., & Madsen, R. (1985). *Habits of the heart.* New York: Harper and Row.

Boyd, V. (1992a). Creating a context for change. *Issues . . . About Change, 2*(2), pp. 1–10.

Boyd, V. (1992b). *School context: Bridge or barrier for change.* Austin: Southwest Educational Development Laboratory.

Boyd, V., & Hord, S. M. (1994). *Principals and the new paradigm: Schools as learning communities.* Paper presented at the annual meeting of the American Educational Research Association, New Orleans.

Bridges, W. (1980). *Transitions: Making sense of life's changes.* New York: Addison-Wesley.

Bridges, W. (1991). *Managing transitions: Making the most of change.* New York: Addison-Wesley.

Busick, K. U., & Inos, R. H. (1992). *Synthesis of the research on educational change: Implementation phase.* Honolulu: Pacific Regional Educational Laboratory.

Caine, R. N., & Caine, G. (1997). *Education on the edge of possibility.* Alexandria, VA: Association for Supervision and Curriculum Development.

Darling-Hammond, L. (1996). The quiet revolution: Rethinking teacher development. *Educational Leadership, 53*(6), 4–10.

Deal, T. E., & Kennedy, A. A. (1982). *Corporate cultures: The rites and rituals of corporate life.* New York: Addison-Wesley.

Deal, T. E., & Peterson, K. D. (1990). *The principal's role in shaping school culture.* Washington, DC: U.S. Department of Education.

Fullan, M. G. (1991). *The new meaning of educational change.* (2nd ed.). New York: Teachers College Press.

Fullan, M. G., & Miles, M. M. (1992). Getting reform right: What works and what doesn't. *Phi Delta Kappan, 73*(10), 745–752.

Hall, G. E., & Hord, S.M. (1987). *Change in schools: Facilitating the process.* Albany: SUNY Press.

Hargreaves, A. (1997). Rethinking educational change: Going deeper and wider in the quest for success. In A. Hargreaves (Ed.), *ASCD yearbook: Rethinking educational change with heart and mind* (pp. 1–26). Alexandria, VA: Association for Supervision and Curriculum Development.

Hord, S. M. (1992). *Voices from a place for children*. Austin: Southwest Educational Development Laboratory.

Hord, S. M. (1993). *A place for children: Continuous quest for quality*. Austin: Southwest Educational Development Laboratory.

Hord, S. M. (1997). *Professional learning communities: Communities of continuous inquiry and improvement*. Austin: Southwest Educational Development Laboratory.

Hord, S. M., Rutherford, W. L., Huling-Austin, L. L., & Hall, G. E. (1987). *Taking charge of change*. Alexandria, VA: Association for Supervision and Curriculum Development.

James, L. R., & Jones, A. P. (1974). Organizational climate: A review of theory and research. *Psychological Bulletin, 81*(12), 1096–1112.

Joyce, B., Wolf, J., & Calhoun, E. (1993). *The self-renewing school*. Alexandria, VA: Association for Supervision and Curriculum Development.

Lieberman, A. (1995). Practices that support teacher development: Transforming conceptions of professional learning: *Phi Delta Kappan, 76*(8), 591–596.

Likert, R. (1967). *The human organization: Its management and value*. New York: McGraw-Hill.

Little, J.W. (1982). Norms of collegiality and experimentation: Workplace conditions of school success. *American Educational Research Journal, 19*(3), 325–340.

McGregor, D. (1960). *The human side of management*. New York: McGraw-Hill.

McLaughlin, M. W., & Talbert, J. E. (1993). *Contexts that matter for teaching and learning*. Stanford: Center for Research on the Context of Secondary School Teaching, Standford University.

Rosenholtz, S. (1989). *Teacher's workplace: The social organizations of schools*. New York: Longman.

Schein, E. (1985). *Organizational culture and leadership: A dynamic view*. San Francisco: Jossey-Bass.

Schmoker, M. (1997). Setting goals in turbulent times. In A. Hargreaves (Ed.), *ASCD yearbook: Rethinking educational change with heart and mind*. Alexandria, VA: Association for Supervision and Curriculum Development.

Scott, C. D., & Jaffe, D. T. (1989). *Managing organizational change*. Menlo Park, CA: Crisp.

Senge, P. M. (1990). *The fifth discipline: The art and practice of the learning organization*. New York: Doubleday/Currency.

Wheatley, M. J. (1992). *Leadership and the new science: Learning about organization from an orderly universe*. San Francisco: Berrett-Koehler.

Wheatley, M. J., & Kellner-Rogers, M. (1996). *A simpler way*. San Francisco: Berrett-Koehler.

11

A Systemic View

The Concerns-Based Perspective in Action

You know, using Stages of Concern and Innovation Configurations together is what made the real difference. We could understand what they were concerned about and target our training and coaching around the most important IC Map components.

This change effort was different in so many ways. One of the most important was that the evaluators, the administrators, and all of the lead facilitators were working off the same page. The evaluators wrote their reports using CBAM data, and those of us who were facilitating the change process were trained in using the same concepts. We understood the reports and could use the findings!

This research project represents one of the few times when we had data about implementation at the classroom level, as well as student outcomes. The result is that we now can say that the higher the level and extent of implementation, the higher the student outcomes. This is the difference between being research-based and being research-verified.

One of the central themes in this book is that we are living in a time of change. Change is all around us, and it is not going to go away. We also have emphasized that change is a process, not an event; you cannot simply check it off as if it were another item on a list of tasks. Change is very complex and subtle too, especially in professional fields such as education. Today's educational innovations have many components and heavy emphases on subtle nuances of performance by teachers and students. At the same time, on the surface, many changes appear to be intuitively obvious and simple. The underlying complexities and required user sophistication are not obvious to the lay observer. Of course, we also are emphasizing that change efforts are expensive in time as well as in dollars.

Each chapter in this book has offered research-based and research-verified concepts and tools that can be used to better understand, facilitate, and evaluate change processes. In this chapter we will illustrate some of the ways these change process concepts have been used in combinations to think about, facilitate, and assess change efforts. Concepts such as Levels of Use (LoU) can be useful by themselves; however, their power can be increased when their use is combined with one or two of the other concepts, such as Innovation Configurations (IC).

One important part of the thinking that was proposed in the original writing about the concerns-based approach was to be sure to view the whole as well as the parts. The idea of systems thinking and especially the use of adaptive systems theory were emphasized (Hall, Wallace, & Dossett, 1973). This systemic view has become much more widely accepted recently (see, for example, Reigeluth & Garfinkle, 1994). Thinking about change processes in organizational settings as being *systemic* is important, especially since there are so many pieces and interactive dynamics. Therefore, examples of how to use multiple elements of the CBAM in a single change process will be addressed in this chapter.

The second major agenda for this chapter is to highlight some of the key implications and unaddressed issues related to thinking about, facilitating, and studying change processes. What are the pressing research questions? How can established concepts such as institutionalization be operationally defined using CBAM concepts? What is the ideal system state from a concerns-based perspective? In the second part of this chapter, these and related interesting ideas, issues, and questions will be examined.

FOCUS QUESTIONS

1. How can all three of the CBAM diagnostic dimensions be used at the same time?
2. Can data about implementation using LoU and IC Maps be related to student outcomes?
3. What are next steps for research on facilitating change from a concerns-based perspective?
4. What are some of the significant implications of thinking about the change process from a concerns-based perspective?

Systemic Applications of Elements of the Concerns-Based Adoption Model

In each of the preceding chapters key concepts in the Concerns-Based Adoption Model were introduced and described along with ways that each has been applied in research and change facilitation efforts. Each of these concepts can be very useful by itself for planning, facilitating, researching, and/or assessing change processes.

However, the greatest gain comes from using the concepts in combination, which is what the whole of the CBAM represents.

In Figure 11.1 the different elements of the CBAM are brought together. An explicit assumption in this portrayal is that change in organizational settings needs to be viewed as an *adaptive systemic process.* Rather than having a change agent initiate various actions, or interventions, to influence use of an innovation, CBAM change facilitators are expected first to probe (using formal measures and one-legged interviews) at the individual and group levels. The purpose of this probing is to assess the current system state in terms of Innovation Configurations (see Chapter 3), Stages of Concern (see Chapter 4), and Levels of Use (see Chapter 5). Based on the diagnostic information, the change facilitators then make concerns-based interventions. The diagnosing and intervening process should be ongoing, and interventions should be based on current assessments. In this way facilitating change is *adaptive,* that is, the facilitator continually adjusts the interventions based on the current diagnostic information. This adaptation occurs in the same way that living organisms adapt to their environment or the digestive system adds enzymes when food is introduced. Effective change facilitators adapt in response to what they learn about the current system state.

From a CBAM perspective, change facilitation requires systemic thinking too. Every action can lead to a multitude of reactions and future actions. The more skillful change facilitators are able to anticipate and predict the most likely actions and reactions. They keep in mind questions such as: "If I do *X,* will the staff's SoC

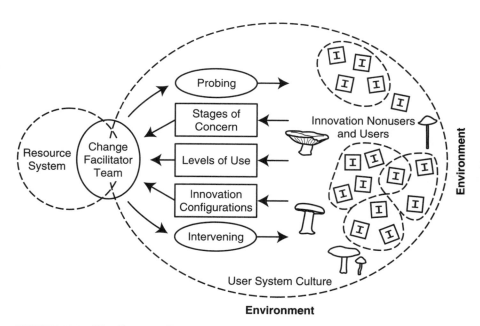

FIGURE 11.1   The Concerns-Based Adoption Model

change? Will the innovation be adapted?" Change facilitators also think out possible scenarios: "This person is likely to talk to her friend, and they will consider *X*." Effective change facilitators use the three CBAM diagnostic dimensions to derive a database for answering these questions. There is strategic as well as adaptive-systemic thinking. Change facilitators look for patterns and use what has been learned from research and theory to anticipate potential developments.

In this chapter, examples of using combinations of various elements of the CBAM to facilitate and to study change processes are presented. In each case, elements of the CBAM were used to learn more about a change process and to plan for future interventions. The Change Principles introduced in Chapter 1 and the key CBAM concepts presented in each of the other chapters are used here in various combinations to illustrate applications and to report on recent findings from research.

The other topic in this chapter is *potholes*—the challenges, problems, crises, disappointments, and setbacks found in all change processes. This term was used in the title of this book, but scant attention has been given to it in the preceding chapters. The reason for saving examination of potholes until the last chapter is that the various CBAM concepts and research findings can now be used to explain their causes and dynamics. Without this background, potholes in the change process would continue to appear to be unpredictable, irrational, whimsical, unexplainable, and uncontrollable. Through the use of CBAM concepts most pot holes can be explained, and many predicted. An important consequence of these analyses of potholes is the consideration of the types of interventions that are necessary to identify them, to fix them, and, more importantly, to prevent their creation in the first place.

Districtwide versus Site-Based Implementation Support

Fortunately, for the most part, school district leaders now understand that supporting implementation requires more than purchasing the materials. At a minimum, a workshop is typically held before the school year starts. These sessions introduce the innovation, its philosophy, and any required materials. Some district leaders have moved further in their thinking and have established year-long and in some cases two- or three-year programs of implementation support. Two such multiyear efforts that have used elements of the CBAM are described below. Interestingly, they both happened to have focused on introducing new approaches to teaching mathematics using manipulative materials, standards, and constructivist teaching strategies. In one district, two designs to implementation support were employed: (1) districtwide workshops and assistance; and (2) a master teacher who was assigned to work half-time as an on-site trainer and coach. In the second district, a third and more intensive variation of districtwide and site-based support was carried out, as master teachers were employed full-time as a districtwide change facilitator team. This action research project included examination of the relationships between extent of implementation and student outcomes.

Case One: Two Intervention Strategies, Districtwide Support versus Site-Based Coaching, and Stages of Concern

In the early 1990s, Larry Bradsby, then coordinator of mathematics for the school district of Jefferson County, Colorado, offered us an interesting research opportunity in which information about Stages of Concern (SoC) might be informative. It seemed that with the support of a foundation grant, the district was engaged in two models of implementation support for teachers who were learning how to teach mathematics a new way, which now would be called standards-based. The two models of implementation support were as follows:

- *Model I—A districtwide approach*: The mathematics coordinator and lead mathematics teachers developed a set of one-day training workshops that were presented throughout the year. Teachers from across the district could attend these sessions. The lead teachers ran a telephone hot line to answer teachers' questions. When requested, the lead teachers would also visit schools, conduct demonstration lessons, and observe classrooms.
- *Model II—A site-based lead teacher approach*: In a few schools, a skilled teacher was assigned to work half-time as a staff trainer and coach. This lead teacher presented the same workshops to his or her site colleagues as were available districtwide. The lead teacher also moved throughout the school to answer questions, help in preparing materials, teach sample lessons, and offer feedback and suggestions.

Stages of Concern Questionnaire (SoCQ) data were collected districtwide, from teachers who had participated in both models, early in the fall and late in the spring of the first year of implementation. Selected SoC profiles, which are presented in Figures 11.2–11.6, offer important insights about effects of the two staff development models.

1. The Model I approach most definitely addressed teacher concerns. The SoC profiles for teachers from two schools that had access to the districtwide workshops and related implementation support are presented in Figures 11.2 and 11.3. It would appear that at the beginning of the year, teachers in School A (Figure 11.2) were very interested in learning more about the new approach to teaching mathematics (high self concerns: Stage 1 Informational and somewhat high Stage 2 Personal). In School B (Figure 11.3), the year began with teachers having high Self and Task concerns. Our inference is that the teachers were early in their attempts to use manipulative materials and the constructivist approach. They wanted to know more (Stage 1 Informational) about how to use the materials (Stage 3 Management), were not comfortable with what they were doing (Stage 2 Personal), and had concerns about how to do it more efficiently (again Stage 3). By the end of the school year, the SoCQ profiles for both schools had changed significantly. (Note that a ten percentile change on any of the Stage of Concern scales generally will be statistically significant.). For both schools, Stage 1 and 2 concerns had decreased.

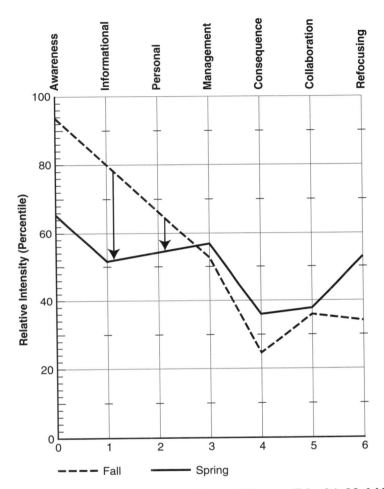

FIGURE 11.2   Change in Nonuser Teacher Stages of Concern (School A, Model I)

2. The SoCQ profiles in Figure 11.4 clearly document an important effect of having dedicated, on-site implementation support (Model II). In School C, self and task concerns did not become aroused! It appears that the lead teacher (i.e., the Second Change Facilitator) at the site was able to address the many Stage 1 Informational and Stage 3 Management concerns early, as they were emerging, and in relevant ways. It would appear also that having frequent personal contact and addressing Stage 1 and 3 concerns resulted in Stage 2 Personal concerns not becoming intense either. In this approach, the daily molehills that are a natural part of change did not grow into mountains as people waited for someone to show up and answer their simple "how-to" questions. The frequent contact by an on-site change facilitator, who understood the logistics of use, resulted in task concerns being addressed immediately. In addi-

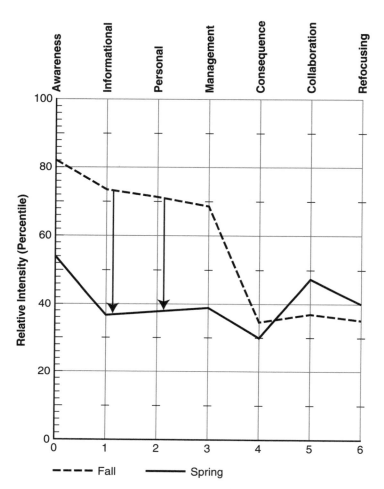

FIGURE 11.3   Change in Early Implementor Teacher Stages of Concerns (School B, Model I)

tion, because the lead teacher had expert knowledge about use of the innovation, in many instances potential task concerns were anticipated and addressed. By being on-site daily and having assigned time to work with teachers, the facilitator could take steps to reduce the possibility of task concerns becoming aroused by pointing out the unforeseen pitfalls and providing the right materials and suggestions in advance.

3. *Pothole Warning*: Sending a single teacher from a site to a districtwide work-shop may lead to the individual's discouragement. Model I's districtwide approach basically extended an open invitation for anyone to attend the training sessions.

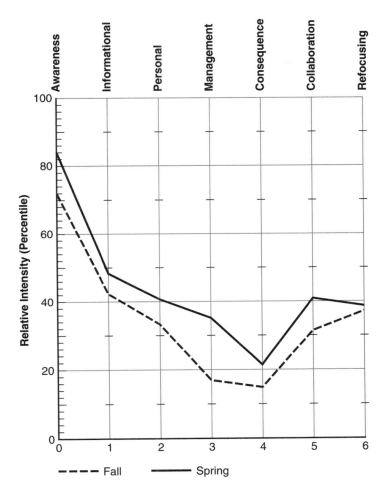

FIGURE 11.4   Change in Teacher Stages of Concern (School C, Model II)

Entire school staffs, groups of teachers from a school, and even individual teachers could and did attend. In the SoCQ data were profiles of several teachers who attended the Model I workshops as individuals; no colleagues from their schools participated. The unfortunate results are reflected in the SoC profiles in Figures 11.5 and 11.6.

Figure 11.5 shows the SoC profile of a teacher who began the school year with high interest in learning more about the new approach to teaching mathematics (Stage 1 Informational concerns). The intensity of the Stage 3 Management concerns

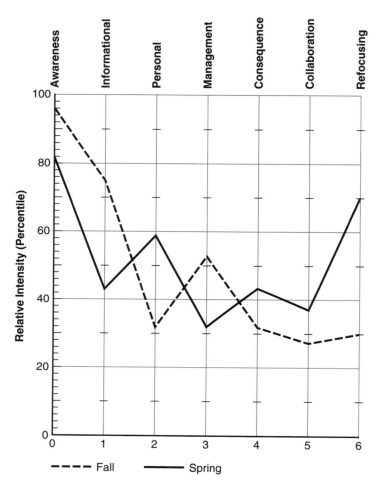

FIGURE 11.5   Change in Stages of Concern of a Teacher with Informational Concerns Who Participated in a Model I Alone

indicates some concerns about the "how-to" process as well. Sadly, the spring SoC profile for this teacher is not what we would hope for following a year of experience and participation in a set of workshops. In the spring this teacher had shifted to more intense Stage 2 Personal concerns and exhibited a strong "tailing up" on Stage 6 Refocusing concerns. Note that many of the Stage 1 Informational concerns must have been addressed, since this stage is considerably lower. This is the picture of a teacher who began the year being open to and interested in learning more about the new approach. However, this teacher ended the year with high personal concerns and strongly held ideas about how things need to be different. Our inference is that this person is now thinking, "I can't do this in my situation." Thus the well-

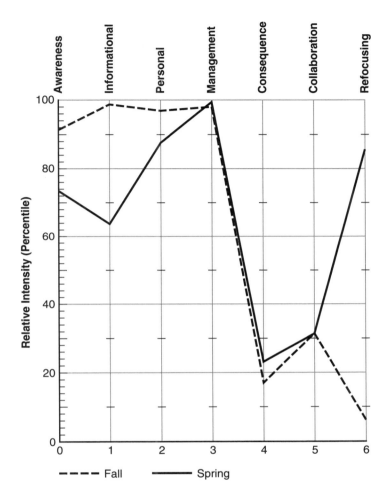

FIGURE 11.6   Change in Stages of Concern in a Teacher with Self and Task Concerns Who Participated in Model I Alone

intended strategy of inviting individual teachers from a school to attend the districtwide workshops and then returning to their school, where they had no colleagues or a principal with whom to share the new ideas, caused the individuals to become discouraged and resistant to using the new approach.

Figure 11.6 reflects a similar story. In this case, it would appear that the teacher had been attempting to do more with manipulative materials in mathematics (high Stage 3 Management) and strongly felt the need for more information (Stage 1). This teacher also had high Stage 2 Personal concerns in the fall. At year's end, however, this teacher too had a strong "tailing up" on Stage 6 Refocusing concerns, high Stage 2 and 3 concerns, and a significant drop in Stage 1 Informational concerns. Here is another case of a teacher who individually attended the districtwide Model I implementation support workshops and then returned to a school without colleagues or a knowledgeable principal with whom to share and discuss the new approach. By the end of the year this teacher's concern profile is very close to the "Big W" (see Figure 4.4). We would expect the person to say: "I have my own ideas about what you can do with this innovation. I cannot (and will not) continue this way with all of these unresolved task concerns." Another positive teacher has thereby lost faith in the innovation and to some extent in him- or herself.

Implications and Recommendations from the Two Models of Implementation Support

A number of implications and recommendations can be drawn from this testing of two models of implementation support:

1. Self and Task concerns can be addressed effectively through districtwide workshops and related support. Clearly Stage 1, 2, and 3 concerns were addressed for teachers who participated as groups and whole staffs from schools. We know from experience and related studies that Model I works well to launch a change process. However, we also have regularly observed that following the first year of implementation, each school site will be at a different point. This appears to be due in large part to the Change Facilitator Style of the principal (see Chapter 7). An implication is that, in the second and subsequent years of implementation support, there should be strategies that address the unique subsystem state of each school. Note this phenomenon is an interesting area in need of further research.

2. The SoC profile data clearly document that assigning a master teacher time to offer training sessions and individual coaching at each site can effectively anticipate and address Self and Task concerns. It is also important that this person has the attributes identified in Change Principle 2 (see Chapter 1). For example, the on-site facilitator must have expert knowledge about how to use the innovation, strong interpersonal skills, and professional creditability with the implementors. Although there have not been treatment group/control group studies on this issue, it seems certain that skilled, specifically assigned site-based facilitators are critical to the success of complex innovations, innovation bundles, and paradigm-shift changes.

3. *Pothole warning*: Sending individual teachers to districtwide workshops does not help the teacher nor the school succeed and can lead to discouragement. There are no colleagues or administrators back at the site who understand what the messenger is saying, nor do they know how to support the person in trying to implement the new way. Tragically, it appears that these individuals are hurt even more than the organization. They tend to blame themselves (raising Stage 2 Personal concerns) and not the organization. They also know firsthand why the change won't work in their situation and how things need to be different ("tailing up" on Stage 6 Refocusing). As a result, these individuals can begin to sound like resistors, rather than the positively interested individuals that they were at the beginning.

4. For teacher implementation success, there must be on-site implementation assistance, with colleagues co-participating and site administrators providing ongoing support. The team concept applies to both those who are attempting to learn about and implement change as well as those who are trying to facilitate it. With the districtwide approach, everyone started from the same point. What follows, especially after the first year of implementation, is individual variation at the adopting sites. Consequently, some strategies and tactics must be designed for the whole system, while others are customized to each specific site.

Case Two: Districtwide Use of Master Teachers, Extent of Implementation, and Student Outcomes

Systemic use of many elements of the CBAM took place in the school district of the U.S. Department of Defense Dependents Schools (DoDDS). In this three-year mathematics implementation effort, the district superintendent clearly worked with the Initiator Change Facilitator Style. She clearly and consistently let teachers, principals, district office staff, and parents know that the new approach to teaching mathematics was a priority. She supported implementation by assigning resources and personnel as well as by providing training for teachers and change facilitators. She also took a direct, frontline role in leadership and in the accompanying action research study (Johnson, 2000). Three master teachers were assigned to work full-time to offer workshops, answer questions, find and organize materials, and to make on-site and in-classroom visits. Principals and district office staff were trained in the new approach to teaching mathematics. Administrators and district office staff also had workshops and coaching sessions on the three diagnostic dimensions of CBAM (SoC, LoU, and IC) and on how to use them in facilitating implementation of the mathematics program. An action research project became an important complementary part of the effort. An IC Map for Teaching and Learning Mathematics was developed (Alquist & Hendrickson, 1999), and shared with teachers and principals. It was used also to systematically assess implementation. In addition, after the mathematics consultants, other district office staff, and the superintendent were trained to research criterion in use of the LoU interview, they became the data collectors for the implementation study.

An important early part of the implementation work in this districtwide change process was developing the first draft of the IC Map. The three mathematics liaisons worked closely with one of the authors of this book across an eighteen-month period to identify clusters, components, and component variations. The 1991 National Council for the Teaching of Mathematics (NCTM) standards and the DoDDS curriculum standards were the guiding framework for identifying IC Map components. The drafts of the IC Map were shared with principals and teachers, thus offering them the first concrete description of the change and of what teachers and students are to be doing.

At the same time that the IC Map was being developed by the mathematics liaisons, all district office staff and administrators had several days of workshops on Stages of Concern, including how to assess the concept and how to conduct one-legged interviews. This allowed those administrators who were interested to customize their daily interventions to the concerns of their teachers. As in most change processes, some used this approach more than others.

The Levels of Use part of this districtwide change process took an unusual direction. As we have pointed out, the superintendent was clearly an Initiator leader. Initially she had been interested in using CBAM concepts as tools to help the mathematics liaisons and principals intervene. However, she also had questions about whether she should commit limited district resources to having three master teachers serve as full-time implementation facilitators. She also faced extreme pressure from certain interest groups to eliminate this new approach to teaching mathematics.

The result of this multifaceted set of interests, questions, and needs was that an action research project began to take shape. By using the three diagnostic dimensions of the CBAM, it would be possible to: (1) monitor implementation progress; (2) develop a common language to talk about change; (3) use diagnostic data to make districtwide, site-specific, and classroom-specific interventions; (4) examine the benefits of having three full-time implementation facilitators; and (5) determine whether this new approach to teaching mathematics made any difference in student outcomes. In other words, in this effort, the "giant leap" from having an innovation to measuring student outcomes would be bridged by first assessing the extent and quality of implementation (Hall, 1999).

Given this systemic agenda, the superintendent and the lead researcher (one of the co-authors) decided that the leadership team, including the mathematics liaisons, the coordinator of staff development, the school improvement liaison, *and* the superintendent, should be trained to research criterion and certified as Levels of Use interviewers. The training was done with eight of ten staff becoming certified and subsequently used to collect LoU data (Thornton & West, 1999).

In analzying several of the key findings and related change process–facilitating experiences of this districtwide systemic implementation effort, keep in mind that this was a collaborative, action research project (Eden & Huxham, 1996). The project was a partnership of practitioners and researchers. The study contributed to advancement of the change effort and new knowledge to the field. There are some caveats, however; for example, only teachers who volunteered were interviewed and had IC Map observations done in their classrooms. There also was limited time for everyone to collect data, since this work had to be done in addition to their regular assignments. Still, the sample size was large, and a number of the findings were quite clear.

Levels of Use interviews were conducted in the spring of the second and third years of implementation. Each year, over 100 of the approximately 140 K–8 teachers volunteered to be interviewed (Thornton & West, 1999). The overall distribution

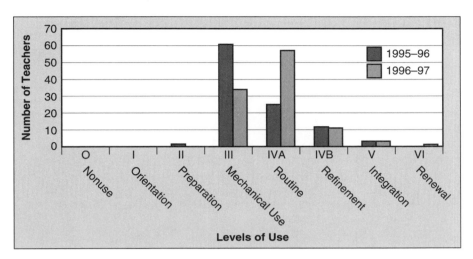

FIGURE 11.7 Levels of Use Distribution after the Second and Third Year of Implementation of a Constructivist Approach to Teaching Mathematics

of LoU for each year is summarized in Figure 11.7. As would be hoped for, especially given the systemwide press, all teachers interviewed were users of the new approach in both the second and third years of implementation. As was reported from other studies in Chapter 5, and would be expected with LoU, the highest proportion of teachers in the second year of implementation were at LoU III Mechanical Use. One implication of this finding is that facilitating the change process was not complete. A tactical decision of the superintendent was to extend implementation support to the third year, including having three full-time mathematics liaisons.

The third-year LoU data documents a decrease in the number of LoU III Mechanical Use teachers along with concomitant increases in LoU IVA Routine users. This trend is in the desired direction. However, the proportion of teachers at higher Levels of Use remained unchanged. Our inference was and continues to be that implementing major paradigm shift innovations, such as a move to constructivist teaching, takes three to five years, even with the best of change facilitation strategies. These data about LoU support this hypothesis.

Another way to use the LoU data is to compare the LoU of teachers who were interviewed in both years (see Table 11.1). There are a number of important trends in these findings. First, all teachers stayed the same or moved "up" in their LoU. The change process thus continued to move forward.

Pothole Warning: A significant number of teachers remained at LoU III Mechanical Use at the end of the third year of implementation. We would hypothesize that such people are not likely to make major progress in what they are doing. Instead, if they can, they are likely to stop using the innovation; no one wants to be

TABLE 11.1   Comparison of Levels of Use after the Second and Third Years of Implementation of a Constructivist Approach to Teaching Mathematics

| | 1996–97 | | | | | |
Level of Use	II	III	IVA	IVB	V	VI
II						
III		14	19	5		
IVA			14	2	2	1
IVB			1	2		
V			1	1	1	
VI						

performing at a Mechanical Level of Use for a long time, for at this level a large amount of effort is expended, little gain is seen, and frustrations are bound to rise.

To help some teachers to move beyond LoU III, we recommended that the site administrator become more active and focused on these teachers so that they could develop greater expertise in using the new approach. Unless concentrated time were spent with these teachers and in their classrooms, they probably would not advance in their use of the innovation. It seemed unlikely that the district level facilitators would be able to make a difference.

How do the LoU ratings relate to the IC Map assessments of implementation? In a number of studies, including this one, we have been able to plot the relationship between teachers being at certain Levels of Use and the IC Map configurations that are exhibited in their classrooms. In this case, as with the others, we have found that teachers at LoU III Mechanical Use tend to use more c and d configurations of the innovation. In other words, on the IC Map, more of their components will be scored toward the right hand side. We also have observed that the a and b variations on the IC Map are observed only in classrooms where teachers are at higher Levels of Use (IVB and higher). These data also indicate that educational innovations are much more complex and subtle than we and our critics admit. These are not easy changes to make. They take time and considerable effort to implement correctly.

In this study of constructivist teaching and learning mathematics, we were also able to examine extent of implementation and its relationship to student outcomes. Without going into all of the technical details, the trends were in the directions of what intuitively makes sense: the higher the Level of Use, the higher the student outcomes. The closer the configurations were to the a variations, the higher the student outcomes (George, Hall, & Uchiyama, 2000).

Pothole Warning: Although these findings seem logical, *the results do not always work out this way*. The extent of implementation and its relationship to outcomes are dependent on a number of factors that can have heavy subjective components. For example, in the case of mathematics, the NCTM and DoDDS Standards were *research-based*; they were the experts' best judgments about what should be done. Until the present study, these hypotheses about best practices were not *research-verified*. Another example of the potential influences of subjectivity is found in the IC Mapping work. If the IC Mapping team is not balanced and careful in developing their consensus selection of components and the wording of each variation, the resultant IC Map may not accurately portray the intents of the innovation. For these and a number of other reasons, we need to be careful about jumping to the conclusion that reaching higher Levels of Use and using practices that are closest to *a* and *b* variations will always result in higher outcomes.

A Sampling of CBAM Research and Evaluation Activities from around the World

One of the major reasons that CBAM constructs, measures, and change-facilitating efforts continue to be so useful and relevant is the number of colleagues in the United States and around the globe who share in this way of thinking about change. Although it is not possible to name every person and every piece of work, we think it is important as well as useful to provide a sampling of research and evaluation from across the spectrum.

Roland Vandenberghe, at the Center for Educational Policy and Innovation at the University of Leuven in Belgium, is a long-term colleague in CBAM research. He has made a number of important cross-cultural contributions and collaborated directly in the development of the Change Facilitator Style Questionnaire. He has done a number of interesting studies of the interventions that school principals make during change processes (Vandenberghe, 1995). Vandenberghe also has been studying micropolitics in schools.

Rudolph van den Berg, at the Catholic Educational Centre in 's-Hertogenbosch, is another long-term colleague and leader of CBAM-related research and change-facilitating work. In addition to his own scholarship, he and his Dutch colleagues established a national network of researchers and change facilitators who share ideas and work related to change. One significant early contribution of our Dutch and Flemish colleagues was their translation of the three diagnostic dimensions into Dutch; theirs were the first studies that confirmed that the constructs were cross-cultural (van den Berg & Vandenberghe, 1981).

More recently, as was described in preceding chapters, Wen Haur Shieh (1996) examined teacher concerns and principal Change Facilitator Style in Taiwan. His findings show that the concerns of teachers in the Chinese culture can be classified into the same Stages of Concern and Change Facilitator Styles.

In a 1997 article Stephen Anderson, University of Toronto, presented a review of many CBAM-based studies from around the world and offered his critique. His review is useful in a number of ways, including his consideration of these applications from a Canadian perspective. He, as do we, advocates for a critical look at what we currently know and for more research on change.

Over the last decade, myriad policies and projects have been initiated with an aim toward improving the quality of education in public schools. There has been a tendency within the educational research community to invent new models of educational change for different policy thrusts rather than drawing upon and extending what has been learned from the past. There has been a tendency within the educational practitioner community to apply research-based models of educational change uncritically. My intent in this article was to revisit one of the most significant and widely applied models of educational change to come out of research on innovation adoption and implementation in education, the Concerns-Based Adoption Model (CBAM). I suggested that CBAM continues to be relevant to understanding teacher change, despite the shifting focuses of school improvement and teacher development policies. I noted that, with few exceptions, the model has been accepted and applied as a matter of fact in the educational research and practitioner community. I argue that despite its intuitive and empirical attraction, CBAM in its present state does not fully explain teacher change in response to innovations in curriculum and instruction. I further argued that education researchers and practitioners who use CBAM concepts and methods should be more critical in their application of the model, in order to further develop and refine the model over time. Using examples of research from the United States, Europe, Australia, and Canada, I illustrated the potential for continuing CBAM theory research and development. There is still much to be learned about the process of educational change among teachers in the organizational context of schools. It is not just a matter of effectively applying what is already believed from past research, nor of continuously inventing "new" descriptive and explanatory models in response to shifting strategic trends of educational change. (Anderson, 1997, pp. 363–364)

CBAM constructs and measures have been applied in medical education as well. Eddy Bresnitz and his colleagues (1997) at the Medical College of Pennsylvania in Philadelphia have employed Stages of Concern, Levels of Use, and Innovation Configurations in implementation of a problem-based learning curriculum and efforts to disseminate technology-based case studies of lung disease to all medical schools in North America. The most extensive use of LoU in medical education has been done by Stewart Mennin and his colleagues at the University of Mexico (Mennin & Kalishman, 1998).

Merrill L. Meehan, at the Appalachia Educational Laboratory (AEL), Charleston, WV, has probably conducted more evaluation studies using CBAM constructs and measures than anyone else. He has been doing such work for nearly twenty years, and also has participated in some of the international gatherings of CBAM researchers. In one recent evaluation report, he reflected on why Levels of Use and Innovation Configurations were germane and particularly useful:

AEL evaluators discussed and debated what they considered to be the most successful aspect of the evaluation procedures employed in the evaluation of the (3-year) earth science project. The discussion quickly boiled down to two prime candidates, the annual impact survey and the annual, dual-purpose IC Map and LoU interviews. The evaluators concluded that the combination IC Map and LoU interviews [was] the most successful aspect/procedure employed in this evaluation. There are several reasons why the evaluators selected the IC/LoU interviews as the most successful evaluation procedure. First, it was a personal contact with participants (high school teachers) each spring. This face-to-face or telephone contact allowed a more personal interaction than the mailed surveys. Second, the efficiency of this dual-purpose interview appealed to the accountability interests of the evaluators. In about a half-hour interview, two major data collection processes were completed with each interviewee. Third, the IC data helped the evaluators establish and describe exactly what the major components of the earth science project were. The third-year IC data should be very helpful to project staff and future teacher enhancement projects in earth science. Fourth, the LoU interview results provided important data on how the earth science teachers actually were using (or not using) the earth science innovation. While the IC Map revealed what the major components of the project were, the LoU revealed *how* the teachers were using those components. The LoU produced operational definitions for eight different Levels of Use. For example, while other data collection procedures may have also discovered that 88% of the teachers were using this earth science innovation, the LoU provided deeper and much richer information about those project users. The LoU evaluation procedure discovered 70% of those users were doing it smoothly in their classrooms or even were trying some changes to improve student outcomes. Only 30% were spending their energies with the management processes of the innovation on day-to-day basis. Fifth, another appealing aspect of the IC/LoU evaluation procedure was that it allowed the earth science project director to interact with the evaluators to make several crucial decisions before the interviews could be started. This work with the client was seen as a very beneficial aspect of this procedure. (Meeham, 1997, pp. 35–36)

There are a number of directions for future research that need to be addressed. We certainly must have a better understanding of the dynamics and relationships between characteristics of interventions and the arousal and resolution of Stages of Concern. One very interesting and important area that requires considerable study is that of organization culture. We have stated that the ideal user-system state is one in which there are continually intense impact concerns, especially at Stage 4 Consequence and Stage 5 Collaboration. We need to study the characteristics of organizations that make it possible for them to have and sustain impact concerns. We also need descriptions of the culture when impact concerns are high. What are the norms, values, symbols, rituals, and stories? What roles and activities maintain an impact-concerned culture?

In our early work, we studied organizational climate. We even developed a very solid climate measure, the School Ecology Survey. But climate is different from culture. Here we are proposing that there be in-depth ethnographic studies of organization culture with special attention to those in which the staff sustain high impact concerns.

Issues and Implications

There are many additional issues and implications that could be presented in this chapter and as part of a concluding discussion. We have selected a few of the most salient. Each of these will make more sense now that you understand CBAM concepts.

What is institutionalization? Institutionalization has been a concept in the change literature for many years. In general, it represents the phase of change process in which the change has been put into place and has become a part of the regular way that things are done. It is possible to use CBAM concepts to provide a more operational definition. We would define *minimum institutionalization* as the time when all, or nearly all, members of the organization: (1) are using the innovation at Level of Use IVA Routine or higher; (2) have resolved their self and task concerns; and (3) are using "acceptable" configurations of the innovation. Minimum institutionalization should be the first strategic objective. Without achieving this platform, sustained use of the innovation is in jeopardy. When Self and Task concerns are not resolved, there will be strong interest in discontinuing or adapting the innovation. There also is an increased probability of the growth of poisonous mushrooms. If people remain at nonuse levels or become stuck at LoU III Mechanical Use, Self and Task concerns are likely to increase. These dynamics lead right back to adapting (and in some cases mutating) the innovation or throwing it away.

In the CBAM perspective, what is an ideal system state? We have emphasized throughout that there are no "good" or "bad" Stages of Concern or Levels of Use. However, this does not mean that there is not an ultimate goal for change processes. In the CBAM perspective, the ideal would be: (1) to have most persons at higher (IVA and above) Levels of Use; (2) to use *a* and *b* configurations of the innovation; and (3) to have intense impact concerns. The optimal organizational culture is one in which the members have high Stage 4 Consequence and Stage 5 Collaboration concerns. They are focused on how they can work together to have the most effect on their clients—students. They not only have the concerns but are *operating* at LoU V Integration. Further, they are striving to use the best (*a* and *b* variations) configurations of the innovation. To achieve this ideal system state requires a number of years (three to five or even longer) and an able Change Facilitator Team with Initiator leadership and skilled Second Change Facilitators.

What about the ethics of change? This is a question that we always raise with our students and clients. One way we phrase it is to ask, "When does change facilitation become manipulation?" After all, we are talking about tools and techniques to get people to change. Unfortunately, little has been said or written about this important issue. Early in our work, we asked Matt Miles (1979) to write a paper and provide us with a seminar on ethics. His thoughts and wise counsel have stayed with us. For example, in reflecting on organization development (OD) consultants, he pointed out critical issues related to the accountability of OD change agents:

> To whom are OD change agents accountable? At one level, as Bermant and Warwick (1978) point out, they are *personally* accountable for their actions, like any person in society. They should not lie, cheat, steal, or engage in similar socially reprehensible actions. And they are *legally* accountable in a very general sense, not only for misdemeanors and felonies, but for items like breach of contract. However, I have never

heard of malpractice litigations being threatened against an OD practitioner (though it has occurred for encounter group leaders).

In any case, litigation is a gross tool for insuring ethical behavior by practitioners. The most central form of accountability is that which OD consultants have toward their *sponsors*, who are paying the bill, in several senses. Sponsors can terminate contracts, or at least revise them, if the program is not functioning as intended. . . . Finally, there is *professional accountability* for OD practitioners, for which at present there are no formal structural supports comparable to those in medicine, law, accounting, and psychology. (Miles, 1979, pp. 8–9)

In the concerns-based perspective, "good" and "bad" are primarily defined in terms of what change facilitators do and do not do. It is neither good nor bad for individuals to have certain concerns profiles, Levels of Use, or configurations. What *is* good or bad is the types of interventions that are made. All interventions need to be *concerns-based*. They need to be related to the concerns of the clients, not the change facilitators. As a simple example, consider a teacher with high Stage 2 Personal concerns. We have heard administrators and others say to these individuals something like, "You should be concerned about students, not yourself." This is a wrong intervention from a concerns-based perspective, for its single effect will be to further raise the teacher's personal concerns. "Good" interventions would be to acknowledge the personal concerns, to attempt to provide additional information to increase understanding, to be supportive, to provide stability, and so on. Our point here is that the change facilitator bears major responsibility for whether teachers have implementation success. Just as in the Japanese management models, if an employee is not doing well, the manager has failed. Making concerns-based interventions increases the likelihood of success for all.

In some ways it may sound like Stages of Concern, Levels of Use, and Innovation Configurations are the same thing. In fact, superficial reading of each of these concepts can lead to uncertainty about how they differ. We will argue, however, that they are orthogonal concepts (see Figure 11.8). Each is an independent dimension of the change process. They address different aspects that can have some parallels. One of the authors has a favorite metaphor to help in maintaining the distinctions, which we present here briefly.

Think of driving a car as the innovation. The early adolescent has an interest in driving and wants to learn more about it (Level of Use I Orientation). During her fifteenth year, she takes driver's education (LoU II Preparation). At some point, she actually sits behind the wheel and drives for the first time. Chances are these early driving episodes are at LoU III Mechanical Use. There is a disjointedness to braking, as full attention is on how to turn properly at the next intersection. With experience, hopefully, she will drive at LoU IVA Routine, not even thinking about what she is doing.

But there is also the concerns dimension of this innovation metaphor. Think about the teenager as she takes that first drive by herself! Stage 2 Personal concerns are intense as she says to herself: "Will I be able to do everything and get back safely? What if I wreck the car?"

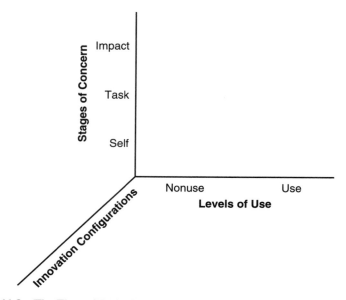

FIGURE 11.8   The Three CBAM Diagnostic Dimensions as Orthogonal, Independent Constructs

Neither of these descriptions addresses Innovation Configurations, which would answer the question of what kind of car is being driven. The response could be that it is a Ferrari F355 cabriolet, or a Chevy Impala, or an old VW beetle. There also are *e* and *f* configurations that can be imagined, such as a bicycle or a child's pedal car. In terms of the interrelationships of each CBAM dimension, no matter what configuration of car is described, any profile of Stages of Concern and Level of Use is possible. The three CBAM diagnostic dimensions are independent constructs. Each informs about a different aspect of individuals and groups before, during, and after a change process.

We would argue that for the greatest success in change, the Change Facilitator Team needs to be knowledgeable about all three diagnostic dimensions and base their interventions on contemporary data about the state of the system in relation to each. Don't forget also that it is possible for individuals and the whole system to move backward! Take our driving example. Just try driving in England. Do those self and task concerns return? What about your Level of Use? Instead of shifting the transmission, how frequently do you try to open the driver's door (LoU III Mechanical Use)? The configuration of the car comes into play too. In England, most of us rent "economical" little cars that have different names and brighter colors than in the United States.

Summary

In this book we have presented key concepts about change, especially as they relate to people and how the process unfolds in organizational settings. Many additional ideas, research findings, and stories could be discussed, but it is time for you, the reader, to use what you have learned. Whether you are a potential user of an innovation, a key change facilitator, or a researcher, the concepts and tools presented here should be of help. We offer one brief caveat and one of our favorite phrases in the way of conclusion.

The Caveat

Earlier in this chapter we touched on the ethics of being a change facilitator. We would like to return to this topic here but with a different emphasis. As dramatic as it may sound, the information presented in this book and other similar texts can be used in very inappropriate and inexcusable ways. In fact, the tools and findings from research in the social sciences are in many ways far more dangerous than what the physicists were doing underneath the football stadium at the University of Chicago in 1940, since social scientists are talking about how to change people, organizations, and social systems. In addition, there are no rules of access to the information. Anyone can pick an idea out of this book, some questionnaire, or any other piece of work, and do with it what they please. There are no codes of conduct. There are no security clearances. What happens from here depends on the integrity and professionalism of the users. We ask that you think often about whether you are being responsible and concerns-based in what you do. Fortunately, the first concerns that are aroused when there is change are self concerns. To a large extent, people will begin a change process by protecting themselves. Only when the innovation and change facilitators are perceived to be safe, will people move to implement the change. Your job is to make sure that self concerns are respected and that the abusive intentions and actions of others are challenged.

A Final Phrase

An important perspective to keep in mind as we are engaged in the change process is summarized in one phrase:

> The road to success is always under construction.

REFERENCES

Alquist, A., & Hendrickson, M. (1999). Mapping the configurations of mathematics teaching. *Journal of Classroom Interaction, 34*(1), 18–26.

Anderson, S. E. (1997). Understanding teacher change: Revisiting the Concerns-Based Adoption Model. *Curriculum Inquiry. 27*(3), 331–367.

Bermant, B., Kelman, H. S., & Warwick, D. P. (1978). *The ethics of social intervention.* Washington, DC: Hemisphere.

Bermant, G., & Warwick, D. P. (1978). The ethics of social intervention: Power, freedom and accountability. In G. Bermant, H. C. Kelman, and D. P. Warwich (1978). *The Ethics of Social Intervention.* Washington, DC: Hemisphere.

Bresnitz, E. A., Ross, M.C., Hall, G.E., & Steigelbauer, S. (1997). A randomized study to assess the facilitation of faculty implementation of computer-based learning in medical education. *Journal of Medical Education Technologies.*

Eden, C., & Huxham, C. (1996). Action research for the study of organizations. In S. R. Glegg, C. Hardy, & W. R. Nord (Eds.), *Handbook of organization studies* (pp. 526–542). Thousand Oaks, CA: Sage.

George, A. A., Hall, G. E., & Uchiyama, K. (2000). Student outcomes and extent of fidelity of use of mathematics. *Journal of Classroom Interaction, 35*(1), 8–25.

Hall, G. E. (1999). Using constructs and techniques from research to facilitate and assess implementation of an innovative mathematics curriculum. *Journal of Classroom Interaction, 34*(1) 1–8.

Hall, G. E., Wallace, R. C., & Dossett, W. (1973). *A developmental conceptualization of the adoption process within educational institutions* (Report No. 3006). Austin: The University of Texas at Austin, Research and Development Center for Teacher Education. (ERIC Document Reproduction Service No. ED 095 126).

Johnson, M. H. (2000). A district-wide agenda to improve teaching and learning in mathematics. *Journal of Classroom Interaction, 35*(1), 1–7.

Kelman, H. C., & Warwick, D. P. (1978). The ethics of social intervention: Goals, means, and consequences. In B. Bermant, H. S. Kelman, & D. P. Warwick, *The ethics of social intervention* (pp. 3–33). Washington, DC: Hemisphere.

Meehan, M. L. (1997). *Comprehensive evaluation of a statewide three-year teacher enhancement project in earth science education.* Paper presented at the annual meeting of the American Educational Research Association, Chicago.

Mennin, S. P., & Kalishman, S. (Eds.) (1998). Issues and strategies for reform in medical education: Lessons from eight medical schools. *Academic Medicine, 73*(9), 546–554.

Miles, M. B. (1979). Ethical issues in OD. *OD Practitioner, 11*(3), 1–10.

National Council for Teachers of Mathematics. (1991). *Curriculum and evaluation standards for school mathematics.* Reston, VA: Author.

Reigeluth, C. M., & Garfinkle, R. J. (1994). *Systemic change in education.* Englewood Cliffs, NJ: Educational Technology Publications.

Shieh, W. H. (1996). *Environmental factors, principals' Change Facilitator Styles, and the implementation of the cooperative learning project in selected schools in Taiwan.* Unpublished doctoral dissertation, University of Northern Colorado, Greeley.

Thornton, E., & West, C. E. (1999). Extent of teacher use of a mathematics curriculum innovation in one district: Years 1 and 2 Levels of Use (LoU). *Journal of Classroom Interaction, 34*(1), 9–17.

Van den Berg, R., & Vandenberghe, R. (1981). *Onderwijsinnovatie in Verschuivend Perspectief.* Amsterdam: Uitgeverij Zwijsen.

Vandenberghe, R. (1995). Creative management of a school: A matter of vision and daily interventions. *Journal of Educational Administration, 33*(2), 31–51.

Stages of Concern Questionnaire

Name _____

Date Completed_____

It is very important for continuity in processing this data that we have a unique number that you can remember. Please use:

Last four digits of your Social Security No.   ____   ____   ____   ____

The purpose of this questionnaire is to determine what people who are using or thinking about using various programs are concerned about at various times during the innovation adoption process. The items were developed from typical responses of school and college teachers, who ranged from no knowledge at all about various programs to many years experience in using them. Therefore, *a good part of the items on this questionnaire may appear to be of little relevance or irrelevant to you at this time.* For the completely irrelevant items, please circle "0" on the scale. Other items will represent those concerns you *do* have, in varying degrees of intensity, and should be marked higher on the scale, according to the explanation at the top of each of the following pages.

　　For example:

This statement is very true of me at this time.	0 1 2 3 4 5 6 ⑦
This statement is somewhat true of me now.	0 1 2 3 ④ 5 6 7
This statement is not at all true of me at this time.	0 ① 2 3 4 5 6 7
This statement is irrelevant to me.	⓪ 1 2 3 4 5 6 7

Please respond to the items in terms of *your present concerns*, or how you feel about your involvement or potential involvement with _____. We do not hold to any one definition of this program, so please think of it in terms of *your own perceptions* of what it involves. Since this questionnaire is used for a variety of innovations, the name _____ never appears. However, phrases such as "the innovation," "this approach," and "the new system" all refer to _____. Remember to respond to each item in terms of *your present concerns* about your involvement or potential involvement with _____.

　　Thank you for taking time to complete this task.

0	1	2	3	4	5	6	7
Irrelevant	Not true of me now		Somewhat true of me now		Very true of me now		

1. I am concerned about students' attitudes toward this innovation.

    0 1 2 3 4 5 6 7

2. I now know of some other approaches that might work better.

    0 1 2 3 4 5 6 7

3. I don't even know what the innovation is.

    0 1 2 3 4 5 6 7

4. I am concerned about not having enough time to organize myself each day.

    0 1 2 3 4 5 6 7

5. I would like to help other faculty in their use of the innovation.

    0 1 2 3 4 5 6 7

6. I have a very limited knowledge about the innovation.

    0 1 2 3 4 5 6 7

7. I would like to know the effect of this reorganization on my professional status.

    0 1 2 3 4 5 6 7

8. I am concerned about conflict between my interests and my responsibilities.

    0 1 2 3 4 5 6 7

9. I am concerned about revising my use of the innovation.

    0 1 2 3 4 5 6 7

10. I would like to develop working relationships with both our faculty and outside faculty using this innovation.

    0 1 2 3 4 5 6 7

11. I am concerned about how the innovation affects students.

    0 1 2 3 4 5 6 7

12. I am not concerned about this innovation.

    0 1 2 3 4 5 6 7

13. I would like to know who will make the decisions in the new system.

    0 1 2 3 4 5 6 7

14. I would like to discuss the possibility of using the innovation.

    0 1 2 3 4 5 6 7

15. I would like to know what resources are available if we decide to adopt this innovation.

    0 1 2 3 4 5 6 7

16. I am concerned about my inability to manage all the innovation requires.

    0 1 2 3 4 5 6 7

17. I would like to know how my teaching or administration is supposed to change.

    0 1 2 3 4 5 6 7

18. I would like to familiarize other departments or persons with the progress of this new approach.

    0 1 2 3 4 5 6 7

0	1	2	3	4	5	6	7
Irrelevant	Not true of me now		Somewhat true of me now		Very true of me now		

19. I am concerned about evaluating my impact on students. 0 1 2 3 4 5 6 7

20. I would like to revise the innovation's instructional approach. 0 1 2 3 4 5 6 7

21. I am completely occupied with other things. 0 1 2 3 4 5 6 7

22. I would like to modify our use of the innovation based on the experiences of our students. 0 1 2 3 4 5 6 7

23. Although I don't know about this innovation, I am concerned about other things in the area. 0 1 2 3 4 5 6 7

24. I would like to excite my students about their part in this approach. 0 1 2 3 4 5 6 7

25. I am concerned about my time spent working with nonacademic problems related to this innovation. 0 1 2 3 4 5 6 7

26. I would like to know what the use of the innovation will require in the immediate future. 0 1 2 3 4 5 6 7

27. I would like to coordinate my efforts with others to maximize the innovation's effects. 0 1 2 3 4 5 6 7

28. I would like to have more information on time and energy commitments required by this innovation. 0 1 2 3 4 5 6 7

29. I would like to know what other faculty are doing in this area. 0 1 2 3 4 5 6 7

30. At this time, I am not interested in learning about the innovation. 0 1 2 3 4 5 6 7

31. I would like to determine how to supplement, enhance, or replace the innovation. 0 1 2 3 4 5 6 7

32. I would like to use feedback from students to change the program. 0 1 2 3 4 5 6 7

33. I would like to know how my role will change when I am using the innovation. 0 1 2 3 4 5 6 7

34. Coordination of tasks and people is taking too much of my time. 0 1 2 3 4 5 6 7

35. I would like to know how this innovation is better than what we have now. 0 1 2 3 4 5 6 7

PLEASE COMPLETE THE FOLLOWING:

36. What other concerns, if any, do you have at this time? (Please describe them using complete sentences.)

37. Briefly describe your job function.

A P P E N D I X 2

SoCQ Quick Scoring Device

Directions for Using the SoCQ Quick Scoring Device

The Stages of Concern Questionnaire (SoCQ) contains 35 items. The scoring of the SoCQ requires a series of operations that result in an SoCQ profile. The following steps should be carried out on the Quick Scoring Device:

Step 1   In the box labeled A, fill in the identifying information taken from the cover sheet of the SoC Questionnaire.

Step 2   Copy the numerical values of the circled responses to statements 1 through 35 in the numbered blanks in the Table labeled B. Note that the numbered blanks in Table B are *not* in consecutive order.

Step 3   Box C contains the Raw Scale Total for each stage (0–6). Take each of the seven columns (0–6) in Table B, add the numbers within each column, and enter the sum for each column (0–6) in the appropriate blank in Box C. Each of these seven Raw Score Totals is a number between 0 and 35.

Step 4   Table D contains the percentile scores for each Stage of Concern. Find the Raw Scale Score Total for Stage 0 from Box C; locate this number in the left-hand column in Table D, then look in the Stage 0 column to the right in Table D and circle that percentile ranking. Do the same for Stages 1 through 6, only match the left-hand column raw score with the corresponding stage.

Step 5   Transcribe the circled percentile scores for each stage (0–6) from Table D to Box E. Box E now contains seven numbers between 0 and 99.

Step 6   Box F contains the SoC graph. From Box E, take the percentile score for Stage 0 and mark that point with a dot on the Stage 0 vertical line on the SoC graph. Do the same for Stages 1 through 6. Connect the points to form the SoC profile.

For interpretation of the SoC profile, refer to Hall, George, and Rutherford (1979), The SoCQ Manual.

SoCQ Quick Scoring Device

A

Date: _____

Site: _____ SS#: _____

Innovation: _____

B

	Stage						
	0	1	2	3	4	5	6
	3___	6___	7___	4___	1___	5___	2___
	12___	14___	13___	8___	11___	10___	9___
	21___	15___	17___	16___	19___	18___	20___
	23___	26___	28___	25___	24___	27___	22___
	30___	35___	33___	34___	32___	29___	31___
Raw Score Totals **C**	___	___	___	___	___	___	___
Percentile Scores **E**	___	___	___	___	___	___	___

D

Five Item Raw Scale Score Total	Stage						
	0	1	2	3	4	5	6
0	10	5	5	2	1	1	1
1	23	12	12	5	1	1	2
2	29	16	14	7	1	2	3
3	37	19	17	9	2	3	5
4	46	23	21	11	2	3	6
5	53	27	25	15	3	4	9
6	60	30	28	18	3	5	11
7	66	34	31	23	4	7	14
8	72	37	35	27	5	9	17
9	77	40	39	30	5	10	20
10	81	43	41	34	7	12	22
11	84	45	45	39	8	14	26
12	86	48	48	43	9	16	30
13	89	51	52	47	11	19	34
14	91	54	55	52	13	22	38
15	93	57	57	56	16	25	42
16	94	60	59	60	19	28	47
17	95	63	63	65	21	31	52
18	96	66	67	69	24	36	57
19	97	69	70	73	27	40	60
20	98	72	72	77	30	44	65
21	98	75	76	80	33	48	69
22	99	80	78	83	38	52	73
23	99	84	80	85	43	55	77
24	99	88	83	88	48	59	81
25	99	90	85	90	54	64	84
26	99	91	87	92	59	68	84
27	99	93	89	94	63	72	87
28	99	95	91	95	66	76	90
29	99	96	92	97	71	80	92
30	99	97	94	97	76	84	94
31	99	98	95	98	82	88	96
32	99	99	96	98	86	91	97
33	99	99	96	99	90	93	98
34	99	99	97	99	92	95	99
35	99	99	99	99	96	98	99

F

Chart — Relative Intensity (100, 90, 80, 70, 60, 50, 40, 30, 20, 10, 0) by SoC Stages (0–6):
AWARENESS, INFORMATION, PERSONAL, MANAGEMENT, CONSEQUENCE, COLLABORATION, REFOCUSING

Concerns-Based Systems International

The SOCQ Quick Scoring Device was developed by Eddie W. Parker and Teresa H. Griffin.

APPENDIX 3

Levels of Use of the Innovation

CATEGORIES

SCALE POINT DEFINITIONS OF THE LEVELS OF USE OF THE INNOVATION	KNOWLEDGE	ACQUIRING INFORMATION	SHARING
Levels of Use are distinct states that represent observably different types of behavior and patterns of innovation use as exhibited by individuals and groups. These levels characterize a user's development in acquiring new skills and varying use of the innovation. Each level encompasses a range of behaviors, but is limited by a set of identifiable Decision Points. For descriptive purposes, each level is defined by seven categories.	That which the user knows about characteristics of the innovation, how to use it, and consequences of its use. This is cognitive knowledge related to using an innovation, not feelings or attitudes.	Solicits information about the innovation in a variety of ways, including questioning resources persons, corresponding with resources agencies, reviewing printed materials, and making visits.	Discusses the innovation with others. Shares plans, ideas, resources, outcomes, and problems related to use of the innovation.

LEVEL 0 NON-USE

State in which the user has little or no knowledge of the innovation, no involvement with the innovation, and is doing nothing toward becoming involved.	Knows nothing about this or similar innovations or has only very limited general knowledge of efforts to develop innovations in the area.	Takes little or no action to solicit information beyond reviewing descriptive information about this or similar innovations when it happens to come to personal attention.	Is not communicating with others about innovation beyond possibly acknowledging that the innovation exists.
	0	0	0

DECISION POINT A — Takes action to learn more detailed information about the innovation.

LEVEL 1 ORIENTATION:

State in which the user has acquired or is acquiring information about the innovation and/or has explored or is exploring its value orientation and its demands upon user and user system.	Knows general information about the innovation such as origin, characteristics, and, implementation requirements.	Seeks descriptive material about the innovation. Seeks opinions and knowledge of others through discussions, visits or workshops.	Discusses resources needed in general terms and/or exchanges descriptive information, materials, or ideas about the innovation and possible implications of its use.
	I	I	I

DECISION POINT B — Makes a decision to use the innovation by establishing a time to begin.

LEVEL II PREPARATION

State in which the user is preparing for first use of the innovation.	Knows logistical requirements, necessary resources and timing for initial use of the innovation, and details of initial experiences for clients.	Seeks information and resources specifically related to preparation for use of the innovation in own setting.	Discusses resources needed for initial use of the innovation. Joins others in pre-use training, and in planning for resources, logistics, schedules, etc., in preparation for first use.
	II	II	II

DECISION POINT C — Changes, if any, and use are dominated by user needs. Clients may be valued, however management, time, or limited

LEVEL III MECHANICAL USE

	KNOWLEDGE	ACQUIRING INFORMATION	SHARING
State in which the user focuses most effort on the short-term, day-to-day use of the innovation with little time for reflection. Changes in use are made more to meet user needs than client needs. The user is primarily engaged in a stepwise attempt to master the tasks required to use the innovation, often resulting in disjointed and superficial use.	Knows on a day-to-day basis the requirements for using the innovation, is more knowledgeable on short-term activities and effects than long-range activities and effects, of use of the innovation.	Solicits management information about such things as logistics, scheduling techniques, and ideas for reducing amount of time and work required of user.	Discusses management and logistical issues related to use of the innovation. Resources and materials are shared for purposes of reducing management, flow and logistical problems related to use of the innovation.
	III	III	III

DECISION POINT D-1 — A routine pattern of use is established. Changes for clients may be made routinely, but there are no recent changes outside

LEVEL IV A ROUTINE

Use of the innovation is stabilized. Few if any changes are being made in ongoing use. Little preparation or thought is being given to improving innovation use or its consequences.	Knows both short- and long-term requirements for use and how to use the innovation with minimum effort or stress.	Makes no special efforts to seek information as a part of ongoing use of the innovation.	Describes current use of the innovation with little or no reference to ways of changing use.
	IVA	IVA	IVA

DECISIONS POINT D-2 — Changes use of the innovation based on formal or informal evaluation in order to increase client outcomes. They must be recent

LEVEL IV B REFINEMENT

State in which the user varies the use of the innovation to increase the impact on clients within his/her immediate sphere of influence. Variations are based on knowledge of both short- and long-term consequences of client.	Knows cognitive and affective effects of the innovation on clients and ways for increasing impact on clients.	Solicits information and materials that focus specifically on changing use of the innovation to affect client outcomes.	Discusses own methods of modifying use of the innovation to change client outcomes.
	IVB	IVB	IVB

DECISION POINT E — Initiates changes in use of innovation based on input of and in coordination with what colleagues are doing.

LEVEL V INTEGRATION

State in which the user is combining own efforts to use the innovation with related activities of colleagues to achieve a collective impact on clients within their sphere of influence.	Knows how to coordinate own use of the innovation with colleagues to provide a collective impact on clients.	Solicits information and opinions for the purpose of collaborating with others in use of the innovation.	Discusses efforts to increase client impact through collaboration with others on personal use of the innovation.
	V	V	V

DECISION POINT F — Begins exploring alternatives to or major modifications of the innovation presently in use.

LEVEL VI RENEWAL

State in which the user reevaluates the quality of use of the innovation, seeks major modifications of or alternatives to present innovation to achieve increased impact on clients, examines new developments in the field, and explores new goals for self and the system.	Knows of alternatives that could be used to change or replace the present innovation that would improve the quality of outcomes of its use.	Seeks information and materials about others innovations as alternatives to the present innovation or for making major adaptations in the innovation.	Focuses discussions on identification of major alternatives or replacements for the current innovation.
	VI	VI	VI

Procedures for Adopting Educational Innovations Project. Research and Development Center for Teacher Education, University of Texas at Austin, 1975, N.I.E. Contract No. NIE-74-0087.

CATEGORIES

ASSESSING	PLANNING	STATUS REPORTING	PERFORMING
Examines the potential or actual use of the innovation or some aspect of it. This can be a mental assessment or can involve actual collection and analysis of data.	Designs and outlines short- and/or long-range steps to be taken during process of innovation adoption, i.e., aligns resources, schedules activities, meets with others to organize and/or coordinate use of the innovation.	Describes personal stand at the present time in relation to use of the innovation.	Carries out the actions and activities entailed in operationalizing the innovation.
Takes no action to analyze the innovation, its characteristics, possible use, or consequences of use.	Schedules no time and specifies no steps for the study or use of the innovation.	Reports little or no personal involvement with the innovation.	Takes no discernible action toward learning about or using the innovation. The innovation and/or its accouterments are not present or in use.
0	0	0	0
Analyzes and compares materials, content, requirements for use, evaluation reports, potential outcomes, strengths and weaknesses for purpose of making a decision about use of the innovation.	Plans to gather necessary information and resources as needed to make a decision for or against use of the innovation.	Reports presently orienting self to what the innovation is and is not.	Explores the innovation and requirements for its use by talking to others about it, reviewing descriptive information and sample materials, attending orientation sessions, and observing others using it.
I	I	I	I
Analyzes detailed requirements and available resources for initial use of the innovation.	Identifies steps and procedures entailed in obtaining resources and organizing activities and events or initial use of the innovation.	Reports preparing self for initial use of the innovation.	Studies reference materials in depth, organizes resources and logistics, schedules and receives skill training in preparation for initial use.
II	II	II	II

experimental knowledge dictate what the user does.

ASSESSING	PLANNING	STATUS REPORTING	PERFORMING
Examines own use of the innovation with respect to problems of logistics, management, time schedules, resources and general reactions of clients.	Plans for organizing and managing resources, activities, and events related primarily to immediate ongoing use of the innovation. Planned-for changes address managerial or logistical issues with a short-term perspective.	Reports that logistics, time, management, resource organizations, etc., are the focus of most personal efforts to use the innovation.	Manages innovation with varying degrees of efficiency. Often lacks anticipation of immediate consequences. The flow of actions in the user and clients is often disjointed, uneven and uncertain. When changes are made, they are primarily in response to logistical and organizational problems.
III	III	III	III

the pattern.

ASSESSING	PLANNING	STATUS REPORTING	PERFORMING
Limits evaluation activities to those administratively required, with little attention paid to findings for the purpose of changing use.	Plans intermediate and long-range actions with little projected variation in how the innovation will be used. Planning focuses on routine use of resources, personnel, etc.	Reports that personal use of the innovation is going along satisfactorily with few if any problems.	Uses the innovation smoothly with minimal management problems; over time, there is little variation in pattern of use.
IVA	IVA	IVA	IVA
Assesses use of the innovation for the purpose of changing current practices to improve client outcomes.	Develops intermediate and long-range plans that anticipate possible and needed steps, resources, and events designed to enhance client outcomes.	Reports varying use of the innovation in order to change client outcomes.	Explores and experiments with alternative combinations of the innovation with existing practices to maximize client involvement and to optimize client outcomes.
IVB	IVB	IVB	IVB
Appraises collaborative use of the innovation in terms of client outcomes and strengths and weaknesses of the integrated effort.	Plans specific actions to coordinate own use of the innovation with others to achieve increased impact on clients.	Reports spending time and energy collaborating with others about integrating own use of the innovation.	Collaborates with others in use of the innovation as a means of expanding the innovation's impact on clients. Changes in use are made in coordination with others.
V	V	V	V
Analyzes advantages and disadvantages of major modifications or alternatives to the present innovation.	Plans activities that involve pursuit of alternatives to enhance or replace the innovation.	Reports considering major modifications to present use of the innovation.	Explores other innovations that could be used in combination with or in place of the present innovation in an attempt to develop more effective means of achieving client outcomes.
VI	VI	VI	VI

Reprinted from Hall, G.E., Loucks, S.F., Rutherford, W.L. & Newlove, B.W. Levels of Use of the Innovation: A framework for analyzing innovation adoption. *The Journal of Teacher Education.* 1975. 26(1), 52–56

APPENDIX 4

Six Dimensions of Change Facilitator Style

Cluster I: Concern for People

The first cluster of CF Style behaviors deals with how the principal, as the change facilitator, addresses the personal side of change. People have feelings and attitudes about their work and about how a change process is going. They have personal needs, too. Day to day, facilitators can monitor, attend to, and affect these concerns and needs in different ways and with different emphases. For example, it is possible to spend little time directly addressing the feelings of others or to become preoccupied with listening and responding to each concern that is expressed. The emphasis can also be on attending to individual concerns as they are expressed daily or on focusing on the more long-term needs of all staff, with attention to individual concerns on an as-needed basis.

The Concern for People cluster is composed of two dimensions that weigh the degree to which the moment-to-moment and daily behaviors of a facilitator emphasize *social/informal* and *formal/meaningful* interactions with teachers. The Social/Informal dimension addresses the extent to which the facilitator engages in informal social discussions with teachers.

Social/Informal   This dimension addresses the frequency and character of the facilitator's informal social discussions with teachers and other staff. Many of these discussions may not be even remotely related to the work of the school or a specific innovation. Facilitators who emphasize this cluster engage in frequent social interactions. They attend to feelings and perceptions by emphasizing listening, understanding, and acknowledging immediate concerns, rather than providing answers or anticipating long-range consequences. There is a personable, friendly, almost chatty tone to the interactions. When concerns are addressed, it is done in ways that are responsive rather than anticipatory.

Formal/Meaningful   This dimension addresses brief, task-oriented interactions that deal with specific aspects of the work and the details of the innovation implementation. Facilitators are centered on school tasks, priorities, and directions. Discussions and interactions are focused on teaching, learning, and other substantive issues directly related to use of the innovation. Interactions are primarily intended to support teachers in their school-related duties, and the facilitator is almost always looking for solutions that are lasting. The interactions and emphases are not overly influenced by superficial and short-lived feelings and needs. Teaching and learning activities and issues directly related to use of the innovation are emphasized.

Cluster II: Organizational Efficiency

The work of the organization can be facilitated with varying degrees of emphasis on obtaining resources, increasing efficiency, and consolidating or sharing responsibilities and authority. Principals can try to do almost everything themselves, or they can delegate responsibility to others. System procedures, role clarity, and work priorities can be made more or less clear, and resources can be organized in ways that increase or decrease availability and effectiveness. In this cluster the principal's administrative focus is examined along two dimensions—*trust in others* and *administrative efficiency*.

Trust in Others   This dimension examines the extent to which the facilitator assigns others tasks of locating resources, establishing procedures, and managing schedules and time. When there is delay in making decisions, administrative systems and procedures are allowed to evolve in response to needs expressed by staff and to external pressures. The assumption is that teachers know how to accomplish their jobs and that they need a minimum of structuring and monitoring from the principal. As needs for additions or changes in structures, rules, and procedures emerge, they are gradually acknowledged and introduced as suggestions and guidelines rather than being directly established. Formalizing procedural and policy change is left to others and to time.

Administrative Efficiency   This dimension addresses the extent to which establishing clear and smoothly running procedures and resource systems to help teachers and others do their jobs efficiently is a priority. Administration, scheduling, and production tasks are clearly described, understood, and used by all members of the organization. Emphasis is placed on having a high level of organizational efficiency so teachers can do their jobs better. As needs for new structures and procedures emerge, they are formally established.

Cluster III: Strategic Sense

To varying degrees, principals are aware of the relationship between the long-term goals and their own monthly, weekly, daily, and moment-to-moment activities and those of their school. Some principals are more "now" oriented and treat each event in isolation from its part in the grand scheme, while others think and act with a vivid mental image of how today's actions contribute to accomplishing long-range aspirations. Some reflect about what they are doing and how all of their activities can add up, while others focus on the moment. Principals also vary in the degree to which they encourage or discourage the participation of external facilitators and in how they prescribe their role in the schools. This cluster examines the principal's strategic sense according to two dimensions: *day-to-day* and *vision and planning*.

Day-to-Day At the high end of this dimension, there is little anticipation of future developments, needs, successes, or failures. Interventions are made in response to issues and needs as they arise. Knowledge of the details of the innovation is limited, and the amount of intervention with teachers is restricted to responding to questions and gradually completing routine steps. Images of how things could be improved and how more rapid gains could be made are incomplete, limited in scope, and lacking in imagination. There is little anticipation of longer term patterns or consequences. External facilitators come and go as they wish and spend an extraordinary amount of effort advising the principal.

Vision and Planning The facilitator with a high emphasis on this dimension has a long-term vision that is integrated with an understanding of the day-to-day activities as the means to achieve the desired end. The facilitating activity is intense, with a high degree of interaction related to the work at hand. There is depth of knowledge about teaching and learning. Teachers and others are pushed to accomplish all that they can. Assertive leadership, continual monitoring, supportive actions, and creative interpretations of policy and use of resources to reach long-term goals are clear indicators of this dimension. Also present is the ability to anticipate the possible systemic effects of interventions and the broader consequences of day-to-day actions. Effects are accurately predicted, and interventions are made in anticipation of likely trends. Moment-to-moment interactions with staff and external facilitators are centered on the present work within a context of the long-range aspirations. The focus is on completing tasks, accomplishing school objectives, and making progress. External facilitators are encouraged to be involved in the school according to the principal's perception of their expertise and value.

For additional information see: Hall, G. E., & George, A. A. (1999). The impact of principal change facilitator style on school and classroom culture. In H. Jerome Freiberg (Ed.), *School Climate: Measuring, Improving and Sustaining Healthy Learning Environments.* Philadelphia and London: Falmer Press. pp. 165–185.

INDEX